Praise for *This Is Your Year*

I've worked with and observed Shelly Aristizabal for the past several years. She is a tenacious leader with a heart for people. I'm confident that by applying the principles outlined in Shelly's book, you will be able to more quickly achieve your dreams.

DALLIN A. LARSEN
FOUNDER, CHAIRMAN & CEO, MONAVIE

A perfect daily resource for women. A little bit of Shelly each day is bound to keep you motivated and on track. Shelly's action tips take you beyond her inspiring words to actually "doing" with the result of "being" all you want to be.

LINDA RENDLEMAN, MS
BUSINESS WOMEN CONNECT, INC., WOMEN LIKE US FOUNDATION

Shelly Aristizabal will take you on a very important journey. Some people say I'll believe it when I see it. But the truth is, you'll see it when you believe it! When you truly believe that you have potential, value and purpose, that is when you will begin to make those things become true in your life. You may not have proof, but it is your strong belief in yourself that will allow you to access your own brilliance. Shelly's book will help the reader to believe that this is their year, and will provide the tools to "Design the Life of Your Dreams!"

WINN CLAYBAUGH
AUTHOR OF *BE NICE (OR ELSE!)*, DEAN AND COFOUNDER OF PAUL MITCHELL SCHOOLS

We are privileged to call Shelly our friend. As an accomplished woman, Shelly is an inspiration to many through her wisdom and rich life experience. Shelly provides proven strategies to give you the keys to unlock and succeed at a higher level in your life. In her ground-breaking book you will be challenged to live each day with purpose and passion. Let Shelly assist you in how to discover, develop, and deliver your God given dreams so you can live up in a down world.

REX & KATRINA CRAIN
LIFE COACH, SPEAKER, AND AUTHOR OF *LIFE LIFT*

One year from today your life can be dramatically better! This book can take you there . . . step by step. My friend Shelly Aristizabal's book *This Is Your Year* is an excellent companion to improve your overall life every day. As I read this book I found myself encouraged, challenged, and presented with abundant ideas to reshape my life for the better. I highly recommend it!

JOHN MASON
AUTHOR OF NUMEROUS NATIONAL BESTSELLING BOOKS,
INCLUDING *AN ENEMY CALLED AVERAGE*

Claudia —
Live Your Dream!
Shelly

This Is Your Year

To Design and Live the Life of Your Dreams

Shelly Aristizabal

ISB

DALLAS • ATLANTA • NASHVILLE • LOS ANGELES

THIS IS YOUR YEAR

Copyright © 2012 by Shelly Aristizabal

Published by
ISB Publishing
2128 Boll Street
Dallas, TX 75024 USA

All rights reserved. No part of this book may be reproduced or transmitted in any form or by any means, electronic or mechanical, including photocopying and recording, or by any information storage and retrieval system, without permission in writing from the publisher, except for brief quotations in critical reviews and articles.

ISBN 978-1-93-771707-0

Printed in the United States of America
10 9 8 7 6 5 4 3 2 1

I wish to dedicate this book to

My Foundation
Edwardo, your love, belief, and support lifts me to greatness!

My Motivation
Nicolas, I admire the wonderful man and servant leader that you are becoming.

My Inspiration
Spencer, you challenge me, and your natural talent inspires me like no one else ever has.

My Celebration
Alexander, your wit and intellect astounds me—you are my joy!

My Dream Come True
Emma, you are beautiful inside & out; I delight in my angel from heaven!

A Gift of Love
Grandma Betty Holton, thank you for your positive attitude and unconditional love.

A Gift of Strength
MaMa Dortha Wilson, thank you for being the major influence of my life, for your unconditional love, and teaching me by example strength and faith in God.

In loving memory of my grandfathers: C. R. Wilson, Harold Holton, and John Pryor.

Acknowledgments

I WOULD LIKE TO acknowledge the many people I surround myself with who have made this book possible. Thank you so much!

John Mason, my writing coach, for his patience, guidance, and positive influence.

Joshua Lease, my editor, for his editing and thoughtful revisions and additions.

Lee Gessner, my publisher and support team.

Mary Sanford, for adding just the right design touch.

David Trumble, your artistic ability and insight are gifts you share with the world!

Amy Ryan Photography, your talent makes me look fabulous!

Katrina Crain, for launching my hidden passion to write.

Steve and Gina Merritt, my mentors in business and eternal life!

Brig and Lita Hart, for sharing your faith and wisdom.

Tony Fannin, you encouraged me to be somebody without a safety net.

Nicole Flothe, thank you for being my friend and website designer

Uncle Dan and Aunt Retta Canter, for support in many ways.

Patty Dresser, I treasure your authentic friendship and honesty.

All my girlfriends, for their enthusiastic support, sentiments, and love during this amazing process.

The many great thought leaders who devote their lives to inspire, motivate, and empower anyone in search of something more.

Introduction

Everybody has a story. Mine is one of birth, being born again, then being given a second chance at truly living my dream life.

I was born and raised in a very small town in Indiana, the eldest of four girls. My parents did the best they could to give us roots and wings—I know there certainly was not a lot of loot for things! I spent most of my childhood on my grandparents' farm with not much to do (outside of gardening and chores). So I spent many hours reading and day-dreaming of when I would be free to explore and travel the world!

My family wasn't much for encouraging a dreamer. The reality was that I needed to study and get good grades so I could get a job to work hard to pay the bills. But I always had this feeling and desire to accomplish something *really great* with my life. I didn't know exactly what I was going to do—as a matter of fact, I envied people who seemed to "just know" that they wanted to be a doctor, lawyer, accountant, or whatever. Looking back, I can now see that God *was* guiding me toward His plan for me all along.

About God—yes, I am a believer. Yes, I do include Scripture and mention God in my book. And, *yes*, I do encourage you to continue on your own personal spiritual journey. Please know I do not intend to "push" my belief on you or offend you in any way. I do know that God is love, and I have written this book in love, trusting that you are reading it now not by coincidence but by divine appointment.

My Miracle

I received my second chance to truly live my dream life in April 2009. I was on a business trip and rushing into a meeting in Wilmington, Delaware, after having been in a traffic jam while driving in from New Jersey. Within minutes of arriving and beginning my presentation, I experienced a shot of pain that lanced through my head and almost knocked me over.

My miracle actually began when I *didn't* have the pain while I was stuck in traffic *and* that there were several doctors at the meeting who immediately diagnosed my problem and called an ambulance.

It is a true miracle that I survived, unscathed, a subarachnoid hemorrhage in my brain (half the people who have one *die*, and 90 percent of those who survive have brain damage). The miracle continued because we were five minutes away from one of the top trauma hospitals in the country, with a specialist on staff who deals with my type of head trauma.

I am so thankful that my husband, Ed, was there with me the two weeks I was in the intensive care unit. He made the phone calls that began the thousands of prayers for my recovery. And now here I am today, alive and well with a desire to share this message of hope and encouragement with you.

What Is Success to You?

How do you define success? I believe success is doing the things you know will benefit you and the people you love. Success is determined by your daily agenda, so today matters—you are either preparing or repairing. I also believe success is based on your personal growth—physically, emotionally, intellectually, spiritually, and financially—and we need to be intentional about it every day.

I am not brilliant. I listen and read and learn from brilliant people. Everything I share with you in this book is some of my favorite thinking done by others. (Please look in the back of this book for my list of "mentors from afar," and I encourage you to learn the life lessons from the greatest thought leaders of all time!) I share these thoughts with you because I feel as though I need to learn the information as much as anyone. I really, really wish I had been exposed to this wisdom when I was in my twenties!

How to Use This Book

Please, don't just read this book. Interact with it. Underline it. Write your own thoughts in the margins and make notes at the back in the space provided. Make it *your* book. Personalize it! The books that have helped me most are the ones that I reacted to, not simply read.

I have included some of the features that I think will help you in this book: A daily quote to remember (and maybe post on your FB status). An Action Step—do these at your own pace (it may help to share this journey with a friend). And every seven days, I give a reminder message to Live Your Dream and keep it in front of you (for this reason, I suggest beginning *Day One* of *Your Year* on a Monday, so that the Living Your Dream will always fall on Sundays throughout the year). Please use the link to my website for more information and activities. Oh, and please have *fun*—this is Your Year and Your Life!

What Will Happen When You Read This Book?

My prayer for you is that you experience the incredible sense of hope, energy, and joy that comes from discovering what God put you on this planet to do. There is nothing quite like it. I am excited for you because I know that great things are going to happen to you. They happened to me, and I have never been the same since I discovered the purpose of my life. Your life is worth taking the time to think deeply about—make this a daily appointment on your schedule.

Perhaps you have heard the often-quoted expression of hope passed on to graduating seniors or newlywed couples: "The future is yours for the taking." Yet we know that some people grab life with enthusiasm and take control of their futures, but high hopes don't pan out for everybody. Happy, successful, fulfilled individuals have learned *how* to live life. And this is my wish for you—that you learn how to live your dream.

You may feel frustrated and discouraged at times while exploring your dream. Don't give up! Don't give up too soon on your dream— and it's always too soon to quit on your dream! Make a minor adjustment or two, and just keep on going. Keep dreaming the dream that God has put into your heart. If it were easy, anyone could do it—your dream is special and unique for you.

Are you ready to live to your full potential? Let's get started! With this book I want to equip you to believe that you can reach your dreams. This is YOUR YEAR, and now you will have the tools to discover, design, and live the life of your dreams.

All my best,
Shelly

This Is Your Year

Dream

*I will give my spirit to everyone . . . your young men will see visions
and your old men will have dreams.*

[ACTS 2:17]

Everyone has a dream. You may not be able to describe it. Maybe you
have forgotten it. You may even think your dream is no longer possi-
ble. But it is there, waiting to be discovered. Try to recall the dreams of
your childhood. Spend a few minutes with a five-year-old, and you
will get the idea of how to let go and really dream! Ask him or her,
"What do you want to be when you grow up?" The ideas come so eas-
ily for a child: a firefighter, ballerina, secret agent, doctor, teacher, and
professional athlete. . . . One of the most important rules of happiness
in life is to do what you love. But discovering that dream, your contri-
bution to the world, that perfect job, or what you are meant to do in
life isn't always so easy.

What I mean by *dream* is following your heart's desires to what
you truly love to do, your passion. Dream *big*, and describe it in detail.
Find something that you want so badly that you wake up in the morn-
ing thinking about it and can't wait to get up and do. Dreams are the
why that drives you—fuel for your soul. Dreams can be big or small,
tangible and intangible. Without vision or a dream, we are not going to
truly *live*; we will only survive. Dare to dream! Your dream may be to
work in a certain profession or live in a particular place. Or your
dream might involve simple things: to have more time to work in your
garden, spend more time with family or friends, have time for walks,
or to read books. Keep a dream journal, and create a dream or vision
board; add to it, and look at if often. Follow your passion, and you will
be following the Dream Giver's vision for creating you: your Purpose.
You are a part of God's Big Dream!

*Action: Spend some time meditating, praying, and thinking about
your life. Purchase a journal and begin writing down your thoughts
and dreams.*

What Do I Love To Do Most?

Every thought we think is creating our future.

[LOUISE L. HAY]

If you are not currently living your dream life, you may have a little nagging feeling that something is missing from your life or perhaps you have the desire to be a part of something bigger than yourself. Have you ever thought about how wonderful it would be to do what you loved to do instead of just *dreaming* about it?

What Do You Love to Do Most?

You need to believe that you were created to achieve something remarkable with your life. Following your dream will draw you toward the kind of life you were born to love! Everybody has a dream, and it is never too late to pursue it. Your dream is somewhere, waiting for you . . . and if you don't pursue it, something important *won't* happen. And when we do pursue our dreams, we may create an opportunity to inspire others to fulfill their dreams.

Take a look at the happiest, most successful people on this planet: they are all doing something they love, creating something they believe in, and living a life of purpose and passion. Do that, and it doesn't matter how much money you make. They are using their dreams to make contributions to the world. What special talents, skills, and gifts do you have to share with the world?

If you spend time thinking about your dreams and passions in life, you are taking the first step toward making them a reality.

Action: Take time to be quiet. This is something that we don't do enough in this busy world of ours. We rush, rush, rush, and we are constantly listening to noise all around us. The human heart was meant for times of quiet, to peer deep within. It is when we do this that our hearts are set free to soar and take flight on the wings of our own dreams! Schedule some quiet "dream time" this week. No other people. No cell phone. No computer. Just you, a pad, a pen and your thoughts.

Use Your Imagination

Dream no small dreams for they have no power to move the hearts of men.

[JOHANN WOLFGANG VON GOETHE]

But what do you do if you don't know what you want to do? What if you don't know what your dream is? This is a common problem, and many people wander through much of their lives without discovering their passions and go from job to job, unfulfilled and miserable. Some of us were not raised in a home where dreams were encouraged. *Get real* was the motto—go to school and get good grades so you can get a job, then get married, raise a family, and work until you die.

Fortunately, we don't have to buy into that reality. Thank God, we have books, teachers, and friends who can inspire us to be an avid dreamer! They can be dreams of traveling all over the globe, making a difference in the world, and yes, even being rich and famous!

Please be encouraged to relax and have fun—literally start dreaming! Anything is possible in your dreams! If you become what you think about, then *thinking* is *creating*. Imagine! Reality is for those who lack imagination.

If time and money were not issues, what would you do? Clear your mind and be creative.

Action: Take a few minutes now to do a few activities that may help you begin to discover your purpose in life. Be honest!

1. *Make a list of ten things you would do for free—to discover your passions.*
2. *Make a list of ten things you are good at—to discover your talents.*
3. *Make a list of ten things you like to do now.*
4. *Make a list of ten things you would like to do someday.*

Need help? Sit down with a friend or family member who you trust to be open and honest with you and ask them to give you feedback.

Enlarging Your Vision

You must conceive it and believe it is possible if you ever hope to experience it.

[JOEL OSTEEN]

There is a story about a man on vacation in Florida with his wife. He was a nice man who had achieved a modest level of success; he was coasting along, thinking he had reached his limits in life. One day, a friend was driving the couple around, showing them the sights. They stopped to admire a gorgeous house on the beach. The property was beautiful, with lush gardens and palm trees in a picturesque, peaceful setting.

As the man gazed at the magnificent home, he commented to his wife and friend, "I can't even imagine living in a place like that."

Right there, something inside him said, *Don't worry. You won't. You will never live in a great place like that.* Startled at his own thoughts, he wondered what that meant.

As long as you can't imagine it, as long as you can't see it, then it is not going to happen for you, he thought. The man correctly realized that his own thoughts and attitudes were condemning him to mediocrity. He determined then and there to start believing better of himself, and believing better of God.

Have you limited yourself by thinking too small, condemning yourself to a life less than your dream? It's time to set your sights higher!

Action: We have to conceive it on the inside before we're ever going to receive it on the outside. Think BIGGER than you ever dared to before!

Vision/Dream Board

The future belongs to those who believe in the beauty of their dreams.

[ELEANOR ROOSEVELT]

Now that your creative juices are flowing, let's have some fun. Your dream life can begin today, and it is about being, doing, and having what you want. And it is very unique to you. What kind of car do you want to drive? What house do you want to live in, and where is it? How will you look, how much will you weigh? What trips will you take, and who will you meet along the way?

We are going to create a Vision/Dream Board. You can make it as simple or elaborate as you like. This is a great family activity, a perfect way to share your dreams with the ones you love and you get to hear the dreams placed in their hearts!

Action: Gather supplies—poster board, photos, stickers, scissors, glue, magazines, etc. Cut out pictures of the images you want to create for your life, and then put them on the board. Write down your thoughts and even put dates for short-term dreams and long-term dreams!

Your Big Dream

> *We all have our own life to pursue, our own kind of dream to be weaving. And we all have some power to make wishes come true, as long as we keep believing.*
>
> [LOUISA MAY ALCOTT]

Think about your dream often. Write it down and begin making plans on how you will begin to live your dream life. What will it take to discover and follow your dream? Do you need to have some financial freedom to pursue your dream? Make some hard choices, difficult changes, and maybe even big sacrifices now to provide yourself some personal freedom later. Most importantly, you may need to step outside of your comfort zone. To achieve what you have never achieved, you must do what you have never done. Are you willing to do what it takes to pursue the life of your dreams? Anything less is hardly living at all.

You have a Big Dream. God has put a driving passion in you to do something special. Why wouldn't He? You are created in His image—the only person exactly like you in the universe. No one else can do your dream. Isn't it time to begin? You've waited long enough. Your dream is beating in your chest. Do you feel it? Tell your friends that you are about to begin the journey of your life! Get ready for your dream to come alive! *Dream! Believe! Achieve!*

Action: Hang up your Vision/Dream Board where you will see it every day. Continue writing in your Dream Journal Daily.

Living Your Dream

All human beings are also dream beings. Dreaming ties all mankind together.

[JACK KEROUAC]

Self-Discovery

Be real. Know where you are in order to get where you are going. If you were told you needed to be in Phoenix, Arizona, to collect a million-dollar reward in four days, the most important bit of information you need to know would be where are you now in order to follow a map to Phoenix! Self-discovery can be difficult at times, but it is very important to know where you are to get to where you want to be.

Take inventory of your assets and liabilities. *Plan, do, review,* and *examine* your past successes and failures.

What are your past successes, and where did you come up short? What has worked for you, and what has not? What are some good decisions and some bad decision, and how you have learned from them?

List one hundred things you've learned, accomplished, achieved, or done successfully in your life before today. If you get stuck, refer to the social, personal, economic, career, and health categories to stimulate ideas. Don't stop until you list has all one hundred successes! I know you can do it!

Live to Your Potential

> *Our deepest fear is not that we are inadequate. Our deepest fear is that we are powerful beyond measure. It is our light, not our darkness that most frightens us. We ask ourselves, Who am I to be brilliant, gorgeous, talented, and fabulous? Actually, who are you not to be? You are a child of God. Your playing small does not serve the world. There is nothing enlightened about shrinking so that other people won't feel insecure around you. We are all meant to shine, as children do. We were born to make manifest the glory of God that is within us. It's not just in some of us; it's in everyone. And as we let our own light shine, we unconsciously give other people permission to do the same. As we are liberated from our own fear, our presence automatically liberates others.*
>
> [MARIANNE WILLIAMSON]

Now ask yourself the questions, What on earth am I here for? and What is my purpose in life? Of all the great pursuits of life, this could be the most important! Some believe every virtue, treasure, and reward in life is obtained through the quest to live your potential. Potential is what you can become, the *best* possible version of yourself. When you know God's purpose for your life and understand the big picture, then all the pieces of your life fit together. When you are doing something you feel is meaningful and makes you happy while you are doing it, then you are following your purpose and living your potential.

Some call it mojo or the positive spirit of what you are doing. Who are you? What are you good at? What do other people think you are good at? Dare to dream about what you can achieve. Many people lock their greatness away, afraid of their own vast potential. It is said that the greatest waste in the world is the difference between what we are and what we are capable of doing and becoming.

So what are you becoming?

Action: If you knew that you could not fail, complete this statement: "My name is _____, my life is _____."

Your Purpose

When you are inspired by some great purpose, some extraordinary project, all your thoughts break their bonds: Your mind transcends limitations, your consciousness expands in every direction, and you find yourself in a new, great, and wonderful world. Dormant forces, faculties, and talents become alive, and you discover yourself to be a greater person by far than you ever dreamed yourself to be.

[PATANJALI]

Where do you start? By realizing your greatness! You will only be truly happy when you are living up to your strengths, courage, and capabilities. Listen to your heart. That is where God places your bundle of desires, hopes, interests, ambitions, dreams, and affections for you to discover.

We are sometimes envious of people who "knew what they wanted to be when they grew up"—doctors, firefighters, teachers, inventors, etc. Do you know that you don't want to stay where you are, and you feel a calling to get out in the world? Sometimes you discover what you do want by knowing what you *don't* want! That's OK.

Today, the average life span is 25,550 days. That is how long you will live if you are typical. It may be a good use of time to spend a few of those days reflecting, praying, and reading to help you discover how to *live to your potential*. It may be just what you need to unlock the passion inside of you!

You were put on earth to make a contribution. Discover your passion, and live to your potential. Invest in your passions. Follow that still small voice inside of you, and be comforted in knowing God has a plan for your life. I know that when you ignite that flame of potential, it will set you afire to live the life you are meant to live.

Action: Think about what really thrills you. When you are quiet, think about those things that really get your blood moving. What would you LOVE to do, either for fun or for a living? What would you love to accomplish? What would you try if you were guaranteed to succeed? What big thoughts move your heart into a state of excitement and joy?

The Source of Your Dream

Depend on it: God keeps his word.

[ROMANS 3:4]

Find your *why*. The only way to find your vision, your purpose, and your *why* is to open up to God. The *why* is the fuel that powers your goals and gives meaning to your accomplishments. Believe—your purpose in life is not about you.

The purpose of your life is far greater than your own personal fulfillment, your peace of mind, or even your happiness. It is far greater than your family, your career, or even your wildest dreams and ambitions. If you want to know why you were placed on this planet, you must begin with God. You were born by His purpose and for His purpose.

God has spoken certain things concerning you. Those things are His will and His purpose for your life. Your job is to recognize them, believe them, carry them within you, and speak them often because they give you a tremendous advantage.

It is important to remember that God placed your dream in your heart. He designed you to complete that dream as part of His Big Dream, and He will be with you to guide you along the way.

Action: Consider the source of your dreams; look deep within. Who are you trying to impress?

Comfort Zone

It is not because things are difficult that we do not dare, it is because we do not dare that they are difficult.

[SENECA]

Why is it that so many do not follow their dreams? It is very scary to leave your familiar comfort zone. You will face many challenges and obstacles along the way. You may be surprised to find the people you care about the most may not be the most supportive of your decision to leave your comfort zone and pursue your dream life. When you leave your comfort zone, you really shake up theirs. The people closest to you all have something to lose if you go forward. We are back to asking, "Who do you want to please?"

Get over the idea that your friends and family have to agree with you in order for your dream to be real. Refuse to put your dream on hold, waiting for everybody to get on the same page with you. You can't wait until others become comfortable with your dream before you pursue it.

There will be times when you want to give up. You may feel that you have lost your way. You may experience delays and feel angry and alone. This is the time to find support in like-minded people. Get encouragement from positive, successful people who will remind you to keep the faith.

Action: Ask yourself: What do I need to do today to have the life I want a year from now?

Where You Are and Where You Want to Be

Let go of the past and go for the future. Go confidently in the direction of your dreams. Live the life you imagined.

[HENRY DAVID THOREAU]

As you begin to gain some clarity about where you want to be in life, it is important that you also look at your current reality. The road to your dreams starts here. In order to design a successful strategy for getting what you want, you need to know two things: where you are and where you want to be.

The importance of making an honest assessment of where you are now can't be stressed enough. Starting with inaccurate information will lead to erroneous decisions about what has to be done and how far you have to go to reach your dream. For example, where are you currently with respect to the personal, professional, health, and family aspects of your life? What concerns do you have in these areas? Do you worry that going for your dream will take more time than there is available? Perhaps you don't believe it's possible to make your dream come true. All this is part of your reality too.

Fortunately, your positive attitude and beliefs also will arise—that is, you do believe your dream is possible. It's something you've always wanted, something to which you're committed, and something you know you can have. But first, let's take a little inventory of your life.

Action: Visualize in your mind a picture of your life right now. Then use your imagination to create a picture of yourself living your dream life.

Positioning Yourself

Never mistake motion for action.

[ERNEST HEMINGWAY]

Action: List where you are in each of the areas of your life compared to where you want to be with respect to your dream. Be brutally honest; you can't know where you want to go until you know with certainty where you are now. Don't judge; just write it all down.

Category	Where I Am Now	Where I Want To Be
Personal		
Professional		
Family		
Friends		
Health		
Well-Being		
Financial		
Fun		
Recreation		
Relationships		
Fitness		
Community		

Living Your Dream

> *Dream and give yourself permission to envision a YOU that you choose to be.*
>
> [JOY PAGE]

Living on Purpose

Really think about what you want from life, what you want your life to be like, and what kind of person you want to become. A Big Dream and your goals will give you directions toward your destination in life.

Consciously looking at your life as it is today, speculating about what your life might become in the future, dreaming about the kind of life you really want, and then creating a plan to create that life are the keys to giving your life direction. That is what makes a life worth living! You can create the kind of life you desire!

Essential Skills of Goal Achievement

A dream without a plan is just a wish.

[LARRY ELDER]

How big of a game do you want to play? Do you really want to fulfill the dreams God has placed in your heart? Not the dreams and goals you fantasize about or occasionally think about every now and then or just simply hope for, but God's dream. These are dreams and goals that will create passion in your life and move you into daily, monthly, and yearly **action**. Dreams are goals that bring emotion because of the clear sacrifices that we make preceding long-hoped-for victories. Yes, dreams and goals create miracles and accomplishment. And equally important, dreams and goals can create balance, priorities, and life-enhancement.

A well-known study of the Harvard University class of '53 revealed that only 10 percent of the students had established any goals at all, and that only 3 percent of the men and women in that class had written their goals down on paper. Twenty years later, the researchers again interviewed those very same former class members. They were involved in their careers and had families now. The 3 percent who had written down their goals two decades earlier were now worth more in economic terms than the entire remaining 97 percent of the class *combined!* Of course, financial success isn't everything, but this study clearly shows the results of writing down your goals.

Action: Today, take some time to REALLY reflect about your dreams. How do you see yourself a year from now? What about three years, five years, even ten years from now? Review your past successes. This will help you realize that God has designed you already equipped with everything you need to be successful at anything you desire. Seriously reflect on those goals and dreams that God has designed truly unique to you. Make a list of fifty items you would like to accomplish in the next ten years. Write down everything—from organizing your closet, to starting your own business, to writing a book, to owning your own private jet!

Smart Goals

Men do less than they ought, unless they do all that they can.

[Thomas Carlyle]

A useful way of making goals more powerful is to use the SMART mnemonic. While there are plenty of variants, SMART usually stands for:

S	Specific
M	Measurable
A	Attainable
R	Realistic
T	Timely

Writing down your goals forces you to visualize them. It also creates emotional commitment. Be sure to include a deadline and the steps you will take to achieve your goals. If you set your goal for the cause, the effect will take care of itself. For example, rather than writing, "I want to lose weight," it is better to write, "I will lose ten pounds by June 1 by eating healthy foods and exercising daily." Another example is rather than writing, "I want to make more money at my job," it is better to write, "I will get a $10,000 increase in pay by June 1, and I will add value to my company by coming in earlier every day."

Tomorrow, be prepared for six goal-setting questions for you to ask and answer over and over again. Have a pad of paper, and be prepared to write out your responses. This piece of paper will represent your future goals. Look at it every day, and shape your life the way you see it on that paper.

Action: What are the top ten things that you really, really want out of life?

Identify Your Goals

Discipline is the bridge between goals and accomplishment.

[JIM ROHN]

What are your five most important values in life?
This question is intended to help clarify what is really important
. . . and what is not so important.

What are your three most important goals in life, right now?
Take thirty seconds to allow your subconscious mind to sort out
your many goals quickly. Your top three will pop into your con-
scious mind. Write them down.

**What would you do and how would you spend your time if you
learned today that you only had six months to live?**
When your time is limited, you become aware of who and what
you really care about.

**What would you do if you won ten million dollars cash, tax free, in
the lottery tomorrow?**
This will help you decide what you'd do if you had all the time
and money you need, and if you had virtually no fear of failure at
all.

**What have you always wanted to do but been afraid to attempt?
What if you knew you could not fail?**
Fear of failure can keep us from attempting the very things that
will bring us the most fulfillment.

**What do you most enjoy doing? What gives you your greatest feeling
of personal satisfaction?**
You will always be happy doing what you most love to do, and
what you most love to do is invariably the activity that makes
you feel the most fulfilled.

Action: Enjoy this process of self-discovery.

Goal-Setting Strategy

The invariable mark of a dream is to see it come true.

[RALPH WALDO EMERSON]

Decide exactly what you want your life to look like—ninety days, one year, five years, twenty years, and even one hundred years from now.

Income

Lifestyle

Health

Net Worth

Legacy

Write it down. Have a deadline. Identify obstacles you will overcome.

"I am not _____ already because _____."

Identify the skills you will need to develop. Make a list of people and associations to turn to. Do something *every day* toward your goals. Visualize yourself as if you have already achieved your goals.

Action: Don't stress about answering all the questions in one session. Take a walk and clear your mind and come back later to finish.

Goal Achievement Blueprint

Determine the thing that can and shall be done, and then we shall find the way.

[ABRAHAM LINCOLN]

Goal: _____ **Deadline:** _____

With your goal in mind, answer the questions below. Include as much detail as possible for each of your answers.

- Why is this goal meaningful to me?
- Who has successfully accomplished the same (or similar) goal and can help me strategize to overcome the obstacles I will encounter?
- Who can encourage me to stay on track and help make me accountable?
- What organization or group of people can I connect with that can help me achieve my goal?
- What can I do now to research and create a methodology that will help me succeed?
- How can I eliminate distractions and focus on doing something every day that will cause me to make progress toward accomplishing my goal?
- What can I do to add fun and competition to the equation and at the same time advance me toward my goal?
- How does realizing this goal set me up for even greater success?

Action: Have fun with this and get excited about your future!

Micro, Mini, Maxi Goals

If you want to be happy, set a goal that commands your thoughts, liberates your energy, and inspires your hopes.

[ANDREW CARNEGIE]

It starts with the dream. Determine to dream with a definiteness of purpose to achieve it. Let's take writing this book for an example. The dream is to write and publish *This Is Your Year* with the maxi goal to complete it within a year.

Then break it into specific micro and mini goals. A micro goal is a daily goal of completing a specific number of pages per day. I will accomplish mini goals by writing a minimum number of days per week. I will accomplish writing a certain number of pages per month, so I will have the book written in twelve months.

If your dream has a financial incentive attached to it, then follow the steps below to help you visualize and focus on your dream!

- Determine an exact amount of money you desire.
- Determine exactly what you intend to give in return for the money you desire.
- Establish a definite date when you intend to possess the money.
- Create a definite plan to carry out your desire, and start now.
- Write it all out in a Statement of Desire.
- Read your written statement aloud, twice daily, once in the morning and once in the evening.
- As you read your statement, see and feel and believe yourself already in possession of the money.

Action: What maxi goal can you break into micro and mini goals to accomplish?

Living Your Dream

A goal is a dream with a deadline.

[NAPOLEON HILL]

Do You Have Something Better to Do?

It may be a bit frustrating to realize that our dreams are far away from where we are right now. When we focus on the distance between where we are now and where we want to be, it can be easy to throw in the towel and give up before we even begin. Chances are that's just the kind of thinking that's held you back from living the life of your dreams until now.

The fact is you won't achieve your dream life overnight. It's going to take some time and hard work to bring your dreams to fruition. But do you have something better to do in the meantime?

Time is going to keep on ticking by, and you're going to get a little bit older every day. Eventually, one day, you will die—just like the rest of us. In the meantime, you can focus on the life you'd like to live—creating goals, reaching to achieve them every day, and growing ever closer to the ultimate dream life you desire.

How do you eat an elephant? One bite at a time, of course!

Commitment

Be impeccable with your word. Speak with integrity. Say only what you mean. Avoid using the word to speak against yourself or to gossip about others. Use the power of your word in the direction of truth and love.

[DON MIGUEL RUIZ]

Making a commitment to your goals and dreams could mean you are a person who will "do what you say and say what you mean" whether conditions are optimal or conducive for keeping your word—or not.

Many people make ridiculous excuses for why they don't want to commit. Commitment is doing what we say we're going to do. It's that simple. However, the "doing what we say we will" really isn't the problem, because most people just don't commit to anything!

Just think about the number of people you know who never even make New Year's resolutions. It is more convenient to not make a promise they can't keep, so as a result they are never going to accomplish much of anything.

How big a game do you want to play? Life seems to work in proportion to the size of the promises we make and our ability to make good on them. Make bold promises to yourself—and keep them.

Action: Say what you are going to do. Declare it without fear or doubt—or say it with fear and doubt—but make the statement anyway. Do it even if you are afraid!

You Can Either Make Reasons or Results

It is not fair to ask of others what you are unwilling to do yourself.

[ELEANOR ROOSEVELT]

Till death do us part. For better or for worse. In sickness and in health. For richer or poorer. If you are married, recall and contemplate the above phrases in the average wedding vows. With the current divorce rate being over 50 percent, do the words really mean anything?

When you have a Big Dream, you are no longer an average, ordinary person. Making excuses and being reasonable won't get you to the extraordinary level you desire to fulfill your goals and dreams.

American football coach Vince Lombardi frequently told his players before a game: "In a few hours we'll all be back in here, and you'll either have reasons or results. What is it going to be?" It's no accident that he coached Super Bowl championship teams. It didn't matter if it snowed or if their star quarterback broke his arm—those were just reasons. The players were committed to *results* instead of being average and being *reasonable.*

Wherever you are, that's the place to start. Say it, and begin taking steps. When you put your thoughts into words, you set wheels in motion that are moving you toward your goal.

Action: Reflect on the commitments you have made in your life. Are you committed to pursuing your dreams?

A Matter of Life and Death

> *Sustainability isn't about the quick fix or the cheap solution. Generally it means making a commitment and trying, as best we can, to honor it. In any worthwhile enterprise, from protecting the environment to preserving a relationship, we are going to encounter difficulties. The good life is not a problem-free life. In point of fact, the process of overcoming adversity often produces some of the most rewarding experiences we will ever have. Human beings need to be challenged to "test their mettle," as it were. Throwing in the towel at the first sign of trouble or small inkling of distress may be the easy thing to do, but it doesn't help our self-concept. Most of life's troubles can be overcome if we are willing to work through them with patience.*
>
> [MICHAEL A. SCHULER]

It is a common theme in many action movies to have a warrior commit his life to his cause. He appears to have a fundamental way of being, when he makes a vow to win that is a matter of life and death. Have you ever seen a fighter with nothing to lose? That person is incredibly fierce and goes full out—with complete commitment. He is willing to die for his cause, his purpose for living!

Action: What in life would you actually die for? What values do you believe in so strongly that you'd give up everything rather than sacrifice those values? Can you think of anything right now that's actually worth dying for? How far would you actually go to prove your devotion to your heart's most passionate purpose?

What Are You Committed To?

You have to pay the price. You will find that everything in life exacts a price, and you will have to decide whether the price is worth the prize.

[SAM NUNN]

Some people are committed to looking good, so they don't make agreements that they might not be able to follow through on. Others are committed to just being comfortable; they refuse to push higher or go any further than they are right now if it means leaving their comfort zone. They let their *good* stand in the way of their *spectacular.*

Other people are committed to being right, so they won't make agreements that might put them in the position to make them appear wrong. Still others won't make agreements in order to be accepted— they won't agree to large goals because those who don't want to work hard may shun them.

Consider that by being more, you can actually do more for others and truly make a contribution to those around you. The basis of life is the commitments we make to ourselves and others. Making a commitment to pursue your goals and dreams will produce a chain reaction of activity around you.

Action: What is the biggest agreement you've made and kept? What new and bigger agreement can you make and keep?

What Price Are You Willing to Pay?

The most important thing is to be able at any moment to sacrifice who you are for what you could become.

[CHARLES DUBOIS]

There are prices and benefits for everything. The prices to be paid for doing your business successfully—or what you have to invest or give up—are not always so obvious and, in fact, are often hidden. If you don't know the price, it's usually higher than you want to pay.

How much are you willing to pay to see your dream fulfilled? The problem is most people would like a huge return . . . without having to pay for it. You must be willing to pay the price, because oftentimes the cost of *not* doing something is hidden *and* far more expensive than you may think.

Action: Write down two things that are very important to you that you want to create. Perhaps it is a rewarding relationship, growing your business, a certain waistline, or making a positive difference in your community.

Ask yourself: How much time will this take? How uncomfortable will I need to allow myself to be? How much money will it take?

Now, what are you willing to pay to get that? Begin building up your willingness to pay the price. This is a giant step toward achieving your result.

Accountability

Even the knowledge of my own fallibility cannot keep me from making mistakes. Only when I fall do I get up again.

[VINCENT VAN GOGH]

Writing down and then sharing your goals and dreams with a positive, successful person you trust to encourage you will help hold you accountable to sticking to your commitment. When you actually proclaim your desire—say it out loud—it becomes *real!* Choose someone who will be honest and firm with you. Set up regular times to review your progress and achievements. Being accountable to your *committed,* disciplined, and then sustained action is the final ingredient in the miracle process of materializing any achievement you can conceive.

Simply writing down goals and sharing them does not guarantee your success. For your goals to be meaningful, you must remain committed to your dream. Determine that you're not just going to *start* your dream, but that you're going to *finish* what you started! In life, there are many starters—but few *finishers!* Deciding to invest some of your time, energy, and financial resources in yourself and your business will determine your level of personal success.

There is a difference between wishing for something and being ready to receive it. In order to receive, you must *believe* to achieve. Remember, no more effort is required to aim high in life, to demand abundance and prosperity, than is required to accept misery and poverty.

Visualize yourself as if you have already achieved your dream life. Then contemplate the price you will pay for *not* achieving your goals and dreams. It is also important to acknowledge and celebrate the small achievements along the way in reaching your big goals. Strive for a balanced mind, body, and soul.

Action: Make the promise to yourself to design your best year ever! No matter how last year was for you—this year could be even better.

Live Your Dream

Dreams are necessary to life.

[ANAÏS NIN]

Focus

Three boys were hiking and came to an open field. They decided to have a contest to see who could walk the straightest line. The first two boys zigzagged through the field. The third boy focused on two trees at the edge of the clearing and walked a straight line.

When you know exactly where you are going and focus on that point, you will go directly to that end.

Without a focus for your direction in life, you will wander aimlessly until you are hopelessly lost and confused. Put the blinders on and zoom in on your goals and dreams!

The Power of Our Thoughts

Life consists not in holding good cards but in playing those you hold well.

[JOSH BILLINGS]

Everything begins with a thought. Thoughts lead to emotions, emotions inspire action, and action creates habits. Habits are your character, which leads to results!

Have you heard the expression, "Be careful of what you wish for, because you just might get it?" Sure you have, and you probably believe it is true. Everything begins with a thought. We have thousands of thoughts every hour of the day, so how do we choose the ones to focus on? Do our thoughts really play a role in our circumstances?

Look around you—everything ever invented, created, and discovered began as a thought in someone's imagination. You begin to realize that *anything* and *everything* in the world begins and happens as a result of the power of thoughts. The predominant thoughts that you choose to think combined with the emotions that these chosen thoughts create will, with unwavering certainty, mold and shape your life physically, financially, intellectually, emotionally, and spiritually.

The power of thoughts—more specifically the power of your individual thoughts—plays a crucial role in determining how *every* event, condition, and circumstance in your life unfolds as a result of their creative power.

Action: Have you ever given much thought to your thoughts—where they come from or the power they have in molding and shaping your life? Today, simply be more conscious of what you are thinking about. Make some notes in your journal.

Thoughts Become Real

You are today where your thoughts have brought you; you will be tomorrow where your thoughts take you.

[JAMES ALLEN]

Although it isn't the power of your thoughts alone that determines how things unfold, your chosen thoughts—combined with the power of emotions that these chosen thoughts—ignite and inspire the *action* to create the results!

Understanding and learning to consciously and intentionally implement the power of your thoughts is a *vital* and necessary component of achieving and experiencing your most sought-after dreams and desires.

When you grasp and begin to really understand how your conscious mind as well as your subconscious mind are infused and interact with God's plan for your life, you begin to get *really* excited about your individual potential and what is available to and for you.

Action: It's not our circumstances that define us; it's what we "think" about our circumstances that creates our attitude.

Begin to appreciate that everything—from the invention of the wheel to the creation of the Snuggie—began as a thought in someone's imagination. They became emotionally attached to this idea, which led them to take the action necessary to see that it was created.

Subconscious Thinking

Great men are those who see that thoughts rule the world.

[RALPH WALDO EMERSON]

There have been books written on how to do practically anything and everything. If your dream is to get rich, marry your perfect mate, live a healthy lifestyle, or become a better manager, you can find several books on the topic and simply read them. The books will give you suggestions on what to do to achieve success, and we should all have success in every area of our lives!

The fact is, most people do not do what they are told to do, or even what they know is good for them. In general, most people behave according to certain fundamental beliefs or subconscious thinking. Your subconscious, or belief system, makes the majority of your decisions. People don't make decisions based on what they know; they make decisions based on what they feel.

Many times people may consciously desire a specific outcome; however, their predominant focus is placed on what they *don't* have or don't want rather than what it is they actually desire to experience. The inevitable result—due to the immutable and unwavering creative power of thoughts and their "unconsciously focused" thoughts, combined with "fear-based" emotions—actually creates *more* of what they *don't* want.

Action: Take a look at the people closest to you. Do you know people who are constantly thinking and speaking about how "broke" or "sick" or "lonely" or "fat" they are, yet they consistently insist they don't want to be "broke" or "sick" or "lonely" or "fat"? What are they getting more of?

What Are You Thinking About?

We become what we think about.

[EARL NIGHTINGALE]

This statement, which almost all philosophers agree on, is at the heart of understanding how our thoughts affect who we are, and it points out the connection between what we think and what we become.

When you examine the logic of this connection, it is apparent that if you become what you think about, then you can experience performance and behavior changes by altering the way you think. Your thought process, therefore, is the point where changes need to happen. It is your thought process that affects how you express yourself and who you become.

To use a gardening analogy, thoughts are seeds and our brain is a garden. Given the right conditions, in a gardening situation, the earth will grow anything—nourishing food or poison.

Much the same as the earth grows what is sowed, so our brains also grow the thoughts (the "thinking seeds") we entertain. Our brain cultivates them and gives them nutrients and sustenance. These thinking seeds ultimately determine who we become, how we deal with issues, how we solve problems, and how we present ourselves. The challenge then becomes how to control what is planted in our brain— how to sow the right thinking seeds.

Action: You can plant the positive thinking seeds by asking yourself the right questions. Questions are the gateway to your brain finding answers. Negative questions always yield undesirable results. When you ask yourself, "Why is everyone so rude?" you will find you run into more rude people. When you ask, "How can I help others be happier?" You will find that you are surrounded by positive, happy people who want to make a difference. Positive questions fill you with a sense of optimism, self confidence, and happiness. Try it!

We Think All Day Long

All that a man achieves and all that he fails to achieve is the direct result of his own thoughts.

[JAMES ALLEN]

One sentence to take out of our dialogue is: "I am just so sick and tired of _____!" As people continually think about anything negative, each of these occurrences is enough to allow the subconscious mind to begin the process of what it is designed to do. It absorbs the "conscious thought" as truth. Depending on the emotional response and intensity of the thought, it stores it as a memory picture and begins the process that will actually cause whatever is consistently held as thought to happen in the physical world. When it is *reinforced with words,* and then emotions attached to it are elevated, it will actually *speed up the process!*

The subconscious mind doesn't exercise the same rational thought process that the conscious mind does. It accepts whatever data it's provided. It's non-discerning. It doesn't differentiate between positive and negative. It doesn't conceive and comprehend the negative. It innocently accepts and records whatever data it's provided.

As a specific example, let's assume someone was consistently thinking about *not* wanting to be broke. Not wanting to be broke can only cause one to continue to be broke. Why? Because it is actually thoughts of abundance and prosperity combined with the emotions that these thoughts create that lead to abundance and prosperity—*not* the absence of being broke.

Bottom line—not wanting to be broke isn't recognized as a good goal by the subconscious. Your subconscious will provide to you just as it is being asked, so think abundance and prosperity!

Action: If you choose to have an abundant, happy, balanced, and harmonious life—the kind and quality of life that the vast majority of people don't have—your predominant thoughts need to be focused on and in harmony with what you desire, not what is lacking.

Be Solution Oriented

> *If one is lucky, a solitary fantasy can totally transform one million realities.*
>
> [MAYA ANGELOU]

One of the keys to abundance thinking is having a solution-oriented mindset. The average person thinks of himself as positive, but he's not solution oriented. You probably know people who begin making all kinds of excuses about everything in their lives. You may have heard something like this example: "I'd like to go back to college to finish my degree, but I don't have the time."

When average people ask themselves, "Can I do this?" they base it on the circumstances they see. In the example above, this person thought about her schedule, and when asked the question, "Can I finish my college degree?" came up negative.

An abundant thinker asks different questions. Ask the question "How can I?" This simple semantics twist changes everything. It will force your mind to create a solution. Ask, "*How can I* get back to college to finish my degree?" and the subconscious will begin searching for an answer.

When you say, "I don't know what to do," you're saying that your conscious mind doesn't know what to do. That's the smallest part of you. Yet average people are victims to their conscious mind. That's all they are aware of. Your subconscious can solve hundreds of problems that your conscious mind can't.

Average people are reasonable. Reason resides in the conscious mind and has a very important function, but it's not to solve problems. Reason looks at circumstances and at your past. But all that your past tells is what beliefs you operated from. The past has nothing to do with what is possible because, luckily, you can change your beliefs.

Action: Take every situation that you are not clear on and ask yourself "How can I . . . ?" Your subconscious will find the answer!

Living Your Dream

> *The major reason for setting a goal is for what it makes of you to accomplish it. What it makes of you will always be the far greater value than what you get.*

[JIM ROHN]

Set a Goal for What It Makes of You

Set big goals that challenge you to ignite the great potential that lies within you. You will know you are pursuing your purpose in life when the dream is much bigger than you. Follow this dream to become the person you were meant to.

Planting the Thought Seeds

People often say that this or that person has not yet found himself. But the self is not something one finds; it is something one creates.

[THOMAS SZASZ]

You may better appreciate the role that the power of your thoughts plays when you learn to *consciously* direct the emotions that your thoughts ignite. Then you begin to both understand and see, in a real and tangible way, what a profound and transformational difference your individual mind power plays in the process.

Developing a crystal clear understanding as to how the power of thoughts impact *every* area of your life will serve to provide not only the desired outcomes experienced in your physical world but also unfailing and timeless wisdom that will *immensely* enhance your mental, emotional, and spiritual growth. It will add to your understanding and provide a sense of peace, well-being, and overall fulfillment in *every* aspect of life as well.

Our thoughts are the seed that will initiate the process for everything to be made "real." But, had the seed never been planted, the harvest would not and could not exist. Once the seed is planted, it does have to be nurtured in order to reach full maturity.

Action: Review your goals and dreams. Spend time each morning when you wake up and a few minutes before you go to sleep thinking about your goals and dreams.

As You Sow, So Shall You Reap

Do not be deceived, God is not mocked; for whatever a man sows, that he will also reap.

[GALATIANS 6:7]

Earl Nightingale's *Sowing and Reaping* contains a powerful and timeless thought. Let's consider the human mind to be much like farmland. The farmer has a choice to plant whatever seeds he wants, and the farmer decides to plant a seed of corn or a seed of weeds. Our minds, like the land, will return whatever we plant.

With water and attention, the soil of your mind will return a wonderful abundance of whatever you plant. The human mind is far more fertile and incredible than the land, but it works the same way. It will accept what we plant—success or failure. A solid, worthwhile goal, or doubts, fear, confusion—whatever thoughts (seeds) we plant, our minds will find a way to produce them.

The good news is we get to decide. What is it you want? Plant your goal in your mind. It is the most important decision you will ever make.

Now, all you have to do is plant your thought seed, care for it, and work steadily toward your goal, and it will become a reality.

Action: The next time someone does something unpleasant to you, ask yourself the question: Are they sowing, or am I reaping?

Seed Thoughts

We are what we think. All that we are arises with our thoughts. With our thoughts, we make the world.

[BUDDHA]

Just as you plant a seed in the soil, it must surely produce a plant of like proportion to the seed that was planted. If you were to plant crabgrass seeds, you certainly couldn't expect to produce a big beautiful oak tree. If you plant crabgrass seeds, you get crabgrass. If you plant an apple seed, you receive an apple tree.

We all know this simple universal principle. Even a young child understands this. So why would it be any different with our thoughts?

By developing an understanding of this simple principle—by becoming conscious of the consistent thoughts that *we* choose to think—we can then go to work on restructuring and implementing the power of thoughts. More specifically, you can go to work on *your thoughts* to begin to create *your life* based on your newly found knowledge and begin producing desired results.

Just as you would plant the apple seed in the ground and receive an apple tree, whatever thought seeds you plant in your mind, you will receive.

No more than you would expect a crabgrass seed to produce an oak tree can anyone expect the seed thought that create doubt, fear, lack, and limitation to produce a harvest of abundance and happiness in your life.

Action: Choose to plant thought seeds that project and create love, joy, peace, fulfillment, contentment, prosperity, etc. You will experience (reap) the harvest of your seeds that harmonize with the original seeds planted.

Thoughts on Wellness

Whatever the mind of man can conceive and believe, it can achieve.

[NAPOLEON HILL]

These same principles are what determine your health and wellness. If your thoughts are constantly focused on health and wellness in your body, you will reap a harvest of health and wellness.

It doesn't matter what the situation or circumstance, whether it is health, finances, relationships, etc. The power of thoughts is every bit as creative in health situations as it is with money matters. The power of thoughts—more specifically the power of *your* thoughts—combined with the emotional response that you choose as a result of these thoughts is equally as creative and powerful in your personal relationships as they are in any other part of your life.

Your control over the power of thoughts can only be determined by your willingness to accept the fact that it's true and become consciously aware of the thoughts *you* choose to think.

CHANGE YOUR THOUGHTS, AND YOU WILL CHANGE YOUR WORLD!

Action: Make a conscious and consistent effort, and you will develop the ability to focus the power of thoughts on creating a life far in excess of any you may have previously conceived or believed was possible for you.

To think Is to Create

With the new day comes new strength and new thoughts.

[ELEANOR ROOSEVELT]

The creative process is fixed, immutable, unwavering, consistent, and *always* perfect. Just like the law of gravity, the law of averages, and Murphy's Law, universal principles are, always have been, and always will be set and fixed. There is no wavering in their perfect and precise operation. You cannot outsmart them, hide from them, or overcome them. They are precise and exact and have existed since the beginning of time itself. They will continue to exist and produce in their precise manner into infinity.

They are not prejudiced in their implementation. It doesn't matter what your spiritual or religious beliefs are, what gender you are, what your age is, or what country you come from. They don't differentiate among people that we perceive as good or bad. They are exact and non-prejudiced in delivering to all, exactly the same, in accordance with the seeds that are planted.

Your knowledge or ignorance of them is of no consequence. They will continue to exist regardless of your awareness or lack of awareness of them. A person's belief or disbelief in their power has no effect on their operation. They will continue to operate exactly as they have since the beginning of time whether you believe in them or not.

Once introduced to or made aware of these principles, you have the *power of choice*—to do with them what you will.

We choose those thought processes. *We* choose the emotions that we experience, and *we* choose whatever events, conditions, and circumstances we create in our lives.

Action: We are always receiving an abundance of something. When you become conscious and choose to recognize the creative power of thoughts, you have the potential as well as the ability to transform your entire world.

Be-Do-Have

If you think you can do a thing or think you can't do a thing, you're right.

[HENRY FORD]

Have you ever noticed that most people live with a *do-have-be* perspective of life? Meaning that they believe that if they *do* the right things, they will have what they desire, and only then will they *be* the person who deserves those things. That can be related to material achievements, but it is also true in regard to relationships, health, and even emotional states that they wish to experience.

Do you know people who have set goals for themselves such as getting a specific kind of relationship? So they set out and *do* what they believe will help them find that "perfect" mate. They do things like go on dates, sign up for Internet dating sites, and follow all the dating advice they can in an effort to *have* the relationship that they desire. They believe that this specific relationship will allow them to *be* happy. Many people take it beyond just being happy and attach a whole list of things that they will be when they finally have that perfect relationship. They will be successful, loving, loyal, open, compassionate, a good lover, and a good partner.

What would happen if you shifted the paradigm to *be-do-have*? By *being* happy, successful, loving, loyal, open, compassionate, a good lover, and a good partner, you will begin *doing* things differently, which will allow you to *have* things you never would have had if you were running the process as a do-have-be paradigm.

Action: Begin to see yourself and to act as if your goal has already been achieved! Write in your journal about how that makes you feel.

Living Your Dream

> *Life is too short to be little.*
>
> [DISRAELI]

Have an Attitude of Gratitude

In order to create abundance, you must first acknowledge and appreciate the abundance you already have. This is an everyday activity you need to incorporate into your routine to set your creative power in motion. Gratitude is the attitude that changes everything.

To be grateful for something is to stop resisting. Resistance pushes away; gratitude and an abundance mindset attract more of themselves to you. Ask yourself daily:

- What are my current assets? (i.e. personal contacts, career, education, experience, time-management skill, etc.)
- What is great in my life right now? (i.e. family, friends, finances, health, resources, community, etc.)
- What's great about me? (i.e. specific skills, personality, passion, ambition, desire, willingness, etc.)

Belief System

They may forget what you said, but they will never forget how you made them feel.

[CARL W. BUECHNER]

The power of thoughts plays a tremendous role in determining the kind and quality of your life—period. The kind and quality of the consistent thoughts you choose define, mold, and shape the kind and quality of your life physically, financially, intellectually, emotionally, and spiritually.

To do anything, you must first believe it can be done. Believing something can be done sets the mind in motion to find a way to do it. Believing something can be done paves the way for creative solutions. When you believe something is impossible, your mind goes to work for you to prove why. The mind is a very powerful thing. When you believe, your mind finds a way to do it, believe, and you start thinking—constructively.

Building belief is having the confidence that you can do whatever you set your mind to do. Knowing *why* you want to live the life of your dreams will give you the confidence to take action.

Action: When you have your vision to live your dream life, you must believe that you will achieve it. Meditate and pray on your vision, and believe in yourself. Ask God for wisdom, guidance, and favor as He expands your territory now that you are pursuing the dream He has placed in your heart.

Is Seeing Believing?

I wouldn't have seen it if I hadn't believed it.
[MARSHALL MCLUHAN]

Faith is defined as "confident belief in the truth, value, or trustworthiness *of* a person, idea, or thing. Belief that does not rest on logical proof or material evidence."

But the conventional wisdom of the world is, "I'll believe it when I see it."

In Matthew 21:22, Jesus says, "If you believe, you will receive whatever you ask for in prayer."

He doesn't say you'll receive them *first* so you can believe them! He says *believe* and you shall *receive*.

We practice believing all day long. We don't think much about believing whether the chair will hold us up when we plop down—we just know. We have faith that the car will start up every time we turn the key—we don't necessarily have to see it happen before we believe that it will.

Believe first that you can do it. Believe in yourself and know that quitting is not an option. Know that you know that you know—you will finish what you have started! Believe first, and *then* receive.

Action: So, what do you believe? Decisions, not conditions, determine our success. Having faith that you can and will fulfill your goals and dreams will give you the confidence to pursue them with passion!

Dream, Believe, Achieve

If you don't believe in yourself, chances are no one else will.

[UNKNOWN]

The story of Roger Bannister is an inspirational one. For many years it was widely believed to be impossible for a human to run a mile (1609 meters) in under four minutes. In fact, for many years, it was believed that the four-minute mile was a physical barrier that no man could break without causing significant damage to the runner's health. The achievement of a four-minute mile seemed beyond human possibility, like climbing Mount Everest or walking on the moon.

Roger Bannister had a dream that he could break the four-minute mile. He set a goal to run the mile in less than four minutes. He trained and worked hard. On May 6, 1954, Roger Bannister was the first man to ever run the mile in less than four minutes.

So what happened to the physical barrier that prevented humans from running the four-minute mile? Was there a sudden leap in human evolution? No. It was the change in thinking that made the difference; Bannister had shown that breaking the four-minute mile was possible. Often the barriers we perceived are only barriers in our own minds. Previous runners had been held back by their beliefs and mindsets. Once that barrier was broken, other runners saw that it was possible. Sixteen runners went on to run a four-minute mile that year.

Action: Remind yourself that you are committed to pursuing your goals and dreams. You believe that you will achieve them. Now, you must be prepared to pay the price and put in massive action. Roger Bannister trained hard to achieve success—write in your journal that you are willing to do what it takes to make things happen!

Limiting Beliefs

There is nothing either good or bad except that thinking makes it so.

[SHAKESPEARE]

Our beliefs and mindsets limit or expand our world. Beliefs have power over us because we treat them as though they're true. Beliefs influence what you attempt or choose not to attempt in life. They determine what you pay attention to, how you react to difficult situations, and ultimately your attitude. Success and failure begin and end in what the mind believes is possible.

The first step you can take in influencing the world around you and realizing your potential is to *change how you think*. If Roger Bannister accepted that the four-minute mile was a physical limitation, he would never have tried to break it. Just like the runners of times past, many of the barriers that hold us back today exist only in our minds.

What are the four-minute miles that are holding you back in your personal and professional life?

Are there any role models you can learn from who are challenging existing limits?

Until we change the consistent, self-limiting thought process that creates our barriers, the exact same results will continue. This pattern will continue to repeat itself over and over and over again until we change the thought process and establish a different belief. This will automatically attract the resources or conditions required and needed for a different outcome!

Action: Again, spend some quiet time exploring the beliefs that have held you back from pursuing your dreams up to this point. How will you change your thought process?

Becoming Aware of Our Beliefs

Insanity: doing the same thing over and over again and expecting different results.

[ALBERT EINSTEIN]

It is possible to become consciously aware of our beliefs and ensure that they drive the kind of behavior that will produce the quality of life we're seeking. It's possible to realize that our beliefs tell us what to do! Once we understand that, we can start putting those beliefs in place that will tell us to have a peaceful, meaningful, enjoyable life—in other words, to achieve our personal best.

It is important that we get in touch with the beliefs and the behaviors that drive our actions. When those behaviors deliver unsatisfactory results, it only makes sense that we ought to change them for the most basic reasons: everyone wants to have satisfactory results in their lives! The only way to effectively change behavior is by changing the belief that's prompting it.

To improve the quality of your life, first identify the current belief, and then recognize the need to change the beliefs that are driving destructive behavior. Finally, do what is necessary to change them.

It is not always easy to do. Once in place, a belief—whether it's good for us or bad for us—can be stubborn and difficult to budge. If we are striving to achieve our personal best in life, both personally and professionally, we must focus on the principle-driven behaviors that will improve our quality of life. When we know what's driving us, then we're in a position to see if it will take us where we want to go. This will offer the freedom to realize our potential.

In identifying certain beliefs, we are not labeling right or wrong. They are correct or incorrect, depending on the behavior they drive and the needs that are satisfied as a result. Principle-driven behavior is driven from within, to establish beliefs that are correct for us, beliefs that in turn will drive behavior that will produce satisfying results in our individual lives.

Action: What do we really want? That's the universal question. Do we want to be a better businessperson, spouse, parent, golfer, or friend? Do we want to have better health, security or self-image? We can achieve any of these by discovering the correct belief to guide us.

Change the Limiting Beliefs

Create a vision and never let the environment, other people's beliefs, or the limits of what has been done in the past shape your decisions. Ignore conventional wisdom.

[ANTHONY ROBBINS]

We can search for correct beliefs in a wide variety of places, both from within and around—people whose success we admire and whose failures we can learn from. People we know personally or not—leaders, athletes, friends, neighbors, and our own family. If we observe their results and find we would like to duplicate them, then our task becomes a simple one of understanding the *belief that drives that behavior* and adopting it as one of our own. We can also identify and avoid the beliefs of those whose behavior we find harmful and unfulfilling.

True freedom comes beyond "borrowing" the beliefs and behaviors we admire in others; it's when we objectively identify our own beliefs that we can be in charge of ourselves. When we know that we have the authority to alter those beliefs that bring us undue stress, unhappiness, pain, and sadness—that lower our quality of life—we're in a position to truly chart our own course.

Understanding our own beliefs and knowing we have the authority to alter those beliefs can result in dramatic feelings of personal control, self-management, contentment, and inner peace. Altering our beliefs—the way we look at life—really can facilitate significant change and meaning in our lives.

Our beliefs, or personal truths, fuel us—they generate our actions or our inactions. Our beliefs can propel and move us—or inhibit and hold us back.

Action: What beliefs fuel you most? List three of your most inspiring beliefs.

Living Your Dream

> *When you have come to the edge of all light that you know and are*
> *about to drop off into the darkness of the unknown, Faith is knowing*
> *one of two things will happen: there will be something solid to stand on*
> *or you will be taught to fly.*

[PATRICK OVERTON]

Guidelines for Pursuing Your Dream Life

- Ink it! Write down all of your dreams and goals.

- Forget reality. If you knew you couldn't fail, what would you do?

- Think big! What's in the BAG? That stands for your Big Audacious Goal! What is that one thing that makes your palms sweat a little when you think of it?

- Say it in the positive. Decide what you want to move *toward,* not away from. Example: "I have a loving, respectful, and intimate relationship with my spouse," not "I want to fix my marriage."

- "I am!" State your goals in the present tense, first person. "I am a millionaire by X (date)," then your creative power will go to work producing what you declare.

- Be sure your goals are YOUR goals!

- Make sure your goals align with your values.

Positive Mental Attitude

It's your thoughts behind the words you speak that create your attitude.

[JEFFREY GITOMER]

What is a positive attitude? The simple definition is that it is the way you dedicate yourself to thinking. Interestingly, that's also the definition of a negative attitude.

A positive attitude comes from within. Positive attitude has nothing to do with what happens *to* you. *It's about what you do with, and how you react to, what happens to you.* Positive attitude comes from your ability to process thoughts in a positive way, regardless of the circumstance.

Our single most significant daily decision is our choice of attitude. It has been said that life is ten percent what happens to us and ninety percent how we respond to it. Your response is your responsibility.

Action: Think about how you wake up in the morning. Internal happiness is the beginning of positive attitude, not the achievement of it. Realize that attitude is your choice, not your circumstance. Attitude is the way you respond to the situation, not the situation itself. You have control over the way you choose and the way you respond.

Attitude Awareness

To think you can, creates the force that can.

[ORISON SWETT MARDEN]

Think about your attitude, and think about what affects it. Think about the things that negatively influence you, the things that bust your positive attitude—they're usually "the little things." It's our *decisions*, not our *conditions* that determine our attitude. Do you have negative things to say about other people? People put others down to build themselves up. Be aware of how you describe others in their absence versus if they are in your presence. Many moms tell their children, "If you have nothing nice to say, say nothing." Check your attitude when you describe situations or things. Do you look to acquiring or doing what will bring you long-term happiness? Most "things" will bring temporary joy, but long-term happiness doesn't come from things, it comes from *attitude*.

Your attitude is tested daily. Life happens. It is easy to have a good attitude on a good day, but you must be determined to have a great attitude—even through a bad time. Decisions, not conditions, determine our attitude.

Action: Take passionate action toward living your life. Don't just make it through the day, really live it! Wring every moment out of it and live each day with passion. Passion and a positive attitude are contagious. Try it; you will find others attracted to you who are just as passionate about life and living!

Attitude Is Everything

Anything your mind can conceive and believe, it can achieve.

[NAPOLEON HILL]

Think negative or think positive—it's a choice and a process. Negative is an instinctive process. *Positive thinking is a learned self-discipline that must be studied and practiced every day.*

To achieve a positive attitude, you must take physical, verbal, and mental actions every day, in every situation. Take the responsibility to control your inner thoughts and emotions. Act instead of reacting. Don't wait until something bad happens and then try to deal with it. Be proactive and make something good happen.

If you put positive in, you get positive results. Make a commitment to read from a positive book *every day*. Turn off the TV and listen to a positive thinker's recordings. Invest your time with positive people, doing positive things to grow your mind. Invest in yourself.

Action: Spend an hour a day learning anything, and in five years, you will become a world-class expert. The question you need to ask yourself is, **What will you invest your time in?**

Your Personal Life Philosophy

The Great Mentor Jim Rohn says:

- Philosophy drives attitude.
- Attitude drives actions.
- Actions drive results.
- Results drive lifestyles.
- If you don't like your lifestyle, look at your results.
- If you don't like your results, look at your actions.
- If you don't like your actions, look at your attitude.
- If you don't like your attitude, look at your philosophy.
- If you have a philosophy of service to others, and if you have a positive attitude, then you can begin to become successful and can begin to take success actions.
- Successful people do what unsuccessful people don't (won't) do. Successful people live outside their comfort zone. Successful people hang around money or things that make money. Successful people are consistent (will be there next year). Successful people stay in the fire. Successful people know how to access information. Successful people are always learning.

Action: Create a few sentences that define who you are or what you want to become, what you do and how you do it.

For example: I want to bring value to myself, my family, and other people. I strive to be the best at what I love to do. I am in it to finish and win it. I have no regrets. I have fun every day.

Smile :) and Laugh :D

Anybody can do just about anything with himself that he really wants to and makes up his mind to do. We are all capable of greater things than we realize.

[NORMAN VINCENT PEALE]

Humor is attractive. A positive attitude can be born from a strong sense of humor. How would someone describe your humor or your sense of humor? Do you think funny first? What is your first thought? How much do you smile?

In seconds, you can turn a blue mood into a good mood with a smile and laughter. Learn to laugh and you will be more positive, especially if you can learn to laugh at yourself.

A simple smile is a powerful atti-tool:

- It displays "positive" without saying a word.
- It shows your warmth.
- It shows your internal feelings externally.
- It shows you're happy.
- It shows you're open.
- It shows you're confident.
- And it sets a tone for the first spoken words.

Your smile is one of the greatest attributes and assets you can possess—and it's *free*. All you have to do is use it every minute of every day.

Action: Funny self-test: What are your first thoughts and responses? How do you react to ordinary situations? What do you say? Can you think funny? Can you create a smile? Can you elicit one? Do you laugh easily and often? Are you happy on the inside?

Attitude Fulfillment

Life isn't about finding yourself. Life is about creating yourself.
[GEORGE BERNARD SHAW]

Fulfillment is the difference between inspiration and motivation.

The benefits of a lifelong positive attitude are internal happiness, gratefulness, and thankfulness. Fulfillment begins with extended internal happiness, combined with a love of what you do, and a pride of accomplishment and achievement—the inner glow of self-assurance that creates an outward, peaceful aura.

What is fulfillment to you? Achieving the highest level in the work you love? Becoming debt free? Creating a Family Foundation Trust? Whatever it is, a positive attitude will lift it to the heights you are hoping for.

Fulfillment is not a one-time thing you get at the end of the rainbow. Fulfillment happens all the time. It's about personal accomplishment, doing something you love to do, or helping others achieve their hopes and dreams.

The attitude fulfillment comes from sustaining it. It comes from having to call on your attitude in a time of need or crisis, and it's there for you. Your attitude is fulfilling when it lifts you up in personal tragedy or helps you through health issues.

Fulfillment is wanting more but being content and at peace with what you have—being internally, and eternally, happy, regardless of circumstance or the people involved.

Action: Positive attitudes breed positive anticipation, which is a strategic advantage in your life. Look at attitude as a gift and a blessing. A gift you can give yourself and the people around you.

Living Your Dream

It is never too late to be what you might have been.

[GEORGE ELIOT]

"Act As If" Principle

Begin to act now as you will act when you reach your goal.

Example: If you were already a millionaire, how would you walk, talk, shake hands, or enter a room? Visualize yourself in the car you will drive, the house you will live in, the vacations you will take, and how much you will give to your church and charities.

If you were already an amazing spouse, how would you talk, listen, and behave?

If you were already your ideal weight, how would you walk, hold your shoulders, dress, groom, and present yourself?

Behave like you have already achieved what you want now and you will certainly become it. The only thing that separates the act from the reality is a few more planetary spins.

Spirituality & God

A faith is a necessity to a man. Woe to him who believes in nothing.

[VICTOR HUGO]

We are all born with a specific purpose to serve the world. We have all been given unique talents and special gifts that allow us the ability to fulfill that purpose. The best use of our life is to use those gifts and talents to be and do what God intended for you. Now, determining your purpose is not always easy for everyone. The best place to start is with prayer.

Most of us are amateurs at understanding the Bible and religion. You didn't create yourself, so it makes sense that the best way to find out how an invention was intended to be used is to ask the Creator or read the owner's manual for that creation's purpose! Please continue on your own personal spiritual journey in your local church, surrounded by like-minded people to fellowship and grow with. Seeking a personal relationship with our Creator, God, and reading the Bible (the owner's manual) is a good idea. He will certainly guide you to fulfill His purpose for you.

Action: "Draw near to God and he will draw near to you." (James 4:8)

The Dream Giver

*All who call on God in true faith, earnestly from the heart, will
certainly be heard, and will receive what they have asked and desired.*

[MARTIN LUTHER]

How do we determine our life's purpose? God places dreams in our
hearts. Everyone has dreams. You may have had dreams as a child that
you lost along the way. You may have a dream right now that seems
impossible to pursue. You may even feel that God forgot to give you a
dream. Often times, as we are pursuing our big dreams, we experience
obstacles and setbacks that make us feel like giving up.

You will know your purpose by following your heart's desire. Are
you willing to trade your ordinary, comfortable life to make an extra-
ordinary contribution and impact on the world? What are you giving
your life in exchange for, in order to bring joy and happiness and ful-
fillment to your life? Do you wish to create a more meaningful life of
significance?

*Action: You playing small does no one any good—what is your Big
Dream?*

What on Earth Am I Here For?

As your faith is strengthened you will find that there is no longer the
need to have a sense of control, that things will flow as they will, and
that you will flow with them, to your great delight and benefit.

[EMMANUEL TENEY]

Asking good questions is a powerful place to begin. The answer might be, *It's not about you.*

Consider the possibility that your purpose of life is much greater than your own personal fulfillment and happiness. It is far greater than your family, your job, or your ambitions. When you begin with God, you realize you were born by His purpose and for His purpose.

People have pondered the meaning of life for thousands of years. We can begin pursuing our dreams when we take our eyes off ourselves—What do *I* want to do? What should *I* do with *my* life? What are *my* goals and *my* dreams for *my* future? Focusing on ourselves may *start* the process, but it will never really reveal God's perfect plan for our lives.

We all struggle with our identity, wondering, Who am I? We all wonder about our importance, asking, Do I matter? Then we consider our impact and want to know, What is my purpose in life?

When you know what God wants you to do, the blessings come from actually doing what you were created to accomplish. What dream in your heart will take you from success to significance?

Action: Take time to pray: "Ask, and it shall be given you; seek and
you shall find; knock, and it shall be opened to you." (Matthew 7:7)

Finding Purpose

Faith has to do with things that are not seen and hope with things that are not at hand.

[THOMAS AQUINAS]

You can easily get confirmation from other people about what you are good at—just ask for honest and open feedback from someone you trust.

Look at your past experiences and results to learn what you are good at. Review your life to make a list of your past mistakes and accomplishments—this will help you determine your specialty. If you are doing what you were designed to do, you will be happy and at peace. What do you truly love to do?

Do not compare yourself to others! You were created to do something totally unique and already have everything you need to accomplish the perfect plan God created you for.

We will have complete joy in our lives when we choose our daily activities based on whether or not the task is in line with the purpose God has for us.

Living for your purpose, on purpose, is the only way to live! Living for your purpose instead of just existing to survive is a powerful paradigm change.

Action: Are you doing what you love to do? Creating your best life takes energy. Your passions will give you the energy to do the work you need to do to create the life you most desire. If you are still contemplating your life's purpose, ask yourself a few questions: What do I have the most fun doing? What do I do that causes me to lose all track of time? What inspires me the most?

Writing Your Mission Statement

Every tomorrow has two handles. We can take hold of it with the handle of anxiety or the handle of faith.

[HENRY WARD BEECHER]

Purpose statement: Writing down your intentions will clarify your purpose and direction for your life. Think about the path for your life, time, and money. This will allow you to connect with your own unique purpose and experience a profound satisfaction as you fulfill it.

Define success for you: Success can be defined as the progressive realization of a worthwhile goal or dream. Define what you believe is important and what really matters. Clarify your roles—purpose will never change. Express how you are unique and what you can do to serve others.

Identify your core values and beliefs: Develop a list of attributes that you believe identify who you are and what your priorities are. Your personal mission statement is an articulation of what you're all about and what success looks like to *you*.

Action: Give yourself some time to consider your purpose and what is truly important to you. Write down all of your thoughts, feelings, and ideas. Tomorrow we will develop your personal mission statement.

Big Questions for A Big Dream Life

Faith is taking the first step even when you don't see the whole staircase.

[Martin Luther King, Jr.]

Asking yourself these questions can help you determine your personal mission statement!

- How will my past successes contribute to my future?
- Can I identify a common theme or pattern in what I do best?
- What will be the center of my life? What am I going to live for?
- What kind of character will I have? What kind of person am I going to be? Be specific.
- What kind of service will I be to my family, my employer, my friends, my community, and the world around me? What abilities, passion, and talents will help me make a difference?
- What does my life communicate? When I narrow my list of core values and beliefs down to the one most important to me, what do I stand for?
- What dreams and goals can I identify that utilize my skills and talents to assist in the progression of my life's purpose?

Action: Write your mission statement. A personal mission statement is personal, but if you want to truly see whether you have been honest in developing your mission statement, share the results of this process with one or more people close to you. Ask for their feedback.

Living Your Dream

I'm not afraid . . . I was BORN for this!

[JOAN OF ARC]

Create Balance

Your goals become the road map by which you navigate the direction of your life. Too often people focus exclusively on one area of their life at the sacrifice of every other area.

Be aware of where you are in all areas of your life to check to see if you are directing your life in a balanced manner. Areas to keep in mind include physical, financial, business, lifestyle, mental, spiritual, family, and relationships.

What good will achieving financial and professional goals be without the health to enjoy it? The key is to be sure you are giving appropriate attention and setting worthy goals in all of the important areas of your life. True achievement and life fulfillment comes when you are happily pursuing success at home and in the marketplace. How will you create and live a healthy lifestyle physically, emotionally, intellectually, financially, and spiritually?

Positive Self Talk

The strongest single factor in prosperity consciousness is self-esteem.
Believing you can do it, believing you deserve it, believing you will
get it.

[JERRY GILLIES]

Positive affirmations (self-suggestion) are a vehicle of communication from our conscious to our subconscious mind. The dominating thoughts of our conscious mind, positive or negative, will influence our beliefs. Our thoughts lead to emotions, and a strong emotional connection will inspire our actions to create results. We can influence the thoughts that enter our subconscious through self-suggestion.

Our five senses are constantly being bombarded with impressions that our conscious mind must sort through—the stimuli get either rejected or passed on to the subconscious mind. So basically, the conscious awareness serves as a type of outer guard to the approach of the subconscious. For example, if a bee lands on your hand, when you see it or feel it, you will have an emotional reaction and leap into action to create the result of getting the bee off your hand.

We have absolute control over the content that reaches our subconscious mind through our five senses. The question we are faced with now is whether or not we *choose* to always *exercise* that control.

Action: Be aware of what you are saying to yourself as you go through your daily activities. Notice your use of self-control (or lack thereof) in certain challenging situations today.

Positive Affirmations

Every moment of one's existence one is growing into more or retreating into less.

[NORMAN MAILER]

Positive affirmations are positive sentences we repeat many times in order to impress upon our subconscious mind and trigger it into action. These sentences describe a situation that we desire to happen, and we repeat them many times—with conviction, attention, and feelings.

As an example, imagine that you are walking with your friends on a track. They are planning to walk twenty laps of the track, something you have never done before. You desire the respect of your friends, and you want to show them that you can walk twenty laps too. You start walking, and at the same time you keep repeating in your mind, "I can do it, I can do it . . ." You keep thinking and believing that you are going to complete the twenty laps. What are you actually doing? You are repeating positive affirmations.

Oftentimes, people repeat *negative* sentences and statements about the diverse situations in their lives, and consequently they bring upon themselves undesirable situations. Affirmations work both ways—to build and to destroy. They are a kind of a neutral power. It is the *way* we use them that determines whether they are going to bring good or harmful results.

Action: Just simply knowing that your thoughts are powerful and you can control what you think about will be a game changer for you. Throughout the day, repeat positive affirmations to yourself. Write how well your day went in your journal.

Creative Visualization

> *Realize that true happiness lies within you. Waste no time and effort*
> *searching for peace and contentment and joy in the world outside.*
> *Remember that there is no happiness in having or in getting, but only*
> *in giving. Reach out, share, smile, and hug. Happiness is a perfume*
> *you cannot pour on others without getting a few drops on yourself.*
>
> [Og Mandino]

Affirmations are similar to creative visualization. The repeated words build mental images and scenes in our minds. The words help to focus us on the goal, object, or situation we want to achieve or create. Frequent repetitions make the subconscious mind accept the words and images as truth, and then they influence and affect the way we think, act, and behave.

The conscious mind—the mind you think with—starts this process, and then the subconscious mind takes charge. This means that the most frequent thoughts that pass through your mind ultimately affect your activities and your life.

Affirmations work like commands we give to a computer. They influence us, other people, events, and circumstances. With our words, we have the power to influence the people we meet, our circumstances, and the events we encounter.

Action: Changing your thought process, saying positive affirmations, and asking the right questions of our subconscious is not always easy. But the more aware you are and the more focused you become, the easier it will be. Say positive words out loud to yourself in your bathroom mirror in the morning and before going to bed every day. This may be awkward at first, but once it becomes a habit, you will be amazed at how powerful you will feel!

Repetition

Even if you are on the right track, you will get run over if you just sit there.

[WILL ROGERS]

Sometimes our affirmations work fast, but more often they need time. Repeating positive affirmations for a few minutes and then thinking negatively *neutralizes* the effects of the positive words. You have to refuse negative thoughts; otherwise you will not attain positive results.

We often repeat affirmations without even being aware of the process. We use them when we tell ourselves that we can't do something, that we are too lazy, or when we believe we are going to fail. The subconscious mind always accepts and follows what we tell it. The same principle is at work when we say to ourselves that we *can* do it as when we say we *cannot,* when we say we are going to succeed and when we keep saying that we are going to fail. It is the same power working both ways. Why not choose the positive over the negative— what do you have to lose?

It may be easier to repeat affirmations that are short and simple. Repeat them when your mind is not engaged in something in particular, such as when you are commuting to work, waiting in line, walking, etc. Repeat them specifically when you wake in the morning and before falling asleep at night.

There should be no physical, emotional, or mental tension while repeating them. The stronger your concentration, the more faith you have in what you are doing, and the more feelings you put into the act—the stronger and faster will be your results.

Action: The power of positive thoughts and words is immense and influences your health, finances, relationships, and overall happiness in life. You can always tell if you are thinking and stating positive affirmations by the way you feel. If you feel deflated, dejected, and devalued, you are probably sending the wrong messages to your subconscious. On the other hand, if you feel positive and optimistic, you are on the right track.

How to Create Positive Affirmations

God is glorified, not by our groans, but our thanksgivings; and all good thought and good action claim a natural alliance with good cheer.

[EDWIN PERCY WHIPPLE]

It is very important to choose only positive affirmations. If, for example, you want to lose weight, do *not* say, "I am not fat, I am losing weight." By saying this sentence, you are repeating to your subconscious mind that you *are* fat. The word *losing* also evokes negative images. It is better to state the positive results you desire by saying, "My body is athletic and weighs the right and healthy weight." Such words evoke positive images in the mind.

It is important to affirm using the *present* tense, not the future tense. Saying "I will be rich" means that you intend to be rich one day—in the indefinite future. You are actually telling yourself that *someday* you will be rich—just not now. It is better and more effective to say (and also feel), "I am wealthy and I live in abundance," and let the subconscious mind work overtime to make this happen now, in the present.

As to results, sometimes they may come fast, and at other times they may take more time to manifest. Achieving results through the power of affirmations depends on how much time, energy, faith, and feelings you invest in your affirmations, on how big or small your goal is, and on how strong your desire is.

By using the power of affirmations, you state what you *want* to be true in your life. You see reality, as you want it to be. For a while, you ignore your current circumstances and your doubts and concentrate on creating a different reality.

Action: Positive affirmations will lead to a positive attitude. A positive attitude is very important to being successful and happy. Have you ever noticed that popular and successful people think and act with a positive attitude? That does more than anything else toward getting you whatever you want out of life, because those who are in positions to make things happen for you will want to be around you and want to work with you to help make your dreams a reality.

Sample Affirmations to Put in Use

You've got to win in your mind before you win in your life.

[JOHN ADDISON]

- I am healthy and happy.
- Wealth is pouring into my life.
- I have many friends and favor with others.
- I am getting wealthier each day.
- My body is the ideal weight and strong.
- I have an abundance of energy.
- I study and comprehend quickly and easily.
- I am calm and relaxed in every situation.
- My thoughts are under my control.
- I radiate love and happiness.
- I am surrounded by love.
- I have the perfect job for me.
- I am living in the house of my dreams.
- I have good and loving relations with my spouse.
- I have a wonderful satisfying career.
- I have the means to travel whenever I want to.
- I am successful in whatever I do.
- Everything is getting better every day.

Action: Having a positive attitude is a choice you make each morning and will make whatever you do easier and more enjoyable. When you believe that each moment is perfect regardless of its outcome, it will help you get through the bad times even stronger and more determined to succeed. Decide today what your positive affirmations will be tomorrow morning.

Living Your Dream

> *Our own Self-Talk creates the words that create the visual pictures for us. All we have to do is begin by creating the right words. When we do, the internal picture of the goal follows naturally.*

[SHAD HELMSTETTER]

Don't Procrastinate One More Minute!

Really do it! Seize the amazing potential that has been dormant inside you; dust off the dreams that have been given to you as your purpose. You have the formula to achieve any outrageous and ambitious dream you can conceive! It is now up to you!

Courageous

> *Be strong, vigorous, and very courageous. Be not afraid, neither be*
> *dismayed, for the Lord your God is with you wherever you go.*
>
> [JOSHUA 1:9]

New things always seem frightening. If we waited until we were no longer afraid before we try to do something we've never done before, we probably wouldn't accomplish much. Successful people know that they need to face their fears with courage and take action *despite* the fear. You can learn to "do it afraid."

You will experience the most thrilling experiences of your life just outside of your comfort zone! Think about the times you have taken that exhilarating ride on a roller coaster or went skydiving or bungee jumping or asked someone out on a date. Were you afraid? Yes! Were you glad you did it? *Yes!*

Need more evidence that a little fear is good to get you going? Just look at the popularity of NASCAR racing, boxing, contact sports, horror movies, and extreme sports. That "need for speed" and excitement is born in us!

Making the decision to pursue your dreams will put you in a position to be afraid, and it will give you the opportunity to be courageous. When you think about pursuing your dream life, do you feel that little tickle of fear/exhilaration in your gut? *Excellent!*

Action: Make a list of the times you have been afraid and were courageous.

Fearless

Things are only impossible until they're not.
[JEAN-LUC PICARD]

Courage is the ability to overcome fear. Let's look at the definition of the word *fear*:

> From the Greek *phóbos,* meaning "fear" or "morbid fear"; a distressing negative sensation induced by a perceived threat. It is a basic survival mechanism occurring in response to a specific stimulus, such as pain or the threat of danger.

In short, fear is the ability to recognize danger and flee from it or confront it, also known as the fight or flight response.

We are not born with courage, but we are not born with fear either. Maybe some of our fears are brought on by our own experiences, by what someone has told us, or even by what we've heard or read. Some fears are valid, like walking alone in a bad part of town at two o'clock in the morning. But once we learn to handle that situation (try to avoid that area of town), we won't need to live in fear of it any longer.

Fears, even the most basic ones, can totally destroy our ambitions. Fear can destroy relationships. Fear, if left unchecked, can destroy our lives. Fear is one of the many enemies lurking inside us.

We can develop the skill of courage to do battle with the enemy of fear. Fight your fears! Build your courage to fight what's holding you back and what's keeping you from your goals and dreams. Be courageous in your life and in your pursuit of the things you want and the person you are becoming.

Action: When you think about pursuing your dream, what are you afraid of?

Some Internal Fears

> *Courage is like a muscle. We strengthen it with use.*
>
> [RUTH GORDON]

Fear of failure or fear of success will keep us paralyzed in mediocrity. *Indifference* is the absence of compulsion to or toward one thing or another. Some people say, "Ho-hum, let it slide. I'll just drift along." But here's one problem with drifting: we can't drift our way to the top of the mountain.

The fear of what others think will cause indecision. *Indecision* is the thief of opportunity and enterprise. It will steal our chances for a better future. This is a fear that will paralyze us and keep us from taking any action.

Doubt is the fear of believing, and doubt will destroy your life and your chances of success. Sure, there's room for healthy skepticism. We can't believe everything. But we also can't let doubt take over. Many people doubt the past, doubt the future, doubt each other, doubt the leadership, doubt the possibilities, and doubt the opportunities. Worse of all, they doubt themselves.

Don't worry—be happy! We all tend to *worry* a little. Just don't let it take control. Instead, let it warn you. Worry can be useful. If you step off the curb in New York City and a taxi is coming, you've got to worry.

Over-caution is the timid approach to life. Timidity is not a virtue (unlike humility—they are different). In fact, it can be an illness. If you give it freedom in your life, it'll conquer you. Timid people don't get ahead in life. They don't advance and grow and become powerful.

Action: Where in your life are you playing it safe?

Strong, Courageous & Firm

> *Be strong, courageous, and firm; fear not nor be in terror before them, for it is the Lord your God Who goes with you; He will not fail you or forsake you.*
>
> [DEUTERONOMY 31:6]

Do you know what it means to be firm? It means to stick to what you know is right without letting anything or anyone talk you out of it. Your dream is yours. *Believe.*

Get real. Face the fears that have been holding you back. Do you want to stay where you are, or do you get a feeling of exhilaration at the thought of living your dream life? Fear is an emotion and *courage is a skill you can learn to conquer fear. Here's how:*

Know that you don't have to be alone. Partnership is powerful! Find a mentor, friend, and accountability partner that will offer you wisdom, guidance, faith, and encouragement along the way.

Pack lightly. You may need to unload some unnecessary baggage that may slow you down before you set off on your journey. Let go of the past and leave your fears at the curb.

Are you properly nourished? Where are you being fed? Feed your body and mind the proper essential nutrients that will prepare you for this wonderful journey. Read, listen, and participate. Don't let your engine run out of fuel just before the finish line. Cut out the hurtful negativity in your life.

You can gain confidence and courage by occasionally looking back on where you've been. Mountain climbers are advised to not look up when they stop to rest; wise climbers look down at where they've been. This will keep you from getting overwhelmed by the "what if's" and psyching yourself out. The courage gained from seeing how far you've come will be the motivation to keep you going.

Action: Follow your path to success. Goals are dreams with a date attached. The goals you set are the map you follow to take you to your dream destination. Successful people follow the map but will make adjustments along the way.

Doing It Afraid

Fall seven times, stand up eight.

[JAPANESE PROVERB]

When you fall—and you will—you must get back up. If you don't you could endanger yourself or your dream. Set your eyes on the prize and keep on going.

It helps to council with someone who has gone down a similar path. It may empower you to realize that you are not the first person to take this on—someone has climbed your mountain before you and if they can do it, so can you!

Enjoy the journey. Yes, during your life's adventure you may have times of incredible difficulty, but it will also be incredibly rewarding. Take time to pause along the way to cherish God's handiwork, admire your own accomplishments, interact with other dreamers, celebrate your successes, encourage others, and reflect on the challenges of the day. Are you enjoying the journey?

Action: Think about your dream life. Why haven't you achieved it? Has fear been holding you back? Why is this dream important to you? What meaning will it add to your life? Now imagine yourself living the life of your dreams. Realize that pursuing your dream life may be the most challenging experience of your lifetime. Expect the best and be prepared to grow and learn throughout the adventure!

F.E.A.R & Risk

> *Success doesn't come to you. You go to it.*
> [MARVA COLLINS]

Let's look at another great definition of fear:

False
Expectations/Evidence
Appearing
Real

Action cancels fear. When facing a challenge or when you feel like you are taking a big risk, ask yourself the following questions:

- What is the worst that can happen if I take on this fearful challenge and fail?
- What is the best outcome I can imagine when I take this on and succeed?
- What is most likely to happen if I go for it?
- If you can survive the worst case scenario, you can get excited about taking on any challenge. This is creating a calculated risk!

Action: Take your biggest "impossible dream" and write down your feelings to the questions above. Are you ready to go for it?

Living Your Dream

There is much in the world to make us afraid. There is much more in our faith to make us unafraid.

[FREDERICK W. CROPP]

Fruit That Lasts

Some days things just seem to go right. We helped our friend talk through an issue that's been bothering her. We encouraged a coworker. The laundry is done. We drew a hopscotch grid on the sidewalk and hopped along with our kids. Inspiration hit, and we tried a new recipe for dinner—and everyone loved it! Why do we find satisfaction from such days?

Perhaps it's because we've been producing "fruit" that lasts. These great days may be few and far between, but they help us cling to what's important.

In her address to the 1990 graduating class of Wellesley College, then–First Lady Barbara Bush said, "At the end of your life, you'll never regret not having passed one more test, not winning one more verdict, or not closing one more deal. You will regret times not spent with a husband, a friend, a child, or a parent."

Love, Joy & Peace

But the fruit of the Spirit is love, joy, peace, patience, kindness, goodness, faithfulness, gentleness, self-control.

[GALATIANS 5:22]

How do you see yourself? How do you look at the obstacles in your way? If we feel we are nothing, it will be hard to accomplish much in life. We will probably shrink back in fear from every challenge.

Faith is being sure of the things we hope for and knowing that something is real even if we do not see it. First, you must imagine yourself living your dream life and make the *decision* to pursue your goals and dreams. Next, you must believe in yourself and have the faith that you are already equipped with everything you need to succeed. Now it is time to take action!

What is it that we must really pursue? Love, joy, and peace. Love is the greatest thing in the world! When we do all things in love, we will find joy in life and have peace in all we do.

Action: To have what you have never had you must do what you have never done! **This Is Your Year** *to create the life of your dreams! Can you do it? YES! Will you?*

Love, Love, Love

A loving heart is the beginning of all knowledge.

[THOMAS CARLYLE]

Love is the greatest thing in life and should be the main focus in everything we do. We seek many things during our lifetime, hoping to find fulfillment in them. But without love, these things fall short of the desired goal. When we put our time and energy into things that do not fulfill us, we feel frustrated.

God is love, and He wants us to love one another. We can only truly love others when we receive the love He has for us. When we know we are loved unconditionally, we will have the confidence to express love to others. How do we best express love?

Love *gives.*

By pursuing the dream God has placed in your heart, you are giving your best gift ever to the world. In the process of fulfilling your dream life, you will "bump" into other people, which may inspire and empower them to begin pursuing their dream!

So, you demonstrate your love to God and to the world by pursuing your goals and dreams.

Action: When was the last time you simply "went with your gut" and made a decision to take action? Trust your instincts; listen to that still small voice inside of you. Ask yourself "How can I do this?" Then, Just Do It!

Joy to the World

When I let go of what I am, I become what I might be.

[LAO TZUE]

It is really easy to find things to worry about. Perhaps if we could learn to laugh a little more, our burdens would be much lighter. In our fast-paced society, we are constantly being updated on all the happenings in the world—with very little good news, it seems. There is not a great deal to laugh about, so we will need to look for things to chuckle about on purpose!

We need to laugh and have a good time as often as possible. You must look for the good around you. What brings you joy? Do you begin each day determined to be joyful and of good cheer?

What you invest your precious time in will determine your joy, peace, satisfaction, and contentment each day. The world is filled with empty people who are trying to satisfy the void in their lives with the latest-model car, a promotion at work, a vacation, or some other thing. Their efforts to find fulfillment in *things* never work. It is sad that so many people waste their entire lives and never realize it.

Be encouraged to find joy in creating the balance in your life—spiritually, emotionally, intellectually, physically, and professionally. Pursuing your dream is a step in the right direction.

Action: In our high-stress, fast-paced society everyday life can create an adrenaline rush! It is not healthy to live this way. Stress will kill you. Where can you reduce pressure and stress in your life? Close your eyes and imagine living your dream life. How does that make you feel?

Joy & Happiness

There are those who give with joy, and that joy is their reward.

[KHALIL GIBRAN]

Laughter is the best medicine. We must consciously nurture and release joy in our lives. Every day we are given is a gift. We should enjoy it fully and not waste it.

Joy is powerful. Find strength in the good around you. When you become a blessing to others and give of yourself, you will naturally feel joyful. When we receive something, we only get the gift; but when we give, we receive the joy of giving. Nothing releases supernatural joy in our lives more than being a blessing to other people.

Selfishness and self-centeredness turn our focus in on ourselves and block our joy, but giving does just the opposite. People are happy when they are reaching out to others. Be a blessing, be happy, and rejoice on purpose, and you will enjoy a life in abundance.

Learn to enjoy where you are on the way to where you're going. You will enjoy the journey when you seek joy and the freedom to laugh and enjoy life, love people, and be unafraid to step out and try new things.

Action: If you're not happy with your life, now is a great time to look at the reasons why. Why are you unhappy? Are you lonely? Disappointed? Scared? Feel rejected? Unworthy? Angry? Harboring regrets? Take a good long look at what you're really feeling. When you acknowledge it, you can change it.

Peace

> *Imagine all the people living life in peace. You may say I'm a dreamer, but I'm not the only one. I hope someday you'll join us, and the world will be as one.*
>
> [JOHN LENNON]

Are you anxious or worried today? Peace of mind must precede peace in every other area of our lives. Think about what you are thinking about. When we allow our minds to wander and we think way too much about everything we have to do, we push ourselves out of peace and into turmoil. We can become overwhelmed when we think about the future and the responsibilities we will have.

We can't change the past, but we can learn from it. We can plan for the future, but in reality we only have today. So be here *now*! Slow down on your way to your destination and let your mind lead you into peace.

When you are in pursuit of your purpose in life and working on fulfilling your goals and dreams, let peace be your guide. People who are living the life of their dreams (or on the way to living their dream life) are happier and experience more joy and peace in life. When you are using your built-in knowledge and resources in the work that you do, you will find peace as you make progress. You will know it is wrong to sit idle and watch life pass by. Idle people do not possess fulfillment in life. Doers will reap the rewards and blessing as they manage their God-given resources.

Action: Anxiety and faith cannot occupy the same space. Peace comes with a strong faith. The process of faith comes as you gain knowledge, with knowledge comes understanding; we acquire wisdom when applying understanding. With wisdom you find the courage to put your faith to work to overcome your fears. Where in your life do you need this most?

Peace of Mind

Happiness is a by-product. You cannot pursue it by itself.

[SAM LEVENSON]

Have you found that when you are at peace with a decision you've made, good comes to you? Nothing is worth anything if we do not have peace. Money, fame, a prestigious job—all are no good if we do not have peace. Do you know people who spend their lives trying to climb the ladder of success, and with every rung they lose more peace because of the pressure? Everything about their lives is consumed with the stress of trying to play all the games to keep the job. Then their health is affected when they don't have peace of mind. Without peace, our lives are full of confusion and chaos, but when we are at peace, we have a good thing.

Follow your heart as you follow your dream and you will find the peace you desire. We will be content and find peace when we make the time for what's important to us, for what we really want to be doing, for spending time with loved ones, and for doing things we're passionate about.

Action: Where in your life can you slow down and reduce stress? Make peace a priority in your life.

Living Your Dream

> *Keep your fears to yourself but share your courage with others.*
>
> [ROBERT LOUIS STEVENSON]

Personal Development

The person you are becoming. Take some time every day to reflect about the person you desire to become one year from now, and then start thinking and acting that way *right now*. You are making an investment in your self and your future when you really apply yourself and commit to personal growth and learning. You can give your best effort and make the decision to do the most important activities in your life on a daily basis.

Relationships

> *Watch your thoughts; they become words. Watch your words; they become actions. Watch your actions; they become habits. Watch your habits; they become character. Watch your character; it becomes your destiny.*
>
> [UNKNOWN]

Relationships are the key to making almost anything happen. They are the foundation to the quality of our lives and to the results we get.

A small boy and girl were building a sand castle on the beach. They spent hours building towers, walls, and a moat. As they were building, the tide crept slowly in. Suddenly, a big wave wiped it all away.

An adult nearby felt sorry for them because of all the work they had put into building the castle, until the two children held hands and ran off together, laughing as they scampered down the beach.

It was then that the adult realized a simple truth: it is fun building empires, but the lasting fun is in having friends you can continue to laugh with and be with long after all that you have spent your life building has washed away.

Action: Make a list of all the people in your life you are thankful for and whom you love.

Relationships Are the Key

We are cups, constantly and quietly being filled. The trick is, knowing how to tip ourselves over and let the beautiful stuff out.

[RAY BRADBURY]

Look around at anything manmade. Consider something small, like a vase holding flowers on your table. How many people do you suppose it took to get that vase to your table? There were people in manufacturing, as well as those in packaging and shipping. Supervisors and secretaries answered phones, salespeople sold the product to stores, and truck drivers delivered. There were those who invested in the company, and on and on. All these people were working in relation to each other with one goal in mind—to get that vase to your table.

Can you begin to see the interconnectedness in life and the importance of mastering relationships? Being "people smart" can make up for a lack of knowledge in many other areas.

Being aware of negative thought processes that are destructive to our professional and personal relationships will allow us to make adjustments in our behavior. The key to achieving high-quality, positive, constructive relationships is learning and growing and changing.

We will take a look at the destructive thought process in relationships—resentment, resistance, and revenge. Being aware that we all think this way starts the process of renewal.

Action: You could make someone's day by simply letting them know you appreciate them in a minute. Give at least one compliment every day!

Resentment

Anger is a person's last desperate attempt to avoid responsibility and blame the situation on someone or something else.

[BRIAN KLEMMER]

Resentment is any negative emotional reaction to what we think has been said or done. Common emotions include: anger, frustration, sadness, jealousy, and hate.

We experience resentment on a daily basis: someone cuts you off in traffic, you don't get a promotion at your job, someone you love gets diagnosed with a disease, and an infinite number of other ways.

Resentment is a natural part of life. In fact, if you do not experience resentment, you are emotionally numb. Thousands of children starve to death every day. How can you not feel resentment, unless you are numb?

Others have been programmed that resentment is inherently bad, so they think there is something wrong with them when they experience resentment. The truth is that resentment occurs in any relationship, no matter how good it is.

The way you handle resentment can turn your life around. It can also destroy if it leads you to *resistance*.

Action: The real question is this: How will you handle resentment?

Resistance

> *I accept relationship itself as my primary teacher about myself, other people, and the mysteries of the universe.*
>
> [GAY HENDRICKS]

Resistance is cutting off communication or putting up a wall. We resist in many ways. For example, if a parent and teen have a disagreement (resentment), and the teen shuts the door to her room and the parent walks away, you have resistance. They are not talking to each other. They are resisting each other.

What you resist persists. Most often, we resist something in order to stay in or gain control. When we are being pushed, we have a natural instinct to push back and say, "It shouldn't be this way." But what you resist persists. It prolongs what you don't want. We always pay a price for resistance!

Think of a time when a boss, employee, parent, child, or lover pushed you. Perhaps they tried emotionally or factually to prove you wrong. When you push back, this only makes matters worse. It prolongs what you don't want.

When we face the reality of the situation and redirect our efforts to find a solution, take the objection ahead and not resist the problem, we can actually create an environment of gaining success for the relationship.

Action: Who or what are you resisting? What price are you paying for this resistance? Think about how you can protect yourself and not resist at the same time.

Revenge

> *Namaste. I honor the place in you where the entire universe resides . . .*
> *a place of light, of love, of truth, of peace, of wisdom. I honor the place*
> *in you where when you are in that place and I am in that place there is*
> *only one of us.*
>
> [MOHANDAS K. GANDHI]

Revenge is the attempt to get even or settle the score. The key word in this definition is *attempt*. You can't really get even, because it is impossible to do so. You can fight back, and the person you are fighting can resent it, resist you, and seek revenge—which you feel you have to resist. It is an endless, destructive spiral. You can't get even.

Resentment, resistance, and revenge hurt *you*. What you put out, you get back. What you sow is what you reap. What goes around comes around. That's the law on the street as well as a divine law.

Do you know children who get mad at their parents and try to get even by getting bad grades or doing drugs? The child pays an incredible price to "get even." When you are operating in resentment, resistance, and revenge you are headed for destruction. Getting upset is unavoidable, but falling into this cycle, you will pay a higher price than you can imagine for this destructive behavior.

Action: Who do you love enough that you will stop the resent, resist, revenge cycle with today?

Solutions

Treasure your relationships, not your possessions.

[ANTHONY J. D'ANGELO]

The solutions are not comfortable; it may mean changing behavior patterns that feel familiar. But why live your life governed by what you feel like doing when you could make choices based on what *really* matters to you?

The giving solution is giving to get yourself out of the resentment, resisting, and revenge cycle. Giving is not about manipulating others; you simply give because you don't want anyone you care for to pay the price of the cycle above. Give because there is a universal law that says what you put out, you will get back—but don't expect it to always come back from the original source.

Imagine being in a sleeping bag in a log cabin and it's snowing outside. The air around you is really cold, and you can see your breath as you peer out. You realize it is so cold because there is no fire in the wood stove.

You look around and notice there is no firewood in the cabin. It is snowing outside, and it is so cold in the cabin you can't will yourself to get up out of your sleeping bag. You try to make a deal with the stove. "Warm me up, and then I will gladly go outside and get some wood."

Sound crazy? We do this frequently in our relationships: "Spend more time with me (stove, warm me up), and I will show more love to you (I'll get some wood)." The other person is thinking, "Become more loving to me, and I will spend more time with you."

Action: If you were going to die today, who would you call, and what would you say? OK—why are you waiting?

Living Your Dream

Trust is the glue of life. It's the most essential ingredient in effective communication. It's the foundational principle that holds all relationships.

[STEPHEN R. COVEY]

Relationships

Cultivate them like a garden. Don't neglect. Can you make a list of people you want to reach out to? Maybe you've been busy and have been meaning to make some calls to people who are important to you. Spend your time on what is most important—building relationships should be at the top of your list. Are you taking care of the people you care most about?

Forgiveness

> *Whatever is begun in anger ends in shame.*
> [BEN FRANKLIN]

Are you haunted by something that happened in your past? Whether someone wronged you or you made a decision you regret, maybe you have unresolved anger or resentment. What you may not realize is that powerful, self-destructive emotions like anger, hate, and resentment can cause you to pay an incredibly high price. Forgiveness is the way to get your power back.

There is power in forgiveness. Forgiving the people who hurt you, even if they don't ask for it, is what you do for *yourself*, not for other people. When you forgive, it doesn't mean that you approve of what's happened. Rather, it means that you're giving yourself permission to move on with your life.

Generally, forgiveness is a decision to let go of resentment and thoughts of revenge. The act that hurt or offended you may always remain a part of your life, but forgiveness can lessen its grip on you and help you focus on other, positive parts of your life. Forgiveness can even lead to feelings of understanding, empathy, and compassion for the one who hurt you.

Forgiveness doesn't mean that you deny the other person's responsibility for hurting you, and it doesn't minimize or justify the wrong. You can forgive the person without excusing the act. Forgiveness brings a kind of peace that helps you go on with life.

Action: Be acutely aware of your thoughts, feelings, and actions. Remember the law of sowing and reaping.

A Different Person

> Forgiveness is to set a prisoner free, and to realize the prisoner was you.
>
> [CORRIE TEN BOOM]

Recognize that feelings of hate, anger, or resentment toward others are the stuff of which emotional prisons are made. You become trapped in an emotional complex of such pain and agony that negative energy begins to dominate.your entire life.

These negative feelings are such powerful influences that once they enter your heart, they are present in all of your relationships. They change who you are, and they contaminate what you have to give. They truly do make you become a different person.

Give some thought to the relationships in your life. You can either contribute to or contaminate these relationships by what you bring to them. If you have unresolved anger or resentment, you must learn that you do not have to be angry just because you have the right to be.

You cannot give away what you do not have. Think about this in the literal sense. No matter how much you might like to, you can't give away a million dollars if you don't have it. Similarly, you cannot give pure and accepting love from a pure and accepting heart if you have neither. If the love in your heart is contaminated with hate and anger, then that is the heart from which all of your emotions spring.

Action: Explore unfinished emotional business and the times you have said, "I can't forgive, because they aren't sorry and they don't deserve or even want my forgiveness." Realize that forgiveness is a choice. You have to choose it.

Choose to Forgive

> *To be forgiven is such sweetness that honey is tasteless in comparison with it. But yet there is one thing sweeter still, and that is to forgive. As it is more blessed to give than to receive, so to forgive raises a stage higher in experience than to be forgiven.*
>
> [CHARLES SPURGEON]

People make decisions based not on the truth, but on *their own perception* of the truth. We know and experience this world only through the perceptions that we create. Our emotional life is based on how we choose to feel. Others can provide an event or behavior for us to react to, but it is up to you to *choose* how you feel about them.

Ultimately, forgiveness of those who have transgressed against you, or those you love, is not about them; it is about you. Forgiveness is about doing whatever it takes to preserve the power to create your own emotional state.

Don't give your power away. The pain of what happened is inevitable, but continuing to suffer is *optional*. The only person you can control is you. By constantly reliving the pain of what happened, you are giving your power away to the person who wronged you.

Don't cling to negative feelings. Anger is nothing more than an outward sign of hurt, fear, guilt, grief, or frustration. While the pain may never completely disappear, forgiveness can help you release the anger and bring those in your life closer to you.

Action: Who do you need to forgive today? Start with yourself.

Real Forgiveness

Anger makes you smaller, while forgiveness forces you to grow beyond what you were.

[CHERIE CARTER SCOTT]

You will know that you have truly forgiven another's trespasses when you don't feel the need to punish by telling other's about what happened. Sometimes we feel the need to share about the perceived injustice because we are afraid the person will get away with it or go unpunished. Give up your vengeance, because we set the standard for our own judgment. "You will be judged in the same way that you judge others" (Matthew 7:2). Can you live with that?

When we show compassion to the one who hurt us, it allows us to give up intimidation. Hurt people want to hurt people, and we usually do this by keeping our distance from the one who hurt us. When we do confront our "enemies," we enjoy watching them freeze and/or twist in the wind as we remind them of their hurtful actions. When we understand the long-term benefits of releasing our pain by forgiving, we set ourselves up to be blessed in so many ways.

Total forgiveness means you won't guilt-trip. Don't forget the grace we receive from God, even though we don't deserve it. Our forgiveness is worthless unless it makes it possible for others to forgive themselves. This will also allow them to save face. For the one who really forgives from the heart, there's no place for self-righteousness. Realize that when you come through the pain and forgive, you will be wiser and stronger.

Action: Forgiveness is a gift you give yourself. It may be therapeutic to write a letter of forgiveness to someone who has died or a person you cannot find. Just writing or saying the words will set you free.

Don't Let the Sun Go Down

Forgiveness is the fragrance the violet sheds on the heel that has crushed it.

[MARK TWAIN]

There is no right timeline for recovery. For some people, making peace happens suddenly and spontaneously. For others, it takes time and effort. You may have to make a conscious effort every day to forgive. To say, "I'm letting this go. I'm not going to invest hatred, bitterness, anger, or resentment in this person anymore." You can find closure in forgiveness.

Real forgiveness is a life-long commitment! You must practice it every day. It is not easy to forgive when others don't acknowledge their offense, but if that's the prerequisite, you may never experience victory! And what you don't forgive, you relive! So, for your own sake, forgive, take back your life, and begin walking in the blessings of freedom.

You can't change the things that happened in your life, but you can decide how you interpret and respond to them. If you didn't receive support when you needed it, give it to yourself now.

Forgiveness is a commitment to a process of change. A way to begin is by recognizing the value of forgiveness and its importance in your life at a given time. Then reflect on the facts of the situation, how you've reacted, and how this combination has affected your life, health, and well-being.

Action: When you're ready, actively choose to forgive the person who's offended you. Move away from your role as victim and release the control and power the offending person and situation have had in your life. As you let go of grudges, you'll no longer define your life by how you've been hurt. You may even find compassion and understanding.

How to & Who to Forgive

The best way to get the last word is to apologize.

[GOD'S LITTLE DEVOTIONAL BOOK FOR WOMEN]

If you're unforgiving, you may pay the price repeatedly by bringing anger and bitterness into every relationship and new experience. Your life may become so wrapped up in the wrong that you can't enjoy the present. You may become depressed or anxious. You may feel that your life lacks meaning or purpose, or that you're at odds with your spiritual beliefs. You may lose valuable and enriching connectedness with others.

Forgive the person who badly hurt you long ago and also the stranger who stepped on your toe in the grocery store. Take those two extremes and forgive them—in addition to everyone in between. Forgive quickly. The quicker you do it, the easier it is! Forgive freely. Forgive means to excuse a fault, absolve from payment, pardon, send away, cancel, and bestow favor unconditionally.

When you forgive, you must own your personal responsibility in the matter, and you must cancel the debt. Do not spend your life paying and collecting debts. Do not try to collect from the people who hurt you, because the people who hurt you can't pay you. Also, forgive yourself for past sins and hurts you have caused others.

Action: Simply put, out of obedience to the Lord, we are called to forgive others as we have been forgiven of our trespasses and sins. Make the choice—a decision to forgive for your own good—and receive the reward of freedom.

Living Your Dream

> *Humanity is never so beautiful as when praying for forgiveness, or else forgiving another.*
>
> [JEAN PAUL]

Decide What You Want and Write It All Down

Create lists, and keep them going. What books do you want to read, who are the people you want to meet, what business and financial plans do you have, where do you want to travel, what experiences would you like to have, where do you want to live, what do you want for your family, spouse, friends, and, most importantly, what do you want to give?

Trust

> *You may be deceived if you trust too much, but you will live in torment*
> *if you do not trust enough.*
>
> [DR. FRANK CRANE]

I love you is arguably one of the most overused and underappreciated phrases. These words have so much power, yet we don't think through the impact of this phrase before we say it. Many people use this phrase as a tool to gain access to certain areas in life. Sadly, after they get what they want, they leave others feeling taken for granted or treated poorly—and the relationship is lost.

Why does this happen? Because trust was broken. The words *I love you* have the power to gain access, but they do not have the power to *keep* you at the point of your desire. Trust can maintain a relationship through many difficult challenges in business and personal relationships. You must know how to trust.

The capacity to trust others and yourself and the wisdom to know when to do so is a powerful attribute that enables you to live an extraordinary life. Love can overlook many imperfections. Trust does not. Trust *demands* perfection. Unlike love, trust must be earned.

What is trust? To trust someone is to rely on the character, ability, and word of that person. What do the words *I trust you* mean? We may trust our children to come home by a curfew and not do illegal drugs. But we wouldn't trust a child to make financial decisions for our business. Trust is item-specific. So *I trust you* is an inaccurate and misleading statement.

Action: Do you easily trust? Are you considered trustworthy?

Why Trust?

The best way to find out if you can trust somebody is to trust them.
[ERNEST HEMINGWAY]

Trust creates the synergistic power of teamwork. Synergy is a scientific phenomenon with the idea that the whole is greater then the sum of the individual parts: 1 + 1 = 3. When people trust each other, they can pool their resources—whether it's money, time, or specific knowledge. This will create a much higher rate of return than they could individually. Without trust, you are condemned to being ordinary.

Without trust, you will be alone; you won't have anyone to share your joy of winning. Some businesspeople either step on others to get ahead or they don't share the recognition. Trust is broken. When that happens, they are alone, and no one is eager to help them. Their power is reduced.

A benefit of trust is efficiency. An individual's ability is limited by the number of hours in a day. By trusting, we can unleash the wondrous power of leverage and get work done, even when we're not working. This allows us to seize opportunities and lift huge burdens. When we have trust and honest feedback, we can make decisions that inspire people to get things done. We can create more together than if we act alone.

When you trust people, you empower them to play at a higher level and make a contribution and a difference. Most people will live up to the trust being placed in them. If you want to make a difference, you must learn to empower others by trusting them. This will produce a feeling of exhilaration in you and them.

Action: Trusting carries risks, but it also returns maximum gains! Who can you trust to help you accomplish your goals and dreams?

Risk/Reward Ratio

He who does not trust enough will not be trusted.

[LAO TZU]

Trust must be earned. We must be responsible and gain a certain amount of knowledge or inner conviction to believe a person is worthy of trust. Trust is built by risking increasing amounts of time, money, authority, feelings, or any other resource. We can be trusting and receive trust by exercising due diligence. This will prevent you from willingly entering into dangerous enterprises expecting to be disappointed.

Before making a commitment to a relationship, it is important to also use due diligence. Evaluate the choices of the person and give his or her honor and integrity some review. Trusting *ourselves* to know what we are able to do and not do is an important part of the formula.

There is a principle called the risk/reward ratio. It simply means that there's no significance without knowing both the risk and the reward involved. If you know that you have a 90 percent chance of losing a $10,000 investment and the return if you win is $1,000,000, you have a high-risk ratio and only a 10 percent chance of seeing your investment bear fruit. You can make a decision whether or not to take the risk with your $10,000.

This same risk/reward formula can be applied to most any decision you face in life, not just money. Money is really just a means of exchange, an illusion to which we give value.

Action: Money is only as real as we make it out to be and is easily replaceable—it's not rare, and it doesn't have an intrinsic value. The paper notes can be easily destroyed by fire or water, or even blown away by the wind. Why risk losing a relationship over money?

Inspect What You Expect

Put not your trust in money, but put your money in trust.

[OLIVER WENDELL HOLMES]

Trust is earned. Some people think that if you check on them, you don't trust them. That is not true. It really means that you are being a good steward over your time, your investments, and the people for whom you're responsible. This scenario will occur between parent and child. The parent will ask the child to perform a particular chore, and it is the parent's responsibility to inspect the situation to ensure that the child has carried through on the task.

Inspecting someone's progress or whether or not they have followed through will actually increase trust when the job is performed as requested. It provides feedback that helps make course corrections. What is at stake and what has been proven? The more a person has proven to you, the less is at stake and the less you should be checking up on him or her. Scuba divers always go with a partner, and they check each other's tanks. It's not that they think the other is incompetent; it's because of the risk involved.

When you give trust, you expect to receive it. We tend to expect trust from the people we truly love even more. We give trust because we desire more intimacy. In life, you never get what you want. You get only what you inspect. Don't expect what you are not willing to inspect. In all of our relationships and dealings with people, you can build trust by simply comparing what was expected to what was actually done. Unclear expectations lead to mistrust.

Action: Don't make assumptions. You can completely transform your relationships when you find the courage to ask questions and to express what you really want. How well do you communicate your expectations to others?

Honesty

Few things can help an individual more than to place responsibility on him, and to let him know that you trust him.

[BOOKER T. WASHINGTON]

Honesty is the foundation of trust. If you are trustworthy, you expect others to be trustworthy as well. It's human nature to expect of others what you expect of yourself. If you are honest, you expect others to be honest. If you are a liar and a thief, it would be unrealistic to expect others not to lie or steal from you. We receive in life what we're willing to put out.

A trust is an equitable right or interest in property distinct from the legal ownership of it: a property interest held by one person for the benefit of another.

According to this definition, a trust is held not for your benefit, but for someone else's. When you live your life thinking about others first, you will maintain trust and people will invest their trust in you—without having to worry about their decision. Keep in mind that there is always a high price to pay when trust is at stake. Make a positive contribution to the relationship—be a giver, not a taker.

Action: It starts with a decision. Trust others and you gain relationships. Relationships will carry you through tough times. That's one benefit of trust.

Invest in Trust

We're never so vulnerable than when we trust someone—but paradoxically, if we cannot trust, neither can we find love or joy

[WALTER ANDERSON]

Trust isn't something to take lightly because the road back from broken trust can be a very long, tiresome, and lonely one. Think "prevention," and develop trust habits now that will become your character now and forever. Do the little things that build trust—and you will receive huge payoffs down the road. Life is about relationships—we need the help, assistance, protection, and love of other people. Here are two things you need to do to build or rebuild trust with someone.

- *Start making commitments and keeping them.* When you make a commitment, you bind yourself to your word. When you keep your commitment, you earn trust.

- *Start making yourself accountable to others.* The more authority you have, the easier it is not to hold yourself accountable, especially to people with less authority. Accountability gives you an ability to have more in your account. It's the only way to have lasting increase in your life, and it's the safest way. Accountability means that you're tracking results.

Action: Be impeccable with your word, and make every effort to build trust in all of your personal and business relationships. The risk in not giving and receiving trust is huge.

Living Your Dream

> *You can't connect the dots looking forward; you can only connect them looking backwards. So you have to trust that the dots will somehow connect in your future. You have to trust in something—your gut, destiny, life, karma, whatever. This approach has never let me down, and it has made all the difference in my life.*

[STEVE JOBS]

Become Valuable

What value do you give to the marketplace? Develop skills to increase your value at your job. Anyone can learn new skills. Read books, listen to programs, attend seminars, and take classes. Any positive move you make from what you are learning will stimulate the value you bring to wherever you get your paycheck. As Jim Rohn says, "Work harder on yourself than you do on your job."

Abundance Mindset

Abundance is not something we acquire. It is something we tune into.
[WAYNE DYER]

One of the first components of an abundant mindset is that you must be willing to pay the price. There is no such thing as a free lunch! When you are willing to invest time, money, effort—and even a possible failure—you will create what you want. If you want to live in abundance, don't look for the easy way, skip steps, or ignore important information.

All things are possible. But first things must come first. You may have a dream to own and manage an apartment building that could earn several million dollars. Be willing to work for a management company and then maybe buy a few houses first. Managing a smaller business can teach you the lessons and develop the skills necessary to expand. Abundance doesn't just *happen*, it occurs in stages. You can't expect to jump to the top rung of the ladder without climbing the bottom rungs. Be willing to pay the price to get where you want to be.

The average person will try to bypass years of learning. Experience can offer real value through volunteering or working jobs "beneath" us, through attending seminars and taking the time to study to develop the skills needed to succeed. There are no short cuts on the road to success.

When something looks like a free lunch and you don't know the price, the real price is usually too high. There is a price for everything. You must know the price, and based on the reward or benefit you can decide if it's worth paying. If it's worth paying the time, money, or energy, then you must be willing to pay the price.

Action: Where do you want to be five years from today? Will you be living an abundant dream life? What steps do you need to take to get there? Write it all down, and study your action plan. What can you do today to get you one step closer to your dream life?

Manifest Abundance

> *The world is full of abundance and opportunity, but far too many people come to the fountain of life with a sieve instead of a tank car . . . a teaspoon instead of a steam shovel. They expect little and as a result they get little.*
>
> [BEN SWEETLAND]

Seeking advice and help from others is wise. Trying to become an expert at everything yourself—that's a waste of time and a way to regress in terms of abundance. The abundant thinker doesn't mind putting out in order to get more back.

People complain about the fees experts charge—financial planners, accountants, plumbers, etc.—and try to save a few dollars by doing the job themselves. If you want to experience abundance, you must realize that your time is valuable and doing too much yourself will take you away from your area of expertise. Are the fees too high? The answer depends on the kind of service you wish to engage. You must pay a true professional well and learn enough to ask the right questions to ensure you have someone qualified to charge a real professional's fee.

Don't sit around counting the pennies you "save" when you could be counting the hundred-dollar bills you'd earned. Before abundance manifests in a tangible way in your life, it must first manifest in your mind. If abundance never takes root there, then you'll probably never experience it.

Action: Do you sweat the small stuff? If you recognize your time as a valuable asset, you won't put it at risk by "stepping over a dollar to save a dime." Does the phrase we don't have time to fix it right once, but we do have time to quick-fix it three times *come to mind?*

Combat the Scarcity Mind-Set

Expect your every need to be met. Expect the answer to every problem, expect abundance on every level.

[EILEEN CADDY]

Scarcity is the position that there's never enough, and it's usually based on the person's assumption that he or she is not enough personally. With almost seven billion people in the world, scarcity begins with the thought, *I'm only one person. I'm not enough.* Then life experiences validate the feeling. This person is the glass half empty—there isn't enough time, there isn't enough money, there aren't enough customers.

To combat this lack mentality, we must realize that abundance is the position in which your wholeness and completeness does not depend on external circumstances.

We are whole and complete at birth because of our spiritual nature and our connection to God. Since God is infinite, we are complete because we are connected to Him. Our wholeness and completeness depend totally on what is inside us—nothing else. Our character, what is inside us, will determine how we obtain our worth. With an abundance mindset, you won't need material things to validate your value.

Action: You may have noticed a number of people who endlessly accumulate more stuff without ever being happy. When a person tries to use material things to fill the hole of satisfaction, it's never enough. The abundance mind-set must precede the manifestation of prosperity in health, relationships, or finances.

Thoughts Become Reality

What is called genius is the abundance of life and health.

[HENRY DAVID THOREAU]

An abundance mentality will create more abundance. Your thoughts are invariably what will always create wealth in your life. And your thoughts will create the right habits that facilitate perpetual wealth. What is your thinking like? Do you have a problem with other people's prosperity? That concern is a reflection of scarcity thinking.

Learn to conquer the subconscious mind before the circumstance occurs. It's our decisions, not our circumstances, that determine our position in life.

Your mind only produces whatever it's focused on. Anchor your vision—and let reality adjust. If you focus on your debt, then you'll inevitably become more indebted. We change beliefs through repetition and emotional involvement. The more emotion is involved, the fewer repetitions we need. The less emotion is involved, the more repetitions we require to change our beliefs.

We all respond to stimuli differently. You may be in a circumstance of financial difficulty at the moment. What would happen if you began thinking that you are wealthy?

Action: Do something that you would do if money were in abundance—for example, go out to eat at a fancy restaurant, splurge on an expensive pair of shoes, or stay in a nice hotel. This will create a real experience of wealth that could possibly get your mind straight and force good times into existence. You deserve it.

Give Your Way to Abundance

When you focus on being a blessing, God makes sure that you are always blessed in abundance.

[JOEL OSTEEN]

Tithing is the practice of giving away the first tenth of your income to wherever you receive your spiritual guidance. Typically, this is your local church, temple, or synagogue. We can put aside the religious aspect for a moment and look at this from an abundance perspective.

We will reap what we sow in abundance. When suffering from a scarcity mindset, the consequent behavior is to hold on to whatever you hold sacred: money, time, or possessions. Do a simple experiment: every time you receive a paycheck, give 10 percent to where you receive your spiritual nourishment. It's a way to acknowledge God as your source.

Tithing puts us in a position to be blessed, but we are still responsible for doing our part and taking action. When you tithe, money is not just going to rain down from the sky. Tithing is the beginning—it combats scarcity thinking.

Understand how the 10-10-80 system works well in the financial realm. Tithe the first 10 percent of your income. Invest the second in yourself for the sole purpose of increasing your net worth. Use the remaining 80 percent to pay for your expenses. This systematic practice of giving and receiving activates the power of compounding interest. It will also send a message to your subconscious that you're worthy of wealth.

Action: Try giving what you want more of. Wish you had more time? Volunteer at a school. Need some money? Give cheerfully. Need more happiness? Smile at everyone!

How Can I?

Your most precious, valued possessions and your greatest powers are invisible and intangible. No one can take them. You, and you alone, can give them. You will receive abundance for your giving.

[W. CLEMENT STONE]

One of the keys to abundance is having a solution-oriented mindset. When average people ask themselves, "Can I do this?" they base it on circumstances they see. *An abundant thinker asks different questions.* "HOW can I do this?" This question forces your mind to create solutions—your subconscious will begin searching for answers.

Consider that there is an infinite number of ways to get across a road—walk, crawl, hop, dance, etc. There's always a way. Your conscious mind uses reason based on past experiences, but your subconscious mind isn't reasonable and can solve problems when you force it by asking, "*How* can I?"

If there's always a solution, how big are you willing to think and allow yourself to dream of possibilities? The truly abundant mind-set is never swayed by the economy and is well grounded in the reality that if you are not living in abundance, then you'll simply have to create it. Those with a true abundant mindset realize that the universe has more than enough resources to go around—enough to make everybody happy and fulfilled. They know there's never a reason to be covetous or envious of another person.

There is no lack. There is more than enough. *You* are more than enough. There is an abundant supply of everything you need. You must build a character of abundance that is deep inside of you. You don't have to think about it—whether circumstances are good or bad, whether you're riding high or low—you think *abundance*.

Action: Take life on. Look for challenging problems to solve. Sooner or later the challenges will squeeze you—that's when character traits will emerge. When you squeeze an orange, juice comes out because that is what is inside the fruit. When life squeezes you, greatness will come out.

Living Your Dream

> *Whatever we are waiting for—peace of mind, contentment, grace, the*
> *inner awareness of simple abundance—it will surely come to us, but*
> *only when we are ready to receive it with an open and grateful heart.*
>
> [SARAH BAN BREATHNACH]

Priorities

Keep a journal of how you spend your time this week. By identifying your priorities and examining how you actually spend your time, you can clearly see there usually is a gap between what you *say* is important in your life and what you *do*. If you are to achieve your dreams and realize the life of your dreams, one of the biggest changes you will need to make in your life—and as you set and work toward your goals—is to more closely align your actions with your priorities.

Focus

Tell me what you pay attention to and I will tell you who you are.

[JOSE ORTEGA Y GASSET]

Focus is the ability to direct your attention, efforts, or activity at a desired direction or object without being distracted. To maintain concentration while we focus on anything takes extraordinary effort in the busy world in which we live. Those who are willing to initiate such attention and maintain it will have the amazing attribute of leverage and produce extraordinary results. Focus is a quality that makes or breaks our ability to achieve greatness.

Focus leverages power, just as a magnifying glass focuses the power of the sun to create heat. The same amount of energy is there with or without the glass. Energy directed through the glass can produce fire.

Life is full of distractions. Very few individuals are willing or able to *really* focus. Most people would be unable to give you an answer if you asked them to describe their purpose in life. Many would have a tough time listing three things they will absolutely accomplish in a day. Their lives are unfocused. Most just plan to work hard and handle what comes up—whatever that is.

One reason we don't learn to focus is the assumption that it requires great amounts of effort and will be difficult in some way. When in reality, it takes average talents, small amounts of time, or minimal resources to make wise decisions, think clearly, and have fun while being focused and relaxed.

Action: How would you rate your ability to focus?

Hit the Target

> *What people say, what people do, and what they say they do are entirely different things.*
>
> [MARGARET MEADE]

To hit a target, it is best to be relaxed and focused. Does that sound like an oxymoron? With so many distractions in life, we wonder how we will get anything done. We all have money and time pressures in life. Urgent phone calls, texts, and emails disrupt work plans; work interferes with relationships; and problems in relationships interfere with our careers. Challenges with kids distract us from the romance in our marriage. A serious illness interrupts *all* plans.

When firing a gun at a target, if you focus on the target but get uptight, you're more likely to miss. If you relax yet are *unfocused*, you'll still miss. If you can learn to be relaxed *and* focused at the same time, you'll win!

Action: To hit your bull's-eye every time, you must cultivate a concentrated focus. No matter how many distractions come your way or how much financial or temporal stress you experience, remain calm and focused on what is important. It takes practice and devotion, but it works.

Die Empty

One reason so few of us achieve what we truly want is that we never direct our focus; we never concentrate our power. Most people dabble their way through life, never deciding to master anything in particular.

[ANTHONY ROBBINS]

What's the point of your life? Why are you here? Knowing the answers will help you focus your life. When you discover your purpose, then it's a matter of not allowing the many distractions of life to sway you from your purpose. You will find when you focus on service or contribution, regardless of your circumstances, your focus becomes laser sharp.

Many of the greatest leaders of our time—such as Mohandas Gandhi; Martin Luther King, Jr.; Nelson Mandela; and Mother Teresa—endured unusual pressure. However, each of them continued to focus on their vision for a better world for everyone. They never wavered. They stayed grounded and centered despite incredible stress.

To achieve greatness, stay true to your focus. Even the slightest distraction could cost many others *their* destinies.

Living life to the fullest with a sense of purpose and urgency is the key to focused living.

Action: If today were the last day of your life, how would you spend it? Who would you be a blessing to? Who would you spend the day with? How would you want to be remembered? Will you die "empty," having given all you have to offer?

Focus on Solutions

If you chase two rabbits, both will escape.
[Unknown]

We must learn to focus on what is actually *effective*—on solutions and not on the problems. Let's review the process of asking the right questions. When we face a challenge and ask ourselves, "Can I?" the answer is based on what's already happened. When we ask, "*How* can I?" even if we apply no more energy, because this question has a different focus, it has enormously different results.

As an example, consider how much we all can get done the day before we go on vacation. It is interesting that we don't really know any more information; we have the same number of hours, yet we can double our performance that day. Why is that, and how does it work?

Maybe if we understood that concept and applied it to every day of our lives, we would be more productive and more beneficial to ourselves and the people around us. Could it be that the day before vacation, we have a game plan and we have accepted responsibility to follow through on it? Think about it: If planning one day can make such a radical difference in that day, what a difference a game plan for *life* would make!

Action: Can you make a decision to concentrate and then maintain your focus to take action? You must forget the past, both your failures and your successes, to create solutions for the future. Never let what matters most suffer for the things that matter least. Focus on what is important!

Be in the Here & Now

He who has done his best for his own time has lived for all times.

There is an old concept called "Be here now," which is related to focus. This simply means that your body, feelings, spirit, and thoughts must all be at the same place at the same time. Have you ever been physically one place but your mind was still at another? That's not being here *now*. Not being here now hurts effectiveness and intimacy. It takes a disciplined mind to be *here now*.

When some people have a problem, they continue to focus on the problem instead of being *here now* to create a solution. Have you ever seen a deer frozen in a car's headlights? Often the car hits the deer because the deer doesn't get out of the way. It's focused on the wrong things—the headlights—so it became distracted from the solution— getting out of danger. The deer could easily outmaneuver the car, but focusing on the wrong thing causes it to become paralyzed by circumstances. Don't let that be the story of your life. Never allow circumstances to impair your focus on what's important.

Action: Focus on your strengths. Do more of what you are good at. Be more of who you really are. If you have a natural aptitude for something, allow yourself to develop that gift. It will make you more successful. Focusing on your strengths will make you better at what you do.

Awareness

> *The future belongs to those who see possibilities before they become obvious.*
>
> [JOHN SCULLEY]

Being able to quickly shift your focus is important—it's an important ability you can develop called *awareness*.

Is it possible to be focused but still be aware of everything going on around us? The answer is yes. In martial arts, for example, your opponent may throw a punch, and you must be focused on responding to that punch, but you must also be aware of what is going on around you. Although two things are happening simultaneously, it is considered singularity of focus.

During the next conversation you have with someone, focus on the person's words. This can be very difficult. Most people are so focused on what *they want to say* that they're anxiously looking for an opening in which to say it. As a result, they don't *really* hear what the other person is saying.

Sometimes we are distracted by a family crisis and are thinking about that as the other person is talking. As you force yourself to focus on what he or she is saying, learn to increase your awareness. You will become aware of not just what the other person is saying but what he or she is *feeling*. You will also be able to feel what is *not* being said—and that's important. You will become aware of the other people around and the overall energy in the room.

Action: Focused listening and focused attention is a skill that anyone can master. It takes practice, but this important skill can be accomplished—and it is worth the effort! Start today!

Living Your Dream

> *The key to success is to focus our conscious mind on things we desire not things we fear.*
>
> [BRIAN TRACY]

Be Prepared

As you prepare to begin the journey to pursue your biggest goals and dreams, you will need to study your specific destination. Depending on where you are headed, you will need different things. Just as someone headed to Florida might need sunscreen while someone headed to the North Pole is more likely to need some warm clothes, so too what you will need for your journey—the skills, knowledge, talents, and resources—vary according to your dream destination. If your dream is to become a physician, the skills, knowledge, talents, and resources you will require will be very different from someone whose dream is to own a yacht and sail around the world, for example.

Take Action

Start doing the thing to have energy to do the thing.

[Bob Proctor]

Powerful motivation comes in understanding that you can achieve anything you truly desire in your heart. It is the knowledge that you are destined to fulfill your every goal and dream that drives you to change. It's the action behind the attraction that makes the wish come true.

The decision is the first step toward change. Regardless of the decision, every change requires some form of action. Do you find it challenging at times to motivate yourself to take action?

Action is the only thing that will overcome fears, inspire change, create momentum, and give you results. You can dwell on, think about, plan, and talk about your goals and dreams all you want—but it is only when you take that first step that you begin to make something happen.

Take a small step! Even the smallest first step will help create momentum toward change. Look at today's quote: you have to "start doing the thing to have energy to do the thing." You can trick yourself into thinking "I'm just gonna start it—it'll only take a few minutes." But once we start it, we can make the decision to finish the task.

Action: You must get focused and clear and create a compelling plan of action toward a goal that is important to you. Have a strategy to follow that creates energy and momentum to propel you to success.

Massive Action Tools

Action speaks louder than words but not nearly as often.

[MARK TWAIN]

As you create your action plan for success, it is wise to find a person who has followed a similar strategy and has already had success. Having a role model or action coach can give you a resource that creates sustainable results that will help you overcome those inner conflicts that typically stop you from taking the massive action necessary to succeed. Don't sell yourself short, find your gift—something that moves you and excites you! The emotional connection will propel you into action.

When you are in alignment with your true desires, and you have the tools available to give you the courage to pursue your goals and dreams, you can overcome and succeed. Don't let excuses take over! If you believe you are lacking resources to achieve your dreams, what you really need is to cultivate *resourcefulness*. Do you have a habit of emotional strength? Do you have courage, creativity, determination, and playfulness? Are you interesting, curious, passionate, and are you stimulating your imagination? All of these qualities allow you to find the resources to get the answers so you can go where you want to go and accomplish your dreams.

Inspiration triggers something that was already inside of you. Inspired life is the ability to find fulfillment and joy in your life. There is a science of achievement—you find out how to get from where you are to where you want to be. Then there is the art of fulfillment—the capacity to feel alive and happy with your life. You have to know what will fulfill you. Humans must grow and have progress to have happiness. And to add meaning to your life, you must make a contribution. Fulfillment makes you feel that your life matters. You must achieve and contribute to experience enjoyment and success in life.

Action: Name three people you admire and who inspire you. Make an appointment to speak with them this week.

Decisions & Destiny

It is decisions, not conditions, that shape your destiny.

[ANTHONY ROBBINS]

Action is the force that creates change and achievement. But decisions create action. Look at the decisions you have made in your life—decisions, not conditions, shape your destiny. If you want new conditions, make new choices; you will find new answers.

What have you done with the choices you have made in your life? Think about the college you chose to attend. This may or may not have been a difficult decision for you, but it has probably created many of your lifelong friendships, impacted your career, and maybe even determined whom you married and where you live now. The simple decisions actually shape your life. Decisions = destiny. Make the decision to determine how fabulous your life is going to be! New decisions create new actions, which create new results. Know that you can design your life!

What do you believe? If you don't like something, change it. When you make the decision, take massive action—that is when things change. There are three decisions we make all the time:

- 🦋 Your focus
- 🦋 The meaning you give
- 🦋 The emotions you feel

Action: You can take control of your decision-making when you understand the importance of focus, meaning, and emotions to create action! Do you focus on your goals and dreams?

Create Action

*Love begins at home, and it is not how much we do . . . but how much
love we put in that action.*

[MOTHER TERESA]

Where focus goes, energy goes. What are you going to focus on—
things you value or things you fear? People have patterns of focus.
What can you control? If you focus on things you can't control (the
economy, the weather, other people), then you live in fear. If you focus
on the things you can control—your thoughts, your mind, your emo-
tions, your decisions, your actions—this is how your actions will cre-
ate change. Do you focus on the past, the future, or the present?

We place meaning on every decision we make—where does your
mind go? Pain or pleasure, is this the end or the beginning? Whatever
meaning you place on something, it becomes a belief to you. You must
come up with an empowering meaning to create a positive experience
about how you feel and what you do. You feel emotions, good or bad,
so then nothing really matters without good meaning.

Emotions filter what you do and how you do it. Are you angry or
happy? Your actions affect what you decide to do.

*Action: Something controls every decision you make. Focus, emo-
tions, even your physical and mental state affects your actions. Con-
ditioning our body to be in the best state of mind the majority of the
time will make a huge difference in the decisions we make. Do you
believe that happiness comes from progress?*

Beliefs & Action

> *Take time to deliberate, but when the time for action has arrived, stop thinking and go in.*
>
> [NAPOLEON BONAPARTE]

Our ability or inability to take action is greatly affected by our beliefs of how things are "supposed" to be. We feel good when things match our beliefs. For example, if you have a belief that life is a test, then that pressure can make things seem difficult for you. If you believe that life is a party, then life is fun and it's all about making connections. We make decisions based on what we believe.

Is there an area of your life that you are really happy with? Write it down. Why are you happy in this area of your life? What is your motive for action? You are happy because your current life conditions in that area match your beliefs of how that should be in life. What is an area of your life you are unhappy with?

Whatever season of life you are in, there are challenges. Why? Because we compare our beliefs (core expectations) of where we think we should be to where we really are. This could cause pain in your life when you are not satisfied and your current life does not match up to your expectations. Being honest with yourself is good; it is how you can close the gap between where you are and where you want to be. This is how you can improve your habits and get a vision and go through the process of change.

Action: In our unhappiness, we still have a choice; we can place blame, we can make a change, or we can accept those things we cannot control. We may need to shift the source of our pain to change our beliefs.

Essence of Your Life

To know oneself is to study oneself in action with another person.

[BRUCE LEE]

What would your life be like if it was exactly how you wanted it to be today? If your life were extraordinary on your terms, what would you do? What would it look like? Describe the essence of your life. What is the ultimate life that you are after?

Everything that happens in your life—what you're thrilled with and what you're challenged by—began with a decision. Your life is the outcome of the decisions you've made and the actions you've taken as a result of those decisions. Different decisions produce different results.

If you want to control the direction of your life, you must consistently make good decisions. It's not what you do once in a while that has an impact on the direction of your life—it's what you do *consistently*. Make decisions today about how you are going to live in the years to come. For your decisions to really make a difference in your life, it's imperative to decide what results you're committed to—and know specifically how these results will transform your life. It's equally critical to decide what kind of person you're committed to becoming. Get clear about what you want to be, do, and have, and what your life will be like after you accomplish this. With that clarity, you'll find it becomes easier to make the kinds of decisions that will move you in the direction you desire.

Action: What are your standards? What will you demand from life? Decide today if you'll accept life as it is or if you'll live your life on your own terms, at the edge and at the highest level.

Living Your Dream

> *Action is a great restorer and builder of confidence. Inaction is not only the result but also the cause of fear. Perhaps the action you take will be successful; perhaps different action or adjustments will have to follow. But any action is better than no action at all.*
>
> [NORMAN VINCENT PEALE]

People to Associate With

Take inventory of the people in your life. What books do they have you reading? What thoughts do they have you thinking? What effect are they having on you? Where do they have you going? What activities do they have you doing?

Knowledge

> *Shall I tell you a secret of a true scholar? It is this: every man I meet is*
> *my master in some point and in that I learn from him.*
>
> [RALPH WALDO EMERSON]

When you think of a knowledgeable person, is he or she book smart, a graduate of Harvard at the top of the class? Maybe a scientist or a brain surgeon is your idea of specialized knowledge. We must understand that specific knowledge in any area of life can provide an edge. The pursuit of specific knowledge *and* a constant eagerness to learn—along with the practical wisdom of applying knowledge to a situation to produce a desired outcome—are character traits to embrace. We will grow as we constantly seek knowledge and seek experts to teach us about topics ranging from technology to finances to relationships to personal development to health to leadership.

For some, low self-esteem can make us think we can't learn. Others can wear a mask of either arrogance that we don't need to learn or complacency from a belief that more learning isn't necessary. Many believe that they are fine and don't desire to learn, yet what are we settling for? Do you have to be broke to want more money? Do you have to hate your job to want something else? Do you have to be on the edge of divorce to want to make your marriage better?

Action: Do you settle for good when you could be creating spectacular? A lifetime goal of learning will keep you young and growing. What good book are you reading? What thought leader's CD are you listening to in your car? What seminar will you attend in the next few months?

Don't Settle

Let the wise listen and add to their learning.
[Proverbs 1:5]

Do dogs like bones? Most of us would think they do, but they don't. Dogs like steak; they settle for bones. Think about a dog family making dinner—you know they would give us the bones and keep the steak for themselves. What happens is that we feed the dog bones, bones, bones . . . until they start thinking they like them.

Dogs begin settling for bones instead of steak. It's not that they dislike bones or that bones are bad, it's that they are settling for bones. Take someone who has been in a good relationship for ten years—a good relationship, not a bad one. What they experience year after year is a good relationship. It is relatively easy then to start settling for a good relationship (bone) instead of trying to create a spectacular relationship (steak).

It's not about changing who you are with. You can make the relationship you are in better. If you have a job, a home, a nice car, and you make a salary that is equal or better than most of your neighbors, it is easy to start settling for a good income instead of creating a spectacular income. Do you believe it is important to pursue excellence and to seek to surpass your current level?

Many people get confused and think, *"If I want more, I must be dissatisfied with what I have."* This is untrue; it equates being motivated to being dissatisfied or ties happiness to dissatisfaction. Crazy, huh?

Action: Where are you settling for ordinary in your life? What action could you take to create spectacular?

Satisfaction & Gratification

> *Feeling gratitude and not expressing it is like wrapping a present and not giving it.*
>
> [WILLIAM ARTHUR WARD]

When we experience *satisfaction*, we feel aligned with our purpose—"This is it, and I'm satisfied." *Gratification* is the feeling of achieving something. "I'm gratified by getting more of something that is better or different than what I already have."

When you know your purpose in life and understand that there are many ways to be in alignment with your purpose, you feel a sense of satisfaction or contentment knowing you are where you are supposed to be. Seeking to *create* something better for yourself, out of that space of satisfaction, will give you the rush of gratification. To have a good balance in life, strive to be content with where you are as you seek to create gratification or to live a more meaningful life.

Having a hunger to learn and grow will allow you to excel at the creation process to draw you closer to your purpose. If we are green when we are growing, when we have "arrived" we are brown and dying. Many people resist the learning process because they fear failure. Trying something new, stepping outside of our comfort zone to learn—even failing—is the process of achieving knowledge. Failure can be the best lesson learned.

A great example of this is a professional athlete. You have heard of athletes talk about being "in the zone." They are masters of adjusting to any circumstance and producing results. At the same time, they love to practice and are always striving for better.

Action: Examine all areas of your life: your family, career, marriage, friendships, spiritual path, etc. Are you green and growing?

The Humble Student

> *Once stretched by a new idea, a man's mind never regains its original dimensions.*
>
> [OLIVER WENDELL HOLMES]

It takes being in a place of humility to understand that no matter how much we know, there is always more to learn. A person with a passion for life and a quest for improvement will thrive, not simply survive. Become someone dedicated to always learning more, because there is always more to learn. Learning can come in various ways when you approach learning as if you are a beginner. Your only worry is how to get better and you are open to where you need to improve.

Receiving feedback without judging the viewpoint right or wrong can be a powerful learning tool. Suppose a child says to her parent, "Daddy, you don't love me." To grow he should think, *That's an interesting viewpoint. Why would she say that? What am I projecting that she would say that? Do I need to change how I express my love?*

When you are committed to growth and development in every area of your life, you will stay determined to search for knowledge, wisdom, and understanding.

Don't be a know-it-all. When we think we know everything, we lose out on knowledge. We can lose passion, effectiveness, and even drift off purpose. We tend to alienate people when we are not open to growth; people shy away and are reluctant to offer their viewpoint.

Action: Life replicates itself. A person being mentored may begin to think they know more and close themselves off from wisdom offered. Appreciate what others have to offer. Always be open to learning.

Specialized Knowledge—the Edge

An investment in knowledge pays the best interest.

[BENJAMIN FRANKLIN]

With an eagerness to learn, we can acquire specialized knowledge. "If only I knew then what I know now" is a statement often used to explain a foolish mistake or regret in light of new information. When the decision was being made, without the benefit of the acquired knowledge, it didn't appear to be foolish. Increased knowledge gives the decision maker an edge.

Why do so few people dedicate themselves to the process of learning? Because growth requires change, and most of us are uncomfortable with change. Gail Sheely writes:

> If we don't change, we won't grow; and if we don't grow, we're not really living. Growth demands the temporary surrender of security. It means a giving up of familiar but limiting patterns, safe but unrewarding work, values no longer believed in, relationships that have lost their meaning. Taking a new step is what we fear most, yet our real fear should be the opposite.

Is there anything worse than living a life devoid of growth and improvement?

Specific knowledge keeps you on the cutting edge of areas such as finance, relationships, health, and spirituality. Learn to ask the right questions and have the courage to apply what you have learned to your life. Knowledge and experience increase insight, and insight leads to foresight, which is the ability to see how things will develop before it happens. This is when your conscious and subconscious are in harmony.

Action: Knowledge becomes power when you put it into action! What did you learn yesterday? How will you apply it to your life?

Wisdom Is Learning from Others' Mistakes

All men by nature desire knowledge.

[ARISTOTLE]

Be willing to pay the price of giving up leisure time to spend time reading, listening, and participating in activities that will help you to grow and learn.

Spend just one hour a day five days a week reading, and in five years you could become one of the most knowledgeable people in any area. It requires *discipline*. Begin now. Set a time and place for regular reading.

Find a time and place that works best for you—and then read consistently. Be a good steward of your time by consciously planning your educational reading time. Remember, "If you don't have a plan, then you plan to fail." Leverage your time. Use your car as a moving university by listening while you drive. Download teaching material to listen as you exercise.

Experiential learning is required to accomplish paradigm shifts or revelations in our belief systems. This means that you must participate in activities in which you have experiences that change your viewpoints. You have a choice to wait for life to hand you the experience you need to enhance your career, relationships, health, and spirituality . . . or to be proactive in the process.

Life is usually the most expensive teacher in terms of time, money, and relationships. Participating in events, workshops, and training sessions is the fastest, cheapest, and most enjoyable way to accelerate your growth.

Action: Invest in yourself as your own company, You, Inc.—your life is your own business—and make the most of it! Establish a budget for personal development; it is a smart thing to do. Become a continual learner.

Living Your Dream

For beautiful eyes, look for the good in others; for beautiful lips, speak only words of kindness; and for poise, walk with the knowledge that you are never alone.

[AUDREY HEPBURN]

Communication

Words are powerful—choose them wisely. You may come along and share your story and shine light on a situation. Choose the best words you can. The imagination can be inspired by words. Words can help people see things they never saw before. Words can build up or break down. Think before you speak.

Basic Life Skills

Whenever you do a thing, act as if all the world were watching.
[THOMAS JEFFERSON]

Success can be defined as the progressive realization of a worthwhile goal or dream. What is success for you? What does it take to succeed? A positive attitude? Well, sure, but that's hardly enough. The Law of Attraction? The Secret? These ideas might act as spurs to action, but without the action itself, they don't do much.

Success, however it's defined, takes *action*, and taking good and appropriate action requires skills. Some of these skills are taught in school; others are taught on the job; and still others we learn from general life experience.

In the next weeks we will go over a variety general life skills that will help anyone get ahead in nearly any area of life, from running a company to running a gardening club. Of course, there are skills specific to each field as well—but these are the skills that translate across disciplines, the ones that can be learned by anyone in any position.

Some people have devoted a lifetime to understanding what makes people happy and successful. The big three are health, wealth, and relationships. People need to find what they really want to do with their lives. We need to figure out how to do scary things that are good for us, break bad habits, let go of bad things in the past, etc. There is a lot to learn!

Action: Determine the level of success that would make you happy in the areas of your health, wealth, and relationships. Write it down in your journal.

Public Speaking

Eighty percent of success is showing up.

[WOODY ALLEN]

The ability to speak clearly, persuasively, and forcefully in front of an audience—whether an audience of one or of thousands—is one of the most important skills anyone can develop. People who are effective speakers come across as more comfortable with themselves, more confident, and more attractive to be around. Being able to speak effectively means you can "sell" anything—products, of course, but also ideas, ideologies, worldviews, and yourself. This means more opportunities for career advancement, bigger clients, or business funding.

Everyone gets nervous before giving a speech. Unfortunately, the more people in the audience, the more important the speech usually is, making any butterflies in your stomach multiply before you begin. Knowing how to keep yourself calm can make a big difference when giving a speech.

Look good and be prepared. Have a great outline, rehearse, and memorize as much of the presentation as you can—this will boost your confidence and help keep you from forgetting in a panic.

Become familiar with the environment where you will be speaking. Where will people be sitting? What potential problems might come up for speaking or displaying information? Get to know the audience as they come in to connect with some friendly faces during your presentation.

Action: Public speaking is often ranked the number one human fear. Yes, most people would rather die than speak in front of a crowd. Remember, action overcomes fear. Practice speaking in front of the mirror, to your pet, children, and family. You may want to try imagining your audience in their underwear—or not!

Writing

Whatever you can do, or dream you can, begin it. Boldness has Genius, Power and Magic in it. Begin it now.

[GOETHE]

Writing well offers many of the same advantages that speaking well offers: good writers are better at selling products, ideas, and themselves than poor writers. Learning to write well involves not just mastery of grammar but developing the ability to organize one's thoughts into a coherent form and target them for an audience in the most effective way possible.

Writing well is about getting the facts right. If you misinform readers about facts, they will consider the rest of your writing to be unprofessional and of poor quality. When writing, try to get the words right first and foremost. It might take a bit of juggling around, but the right word in the right spot is worth more to good writing than almost anything. Do not place a word in text just because it sounds good and you think it will impress readers.

When you start writing, make sure you know why you are writing. What is your goal? If you stick to this throughout the writing process, you should not veer off course. Once you've got this in mind, organize an outline of your written piece. This outline will structure your writing.

Once you've worked out your outline, start writing. The first phase of writing involves getting everything down. Don't worry about spelling or punctuation at this stage. As long as you can read it back, this is fine. The final stage is editing. This is one of the most important phases as it really polishes the piece and gives that final credibility.

Action: Learning how to write well is not rocket science. It is a skill, like any other, that can come with practice and effort. The technology of today offers a tremendous advantage that can allow you to improve your writing skills—use it!

Self-Management

Try not to become a man of success but a man of value.

[ALBERT EINSTEIN]

If success depends on effective action, effective action depends on the ability to focus your attention where it is needed most, when it is needed most. Strong organizational skills, effective productivity habits, and a strong sense of discipline are needed to keep you on track.

Being organized at work, at home, and at play is simply putting into motion a set of systems to manage your time, thoughts, actions, and space. This may include many different types of systems that work for you to organize your desk, your laundry room, your calendar, your family, and yourself.

Developing good organizational skills and time management will definitely take some effort on your part and will not pay off unless you are wholly dedicated to a better and more efficient lifestyle. Some may joke that a plan is a list of things that don't happen, but having a plan can sometimes mean the difference between success and failure in life. It's good to leave some things to chance, but for everything else, it helps to be organized.

Planning your everyday routine in a step-by-step sequence can be a good way to start developing organizational skills. These individual aspects of habit development aid in getting a workable system made to overcome nearly any type of inconvenience and difficulties in your everyday life.

Action: There are training programs available specifically for the development of organizational skills—you can get tips and create your own system that will fit your own style.

Networking

> *If you have built castles in the air, your work need not be lost; that is where they should be. Now put foundations under them.*
>
> [HENRY DAVID THOREAU]

Networking is not only for finding jobs or clients. In an economy dominated by ideas and innovation, networking creates the channels through which ideas flow and in which new ideas are created. A large network, carefully cultivated, ties one into not just a body of people but a body of relationships, and those relationships are more than just the sum of their parts. The interactions those relationships make possible give rise to innovation and creativity—and provide the support to nurture new ideas until they can be realized.

Charles "Tremendous" Jones has said that five years from now your life will be exactly the same except for two things: 1) the books you have read, and 2) the people you have met. Networking is your key to making really interesting, helpful, and powerful contacts.

Develop a plan and a list of people you want to add to your network. Then become an active participant and attend seminars and events where you will have the opportunity to meet those people.

When you do get into a conversation, it is wise to keep focused on the other person rather on yourself. Become a good listener and always remember to smile. Learning to remember and properly pronounce the names of people you meet is not just good manners, it is a good business and networking skill.

Action: A secret to good networking is do what you love to do or would love to learn. If you enjoy sports, for example, join a group that gets together to watch football. You will have fun and meet people with similar interests. Love to read? Join a book club. You will easily connect with like-minded people. So go network!

Critical Thinking

If you think education is expensive, try ignorance.

[DEREK BOK]

We are exposed to hundreds—if not thousands—of times more information on a daily basis than our great-grandparents were. Being able to evaluate that information, sort the potentially valuable from the trivial, analyze its relevance and meaning, and relate it to other information is crucial. Good critical thinking skills immediately distinguish you from the mass of people these days.

Divergent and *convergent* thinking skills are both important aspects of intelligence, problem solving, and critical thinking. Bringing facts and data together from various sources and then applying logic and knowledge to solve problems, achieve objectives, or make informed decisions is known as thinking convergently.

Divergent thinking is thinking outward instead of inward. It is the ability to develop original and unique ideas and then come up with a solution to a problem or achieve an objective.

Divergent and convergent thinking skills are both important to critical thinking. Not only that, they are interrelated.

Deductive reasoning looks inward to find a solution, while divergent reasoning looks outward for a solution. Following the facts and data to determine the answer to a problem is not significantly different than having a spark of a thought and then coming up with a solution. They use some of the same mental processes.

Both require critical thinking skills to be effective. Both are used for solving problems, doing projects, and achieving objectives.

Action: Divergent and convergent thinking skills are two sides to the same coin—of critical thinking. One without the other doesn't make sense. Both start with asking simple questions from a curious mind. You can strengthen your mind by having an insatiable curiosity and strong willingness to learn about the world and the people in it. Get to it.

Living Your Dream

> *Our lives are like a jigsaw puzzle that we piece together. People come into our lives and bring a piece that helps us complete the picture that is our life. You never know when you may be the piece that person needs at a given point in time.*
>
> [HAROLD S. KUSHNER]

WHY: *The Essence of Your Dreams*

What are your true motives for pursuing your dreams? Have you identified the real reason you want to achieve the dreams you have? It is important to recognize that your true desire (WHY) is to achieve the "essence" of your dreams—the feelings the achievement of those dreams will create for you or the kind of experience living those dreams will be like.

Decision-Making

The best way to predict the future is to create it.

[PETER F. DRUCKER]

The bridge that leads from analysis to action is effective decision-making—knowing what to do based on the information available. While not being critical can be dangerous, so too can over-analyzing or waiting too long for more information before making a decision. Being able to take in the scene and respond quickly and effectively is what separates the doers from the wannabes.

Which job should you take? What car should you buy? Should you ask him to marry you? Are you ready for another baby? Is this house right for you, or should you keep looking before you make an offer? Life is full of hard choices; the bigger they are and the more options we have, the harder they get.

As it happens, our brains are fairly binary. They can react very quickly when presented with two options, especially when one is clearly better—stay here and drown in the rising waters or climb onto that big rock and be safe? Easy choice, easy decision.

When presented with more options, though, we choke up. Jump onto the rock or climb the tree? We don't know which is clearly better, and research shows that most people will not choose *at all* when presented with several equally good options.

Practice, experience, and rules of thumb can help us to make those split-second decisions. Fortunately we don't normally face immediate, do-or-die decisions—we usually have the luxury of working through a decision.

Action: What kind of decision-maker are you? Do you get paralysis from analysis? Or do you fly by the seat of your pants? With some new strategies, you can learn to become a skilled, quality, and informed decision maker.

Decision-Making Pros & Cons

Happiness comes when we test our skills towards some meaningful purpose.

[JOHN STOSSEL]

The old chestnut of decision-making is the list of pros and cons. You make two columns on a piece of paper and write down all the positive things that will come of making a choice in one column and all the negative things in the other. In the end, the side with the most entries wins.

But this strategy doesn't take into account the different weight that each positive or negative might have. If one of your pros is "will make a million dollars" and one of your cons is "might get a hangnail," they don't exactly cancel each other out.

Some people counter this problem by assigning point values to each item on their list. A huge income might be worth +20 points, while a tiny risk might be only −1. This helps make a more realistic assessment of your options.

But pros and cons aren't always apparent or obvious, and the whole list-making process doesn't sit well with many people—especially impulsive, "seat-of-the-pants" people who might feel unnaturally hampered by the formality of the pro and con list.

Action: Research other strategies for making big decisions. Not all of them will work for every person or for every decision, but they all have something to offer to help you clarify your thinking and avoid "decision paralysis" while the water rises around you.

Analyze Outcomes

When you have eliminated the impossible, whatever remains, however improbable, must be the truth.

[SIR ARTHUR CONAN DOYLE]

Working through a big decision can give us a kind of tunnel vision, where we get so focused on the immediate consequences of the decision at hand that we don't think about the eventual outcomes we expect or desire.

When making a choice, then, it pays to take some time to consider the outcome you expect. Consider each option and ask the following questions:

🦋 What is the probable outcome of this choice?

🦋 What are the likely outcomes of not making this choice?

🦋 What is the likely outcome of doing the exact opposite?

Thinking in terms of long-term outcomes—and broadening your thinking to include negative outcomes—can help you find clarity and direction while facing your big decision.

Action: Need to make a quick decision? Ask yourself, "What is the worst that can happen if I do this? What is the best possible outcome? What is most likely to happen?" If you can live with all three answers—go for it!

Decisions: Ask Why Five Times

You can hesitate before deciding, but not once the decision is made.

[JOSE BERGAMIN]

The Five Whys are a problem-solving technique invented by Sakichi Toyoda, the founder of Toyota. When something goes wrong, you ask why five times. By asking why something failed, over and over, you eventually get to the root cause.

Here is a great example:

1. Why didn't my car start? *The battery is dead.*
2. Why? *The alternator is not working.*
3. Why? *The alternator belt is broken.*
4. Why? *The alternator belt was well beyond its useful service life and has never been replaced.*
5. Why? *I have not been maintaining my car according to the recommended service schedule.*

Solution: I will start maintaining my car according to the recommended service schedule.

Although developed as a problem-solving technique, the Five Whys can also help you determine whether a choice you're considering is in line with your core values.

For instance: Why should I take this job? It pays well and offers me a chance to grow. Why is that important? Because I want to build a career and not just have a string of meaningless jobs. Why do I not want a meaningless job? Because I want my life to have meaning. Why do I want meaning? So I can be happy. Why? Because that's what's important in life. (Core Value)

Action: Notice that you sometimes have to change how you ask "why" to keep the questions focused inward rather than outward to irrelevant external factors. It wouldn't do any good to ask, "Why does this job pay well and offer me a chance to grow?" since the important thing is that it does, not why it does.

Follow Your Instincts

Asking the right questions takes as much skill as giving the right answers.

[ROBERT HALF]

Research shows that people who make decisions quickly, even when lacking information, tend to be more satisfied with their decisions than people who research and carefully weigh their options. Some of this difference is simply in the lower level of stress the decision created, but much of it comes from the very way our brains work.

The conscious mind can only hold between five and nine distinct thoughts at any given time. That means that any complex problem with more than (on average) seven factors is going to overflow the conscious mind's ability to function effectively, leading to poor choices.

Our subconscious mind, however, is much better at juggling and working through complex problems. People who "go with their gut" are actually trusting the work their subconscious mind has already done, rather than second-guessing it and relying on their conscious mind's much more limited ability to deal with complex situations.

Simply knowing that every decision is a choice, and taking the responsibility for our choices—accepting the consequence, whether a benefit or a price—is the freedom and liberty all humans desire.

Action: Remember, your subconscious mind's "job" is to solve problems for you. When faced with a decision, ask yourself, "How can I make this happen?" Your subconscious mind will go to work to find the way to make it happen!

The Choice Is Yours

> *A decision without the pressure of a consequence is hardly a decision at all.*
>
> [ERIC LANGMUIR]

Whatever process you use to arrive at your decision, your satisfaction with your decision will depend largely on whether you claim ownership of your choices. If you feel pressured into a choice or not in control of the conditions, you'll find even positive outcomes colored negatively. On the other hand, taking full responsibility for your choices can make even failure feel like a success—you'll know you did your best and you'll have gained valuable experience for your invested time.

The important thing is to have a sound process for making decisions. Emotions are often unreliable, particularly with respect to how we will feel in the future. Going with instincts can make you feel good now, but you won't feel good later if consequences show that your instincts didn't really apply to the current decision situation.

A process will help break the decision into smaller parts that can be managed within our cognitive limits. Various techniques and tools can also support the decision maker by reducing the number of required distinct thoughts. However, discipline is required to capture the information used during the process.

Action: Experiment with different techniques to find a decision-making system that works best for you. Use wisdom in making a decision now to gain a positive outcome or reward later.

Living Your Dream

I still find each day too short for all the thoughts I want to think, all the walks I want to take, all the books I want to read, and all the friends I want to see.

[JOHN BURROUGHS]

Be Creative

When you discover the "essence" of your dream, you may discover some very creative ways to realize your dreams. A simple example might be that if you want to be a parent but cannot have children of your own, for whatever reason, you could spend time with children and "parenting" children in any of a multitude of different ways. You could become a preschool teacher, have a daycare in your home, provide foster care, become a Big Brother or Big Sister, work with youth programs, or adopt a child.

If your dream is truly important to you, look beyond the obvious ways to achieve that dream. When one door closes, look for another! Don't give up—*get creative!*

Negotiating

During a negotiation, it would be wise not to take anything personally.
[BRIAN KOSLOW]

Effective negotiation helps you to resolve situations where what you want conflicts with what someone else wants. The aim of win-win negotiation is to find a solution that is acceptable to both parties and leaves both parties feeling that they've won, in some way, after the event.

Be prepared and think through the following questions.

- **Goals:** What do you want to get out of the negotiation? What do you think the other person wants?

- **Trades:** What do you and the other person have that you can trade? What do you each have that the other wants? What are you each comfortable giving away?

- **Alternatives:** If you don't reach agreement with the other person, what alternatives do you have? How much does it matter if you do not reach agreement?

- **Relationships:** What is the history of the relationship? Could or should this history impact the negotiation?

- **Expected outcomes:** What outcome will people be expecting from this negotiation? What has the outcome been in the past, and what precedents have been set?

- **Consequences:** What are the consequences for you and the other person of winning or losing this negotiation?

- **Power:** Who has what power in the relationship? Who controls resources? Who stands to lose the most if agreement isn't reached? What power does the other person have to deliver what you hope for?

Action: Possible solutions: Based on all of the considerations, what possible compromises might there be? Knowing how to compromise is a key component to a healthy and happy relationship of any type.

Empathy

The great gift of human beings is that we have the power of empathy.

[MERYL STREEP]

Empathy is the ability to understand and share the feelings of another.

Q: What do world hunger and bad customer service have in common?

A: The secret to solving them both is empathy and innovation.

Empathy and innovation seem like an unlikely pairing, but together, they're the secret to solving just about everything.

Here's why. You have to care about a problem before you're motivated to solve it. Alexander Graham Bell invented the telephone because his wife was deaf and he wanted to help those who couldn't hear. Empathy for his wife ignited the innovation.

Empathy is about putting your own perspective on pause so that you can experience how the world looks through the eyes of another. With this skill, we then express our values to align with their needs, while innovation is a function of new ideas, risk taking and problem solving to serve that need.

So how do you kick start the empathy/innovation cycle? Simple: take a walk in another's shoes.

We tend to think of empathy as something that softens us. But that's not true. Empathy *empowers* us. Because when you see how the world looks to someone else, you don't diminish your own perspective, you expand it.

Action: You can't be innovative if the only perspective you see is your own. Empathy and innovation—the magic duo that can solve anything.

Research

> *Research is formalized curiosity. It is poking and prying with a purpose.*
>
> [Zora Neale Hurston]

When you need information, where do you go? Your choice of an information source will determine the type of information you receive. With the Internet at our fingertips, we have access to nearly infinite information. When you want to find what you are looking for, you must be able to evaluate the source and the information provided to learn what you are looking for quickly and efficiently.

Nobody can be expected to know everything, or even a tiny fraction of everything. You should be able to quickly and painlessly find out what you need to know. That means learning to use the Internet effectively, learning to use a library, learning to read productively, and learning how to leverage your network of contacts—and what kinds of research are going to work best in any given situation.

When you read, do you learn anything that you can apply immediately to your life, or do the words and ideas just bounce around your brain's pleasure areas for a while before disappearing like so many wisps of morning fog?

Too often we read important stuff—how-to manuals and business and personal development guides—with the same mindset as an entertaining novel. We read to make us feel good about what we've done or what we could do or what others have done, not as an exercise in personal growth.

Action: For more productive reading, try this: Commit to making at least three changes in your life as a result of your reading. As you highlight and take notes, also create "to-do" lists.

Relaxation

Half our life is spent trying to find something to do with the time we have rushed through life trying to save.

[WILL ROGERS]

Practicing relaxation techniques is more than simply chilling out; it is better described as *stress management*. Stress will not only kill you, it leads to poor decision-making, poor thinking, and poor socialization. Working yourself to death in order to keep up and not having any time to enjoy the fruits of your work isn't really "success." It's *obsession*. Being able to face even the most pressing crises with your wits about you and in the most productive way is possibly the most important skill to embrace.

This is a very personal skill to explore. Try a variety of techniques and enjoy the peace that comes with relaxation. Most of the following suggestions are free or low cost and can be done anywhere. The goal is to slow your heart rate, lower blood pressure, slow breathing rate, reduce muscle tension, improve concentration, reduce anger and frustration, and boost confidence.

Use visualization—simply close your eyes and imagine sitting someplace beautiful and happy. Breathe deeply for several minutes. Get some fresh air. Go for a walk and admire the beauty of nature. Be grateful. Get a massage. Do yoga. Meditate for several minutes. Listen to your favorite music. Chat with a trusted friend. Use aromatherapy. Smile.

Action: As you learn relaxation techniques, you'll become more aware of muscle tension and other physical sensations of stress. Once you know what the stress response feels like, you can make a conscious effort to practice a relaxation technique the moment you start to feel stress symptoms. This can prevent stress from spiraling out of control.

Math & Basic Accounting

Eureka, eureka!

[ARCHIMEDES OF SYRACUS]

You don't have to be able to integrate polynomials to be successful. However, the ability to quickly work with figures in your head, to make rough but fairly accurate estimates, and to understand things like compound interest and basic statistics gives you a big lead on most people. These basic math skills will help you to analyze data more effectively—and more quickly—and to make better decisions based on it.

It is a simple fact in our society that money is necessary. Even the simple pleasures in life, like hugging your child, ultimately need money . . . or you're not going to survive to hug for very long. Knowing how to track and record your expenses and income is important just to survive, let alone to thrive. But more than that, the principles of accounting apply more widely to things like tracking the time you spend on a project or determining whether the value of an action outweighs the costs in money, time, and effort.

Action: It's a shame that basic accounting isn't a required part of the core K-12 curriculum. It is never too late to learn the basics! Stimulate your brain today.

Teamwork

Teamwork is the ability to work together toward a common vision. The ability to direct individual accomplishments toward organizational objectives. It is the fuel that allows common people to attain uncommon results.

[ANDREW CARNEGIE]

The concept of teamwork is self-explanatory—a group of people working for one goal, where each individual brings forth his or her skills in a concentrated manner and coordinates it with others' skills to produce a desirable end. One can easily understand how paramount this concept is; almost everywhere one applies for a job, the ability to lead or be a team player is acknowledged as an essential skill and a prerequisite. The importance of teamwork is ingrained in us since childhood. As children, siblings are often taught to work together and share; as students we learn to work on projects together or win games together; marriages are a team effort; and finally our workplaces, where "fitting into the team" is constantly expected. This is not to say that individual talent and skills will go to waste without teamwork— they won't. What teamwork does is to build one's personal skills.

Teamwork enhances our skills of coordination and communication, and in a way it forces us to see the bigger picture, where individualistic dreams have to transcend into collective wants. Trust is vital for holding a team together, especially through failures. Failures are inevitable, but a team's strength lies in how it copes, survives, and paves a winning path. Teamwork in the workplace leads to better learning, work distribution, healthy competition, and immense job satisfaction.

Action: The importance of teamwork is not only reflected in the team's wins but also in individual growth. A team in its true sense cannot be built in a day—every member needs to learn and understand each other, as well as individual limitations. OK, are you a team player?

Living Your Dream

> *People often say that motivation doesn't last. Well, neither does bathing—that's why we recommend it daily.*
>
> [ZIG ZIGLAR]

Don't Rule Out the Impossible!

Do you have any "impossible" dreams? Who defines *impossible* anyway? What is impossible to one person is not impossible to another. Before you limit yourself, consider how many impossible dreams have already come true. It's the stuff that history is made of: Columbus discovering America, the Wright Brothers flying an airplane, Thomas Edison inventing the lightbulb. Were it not for impossible dreams, none of us would be where we are today. *Somebody's* got to achieve the impossible. Why not you?

Renewed Thinking

Feelings change—memories don't.

[JOEL ALEXANDER]

Do you know people with natural-born talent who seem to take it for granted? Their potential for greatness appears clear to us, so why don't they pursue it? Do they struggle with how to take control of the way they think? Are they victims of negative thinking and self talk?

We are sometimes influenced by the words and actions of others or by the environment around us. But remember, what we choose to do with our thoughts is entirely up to *us*.

The apostle Paul gave some very clear instructions about thoughts (Philippians 4:4–12). He advocates some actions we can take to have peace, and each of those things involves our thought life in some way:

- *Prayer.* Go to God first. Don't worry—pray!

- *Rejoice always.* This means to give thanks and praise continually, in all circumstances. Choose to respond to even negative situations in a positive way, thanking God and others for their help. Be encouraging to others with a positive attitude.

- *Live in moderation.* This involves balance in what we eat and drink, how much we sleep and exercise, and how we schedule work and play. This requires creating a plan and making choices.

- *Look for the positive side.* Choose to dwell on thoughts that are true, honest, just, pure, lovely, things of good report, things of virtue, and things that are praiseworthy.

- *Choose counsel wisely.* Think about who would be a good role model, mentor, or teacher for you.

Action: Read Philippians 4:4–12. You may want to write it down in your journal.

Take Thinking to a Higher Level

Yesterday is history. Tomorrow is a mystery. Today is a gift. That's why it's called the present.

[UNKNOWN]

Do you remember the children's rhyme that begins "Pussycat, pussy-cat, where have you been?" The tale relates how a cat went to see the queen, and when it was asked later about the experience, the only thing the cat recalled was that it had seen a mouse under the queen's throne. Very often, we tend to look at one incident, one conversation, one failure, or one aspect of a situation and focus on that to the exclusion of the whole. One fragment of life—limited in time and in space—does not represent the whole.

It's worth repeating: What you focus on the most is what you become. If you concentrate most of your thinking on your problems, you will eventually lose sight of things that are rewarding, encouraging, and uplifting.

We should look at a problem from all angles. Look at people from many vantage points. The truth is every person has a good side—even if it's dormant or not yet realized.

People who dwell on negative thoughts are significantly less content than others. They think they are being realistic by focusing on negative, but they are actually *creating negativity* in their own emotions that will eat away at their peace.

Action: Choose to see the positive traits in other people and in various situations, and you will find it much easier to see the positive in yourself and to feel hope.

A Process of Renewal

Always continue the climb. It is possible for you to do whatever you choose, if you first get to know who you are and are willing to work with a power that is greater than ourselves to do it.

[ELLA WHEELER WILCOX]

You must feed your mind and heart truthful ideas on a daily basis. If you look at garbage long enough, your mind will become a cesspool. Weigh carefully what you read and watch—the images that you put in your mind. Weigh carefully what you listen to, the music lyrics, and the programs you watch.

In order to have positive thoughts, we need to have positive input. We need to be exposed to things that are honorable, beautiful, and godly. If you do, those very traits will begin to characterize you as a person.

Read the Bible consistently. God gives us the instruction and inspiration we need through His Word. He wants us to depend on Him to meet our every need; we need to learn to trust Him in all things at all times.

Read from positive personal development books. The input of positive messages will abide in our minds. We must be determined that we are going to remember it, obey it, and apply it to our personal lives.

Action: To a very great extent, the "you" that you see in your mind's eye is the "you" that you become. Who you think you are becomes who you are. Are you repeating your positive affirmations daily?

Focus on Thinking

In the end, it's not going to matter how many breaths you took, but how many moments took your breath away.

[SHING XIONG]

Guard your thoughts. Choose which problems to concentrate on and what ideas to consider. Choose to discard any idea or fantasy that contradicts what you intuitively know to be good and pure.

Most worries and fears involve things that never come to pass. Take inventory of your worries, anxieties, frustrations, and fears. Then choose not to think worrisome, anxious, frustrating, or fearful thoughts. It's your choice—decide what you focus on!

Some people don't believe that people can *choose* how we think. Believe that you can and practice making good choices. Even if you have thought a particular way about something for decades, you can still change your mind! You do not need to remain stuck in an old way of thinking.

Action: Be aware of what you are thinking. When a negative or worrisome or fearful thought comes to the surface, recognize it for what it is, then direct your focus on something positive. It takes practice and self-control, but you can do it!

Allow Sufficient Time

> *As we grow up, we learn that even the one person that wasn't supposed to ever let us down probably will. You'll have your heart broken, and you'll break others' hearts. You'll fight with your best friend or maybe even fall in love with them, and you'll cry because time is flying by. So take too many pictures, laugh too much, forgive freely, and love like you've never been hurt. Life comes with no guarantees, no time outs, and no second chances. You just have to live life to the fullest, tell someone what they mean to you and tell someone off; speak out, dance in the pouring rain, hold someone's hand, comfort a friend, fall asleep watching the sun come up, stay up late, be a flirt, and smile until your face hurts. Don't be afraid to take chances or fall in love, and most of all, live in the moment, because every second you spend angry or upset is a second of happiness you can never get back.*
>
> [UNKNOWN]

Recognize that the cleansing of your mind is like water flowing over rocks in a river. Over time, the rocks' jagged edges become smooth. Over time, with God's help, you can renew and refine your thinking.

How you see yourself is absolutely critical. All self-appraisal begins with perception. Your perception is the basis for your self-identity and self-esteem. It is the foundation on which you build any relationship. Your self-perception gives rise to your choices and behavior. It is the predictor of your future prosperity and success.

Action: Imagine yourself being your best YOU one day, one week, one month, and one year from now.

Have Faith

If your problem has a solution then . . . why worry about it? If your problem doesn't have a solution then . . . why worry about it?

[CHINESE PROVERB]

You must believe that you can change the way you think and that God will help you in the process. We must know that when we ask God for something, we must believe that we are going to receive what we desire—and that includes receiving the ability to establish a new set of mental habits. Unless you believe, you don't receive. When you do believe, you do receive.

Faith and fear cannot reside in the same space. Choose to live by faith and hope, regardless of how you feel. God's Word doesn't change. Its principles are fixed and applicable to all people of all ages in all nations at all times. Your faith must become as constant as God's Word—unchanging.

Ultimately, faith is far stronger than any mood you may have. Moods change, and emotions can be like a roller coaster. Faith is intended to be steadfast and unwavering.

Every person needs some degree of renewal. No matter how good your behavior, or how pure your thoughts and motives, there is always room for more change, more development, and more improvement. You will never be fully perfected—but you can put yourself in a position to experience greater and greater perfections, which means there is continual room for growth and expansion. Renovate in a way to bring about your best future.

Action: You will know when you are on the path to your purpose in life. You will be excited, happy, content, confident, and at peace. Choose daily to pursue these positive attributes.

Living Your Dream

As your faith is strengthened, you will find that there is no longer the need to have a sense of control, that things will flow as they will, and that you will flow with them, to your great delight and benefit.

[EMMANUEL TENEY]

Desire and Determination Are Your Only Limitations

The only one really limiting you is . . . you! Desire and determination can make the "impossible" very possible. How much do you want to achieve your dreams? How important are they to you?

Some people are more strongly affected by their dreams—or certain of their dreams—than others. The strength and intensity of your dreams—how badly you really want something—will determine how far, to what lengths, and how long you are willing to work to get it.

The Natural Law of Momentum

Enthusiasm is the energy and force that builds literal momentum of the human soul and mind.

[BRYANT H. McGILL]

Newton's Law—The scientific formula for momentum:
M x V = P
Mass (M) x velocity (V) = Momentum (P)

Let's first define *momentum*. Momentum is impetus, force, thrust; it is the energy source that drives something else. It is like an avalanche that builds in magnitude, speed, and potential as it gushes down the slope.

How may people even realize that momentum is a natural law, a universal principle, that exists and operates in our lives whether we believe it or not?

The incredible thing about momentum is that once you understand it and how it applies to your life and personal growth, your chances of success go way up. If you can align your choices, thoughts, and actions with the universal principle—the natural law of momentum—your success rate will go through the roof.

As with all natural laws, though, you can either operate in ways where they serve you—or break you. Remember, principles are not biased; they do not break—we can only break ourselves against them.

Action: Think about this sports analogy: Which team usually wins the game? The best team or the team that has the momentum?

Momentum Awareness

What you feed will grow, what you starve will die.

[UNKNOWN]

A thought to ponder: what you are aware of, you can act on; what you are unaware of acts on *you*. It is certain that you are either acting on momentum right now or momentum is acting on you. It is irrelevant whether you believe it or not—it is happening anyway.

Whatever you give consistent and increasing energy to will build massive momentum in your life. As Blair Singer puts it, "highest energy" wins. This is so true. What you feed grows; what you starve dies. It couldn't be simpler when it comes to momentum.

An old Eskimo story goes something like this:

There was once an old Eskimo who had one black dog and one white dog. Every Saturday, these dogs would fight until one of them was too tired to continue. Some Saturdays the black dog would win, and on others the white dog would win. The odd thing was that the old Eskimo always bet on which dog would win . . . and was always right. Somehow he always knew which one would win.

One day, a young fellow asked the old Eskimo, "How is it that you always bet on the winning dog; how do you always know which one will win?" The old Eskimo replied, "Why, that is easy, son—I just bet on the one I had been feeding all week."

Action: So you see, what you feed—give energy to—will grow, and what you starve will die. What are you giving your energy to?

The Point Revisited

Commitment is the igniter of momentum.
[PEG WOOD]

If you consistently and increasingly feed or give energy to negativity, the negative events in your life will become plentiful and momentous. If you get up every day and whine, complain, and stew about the things you don't have, you will only get more of nothing. Your bank account of *have not* will continue to grow and build magnitude, speed, and potential—just like an avalanche.

Have you ever noticed that the more down you are, the more the universe works to *keep* you down? That's the natural law—universal principle—of momentum at work in your life.

On the other hand, if you consistently and increasingly feed or give energy to positivity, the positive events in your life will become plentiful and momentous. If you get up every day determined to feel happy to be alive, to give thanks for what you have, and to show gratitude for others, you will get even more to be thankful and grateful for. Your bank account of *have* will continue to grow and build magnitude, speed, and potential—just like an avalanche.

Have you ever noticed that the more up you are, the more the universe works to keep you up? That too is the natural law of momentum at work in your life.

Action: Good news! You get to choose your avalanche!

Momentum Application

A great flame follows a little spark.
[DANTE ALIGHIERI]

Most of us would rather give energy to the best things in our life than the worst. We would rather feel more up than down every day of the week.

Now that you understand that momentum is indeed a natural law, a universal principle, it is important that you understand how to apply it to your life and personal growth.

Momentum is a perpetual cycle; it is always going and continues infinitely. Knowing this helps you to understand that the more energy you give to the people, circumstances, and activities in your life, the more energy they will need and the more room they will occupy. This means it is your responsibility to choose your relationships, circumstances, and activities wisely.

To ensure that the momentum in your life is fueled with the proper octane of gasoline, you must make choices that are in line with your core values and grounded in correct principles. Feeding any negativity, whether in your relationships or activities, will only make the negative events more momentous in your life. There is a reason why you are often judged by the company you keep.

Certainly, you may not be a thief, but if you hang out with thieves, you cannot then be truly astonished if others also believe that you too are a thief. It may not be right for others to make that assumption; however, you can certainly see how easy it would be to draw that conclusion considering the company you keep. If you are not a thief, why would you hang out with thieves?

Action: Remember a time when you experienced momentum (both positive and negative) in your life. Write your thoughts in your journal.

Build Momentum

One way to keep momentum going is to have constantly greater goals.
[MICHAEL KORDA]

If you want the right things to build momentum in your life, those are what you have to focus on. The difficulty comes in when life throws you all sorts of curve balls and it becomes nearly impossible to juggle them all. Frustration sets in, then dejection, and ultimately depression, which leads to a negative spiral down into the abyss of despair.

The goal then is to maintain a positive attitude much more often than you do a negative one. This way, you will be able to feed the right things and give energy to positivity. Here are a few tips that can help you maintain a more positive attitude.

- Give thanks every day—Each day you rise and give thanks for life and for the blessings in your life, no matter how small you may think they are. Find new things to give thanks for, and the more you do it, the more you will receive to be thankful for.

- Celebrate all wins—Learn to celebrate all your wins and the wins of others. No matter how small the success, give yourself a pat on the back for having accomplished it. Shout it out—tell someone and truly feel good about it.

- Show gratitude—First of all, show appreciation for you, and then show appreciation for all the people in your life. Show appreciation even for the people who don't like you as much; appreciate the lessons you've learned because of them.

- Be of service to others—Find new ways to be of service to others; it doesn't matter what you do so long as you provide value to someone else with a genuine heart.

Action: The greatest gift that you can ever give to another is you. The thankful, positive, happy, grateful, giving, and loving you.

The Impact

> *Success requires first expending ten units of effort to produce one unit of results. Your momentum will then produce ten units of results with each unit of effort.*
>
> [CHARLES J. GIVENS]

The more you can maintain a positive attitude, the easier it will be for you to focus on more productive and enlightening things. You will complain less and solve more problems. You will whine less and help more. You will take less and give more. You will pout less and do more. All of these things will create positive momentum in your life.

The natural law of momentum simply says that the more force you put behind something—the more energy you feed it—the bigger and faster it gets and the more potential it has on impact.

When you consider this, what are the things you want to stop giving your energy to right now? What are some of the issues that have been plaguing you repeatedly because you kept feeding into them?

When you ponder it a moment, you will come up with a few things almost immediately. Once understood, this principle of momentum will have an immediate, profound, and impactful change in your life. It's not always easy to flip the switch the other way, but try it—it's totally worth it.

Action: Here's to more positively momentous events in your life!

Living Your Dream

If you have the guts to keep making mistakes, your wisdom and intelligence leap forward with huge momentum.

[HOLLY NEAR]

Desire. Determination. Persistence. Perseverance.

The single most critical difference between people who achieve their dreams and people who do not is their level of persistence and perseverance. Those who achieve their dreams continue to work toward them no matter what. In spite of the most daunting obstacles, all the negative people who tell them it can't be done, and numerous "failures" or false starts, the people who succeed in achieving their dreams keep on going and going and going. They refuse to quit, no matter what. They are in it to win it!

Confident Attitude

*You can do anything you wish to do, have anything you wish to have,
be anything you wish to be.*

[ROBERT COLLIER]

You can spot them easily in any group. They have that special "some-thing" that sets them apart. What is it? A sense of direction—an assur-ance that they know where they're going! An awareness of their own abilities! Sincerity! An air of past successes! They have instinct to make eye contact and use body language! In a word, what they have is *confi-dence*!

Confidence is taking your current situation—whatever obstacles you are facing, whatever limitation that may slow you down, whatever chronic condition you may live with, whatever has stolen your dreams, whatever factors in life that tend to push you under—admit-ting you don't like it, and never saying, "I can't cope."

Confidence means having the ability to stand up to any test. You were born for greatness. Confidence is knowing that I will do some-thing great with my life. Confidence is the sense that you can do some-thing beyond the ordinary. You have a seed of greatness inside of you—unique to you. Dream big dreams and think big thoughts.

Action: When do you feel most confident? What makes you feel that way?

Confidence

Nobody can make you feel inferior without your consent.

[ELEANOR ROOSEVELT]

From the quietly confident doctor whose advice we rely on to the charismatic confidence of an inspiring speaker, confident people have qualities that everyone admires.

Confidence is extremely important in almost every aspect of our lives, yet so many people struggle to find it. Sadly, this can be a vicious circle: people who lack confidence may find it difficult to become successful.

After all, most people are reluctant to back a project that's being pitched by someone who is nervous, fumbling, and overly apologetic.

On the other hand, you might be persuaded by someone who speaks clearly, who holds his or her head high, who answers questions assuredly, and who readily admits when he or she does not know something. Confident people understand they are not perfect and don't expect perfection from those around them.

Confident people *inspire confidence* in others: their audience, their peers, their bosses, their customers, and their friends. And gaining the confidence of others is one of the key ways in which a confident person finds success.

Action: Who are the most confident people you know? What makes them that way? The good news is that confidence really can be learned and built. And, whether you're working on your own confidence or building the confidence of people around you, it's well worth the effort.

Where Confidence Comes From

I have strength for all things, in Christ, who empowers me.

[PHILIPPIANS 4:13]

We all experience times of frustration and of being unfulfilled. Without confidence, fear will rule your life. You cannot enjoy life without confidence because you feel cheated out of your destiny, you will live in torment. You were not created to live an insecure, fearful life. Insecure people compare and compete with others, measure themselves against others—not happy to be just who they are. Usually they cannot handle any type of correction.

Turn to your owner's manual (Bible) and say, "I am ready for anything, I am self-sufficient in Christ's sufficiency." You can do all you need to do in life through Christ who strengthens you. You are already equipped with everything you need to pursue your goals and dreams!

Knowing God has the answer gives you the ability to know that you can do everything—confident that God is with you yet with humility.

Weaknesses—know and face them, and know that you are not condemned by them. Stick with what you do well, give up the things that others do well that you don't do well. Put your time into your strengths, not your weaknesses. Humility stops thinking about yourself. Confidence does not come from perfection—it comes from knowing God is with you.

Action: Make a list of your strengths and how you are putting them to good use. Know your weaknesses, but show the world your strengths.

What Is Self-Confidence?

It's not who you are that holds you back, it's who you think you're not.

[UNKNOWN]

Your level of self-confidence can show in many ways: your behavior, your body language, how you speak, what you say, and so on.

Low self-confidence can be self-destructive, and it often manifests itself as negativity. Confident people are generally more positive—they believe in themselves and their abilities, and they also believe in living life to the fullest.

We gain a sense of self-efficacy when we see ourselves mastering skills and achieving goals that are in line with our purpose. This is the confidence that, if we learn and work hard in a particular area, we'll succeed. It's this type of confidence that leads people to accept difficult challenges and persist in the face of setbacks.

This overlaps with the idea of self-esteem, which is a more general sense that we can cope with what's going on in our lives. It also comes from the sense that we are behaving virtuously, that we're competent at what we do, and that we can compete successfully when we put our minds to it.

Some people believe that self-confidence can be built with affirmations and positive thinking. It's just as important to build self-confidence by setting and achieving goals—thereby building competence. Without this underlying competence, you don't have confidence: you have shallow over-confidence, with all of the issues, upset, and failure that this can bring.

Action: Go boldly in the direction of your dreams! This will give you immense confidence. When you have your dreams in front of you, your goals set, you're learning new skills, and you are investing in your personal growth—and all with a positive attitude—nothing can stop you from living the life of your dreams!

Become More Confident

Make the most of yourself, for that is all there is of you.

[RALPH WALDO EMERSON]

Establish your worth. You have creative abilities, gifts, talents, strengths, and weaknesses. You are destined for greatness and success in life—that makes you priceless!

Surround yourself with confidence-boosters, not confidence-busters. Confidence-busters give you the "Charlie Brown Complex." One day Lucy put her hands on her hips and said, "You, Charlie Brown, are a foul-ball off the line-drive of life! You're a fifth putt on the eighteenth green! You're a dropped rod and reel in the lake of life! You're a missed free throw, a shanked nine-iron, and a called third strike! Have I made myself clear?" No surprise, Charlie struggled through life. If you want to have confidence, surround yourself with those who *build you up* and bring out your *best*.

Don't compare yourself to others. Comparisons will leave you feeling like the two cows reading an ad on the side of a passing milk truck: *Pasteurized, Homogenized, Standardized—Vitamin D Added*. One cow looked at the other and said "Makes you feel kind of inadequate, doesn't it?"

Action: You are fully equipped and equal for your life's assignment. Discover your gift, develop it, then go out and share it with the world!

Confidence Breeds Confidence

Many people succeed even when others don't believe in them, but rarely does a person succeed when he doesn't believe in himself.

[DR. JOYCE BROTHERS]

Confidence is contagious! It spreads like wildfire throughout your sphere of influence. You have probably experienced this in sports and in business. The leader's confident attitude creates the excitement and momentum for the team to achieve success!

A confident person is typically a positive person. They not only believe in themselves, they look for the best in others . . . and usually find it. People will generally rise to meet your expectations—words of encouragement can be the wind beneath their wings.

With a confident attitude, you begin to see opportunities all around just waiting to be seized. Ever notice when you focus on solutions, things turn out best for those who *make the best* of how things turn out?

Confident people understand that nothing good happens until we are willing to step forward and take responsibility for our thoughts and actions. Only then can we look ourselves in the eye, discover our strengths and weaknesses, and begin to grow.

Action: Experiment with this concept today! You are pursuing your dream—BE CONFIDENT! When you develop confidence, those around you—friends, family, associates—will increase their confidence levels too. Why? Because confidence breeds confidence!

Living Your Dreams

Honesty is the cornerstone of all success, without which confidence and ability to perform shall cease to exist.

[MARY KAY ASH]

Don't Give Up

How many people give up just a moment too soon and fall short of realizing their goals and achieving their dreams? Did you know that John Grisham's first novel, *A Time to Kill,* was rejected twenty-five times before it found a publisher? What if he hadn't made the twenty-sixth submission? Make up your mind to do it—and then *do it*! You don't lose until you quit.

Understanding Behavioral Styles

Knowing others is intelligence; knowing yourself is true wisdom.
Mastering others is strength, mastering yourself is true power.

[LAO TZU]

Research has shown that most successful people have the trait of self-awareness. They are able to recognize opportunities for success, and this allows them to identify ways of achieving objectives that fit within their behavioral style.

Successful people also understand their own limitations and weaknesses, which helps them make decisions as to where not to focus their efforts and where to devote more effort to their strengths.

People who have an understanding of their natural personality and behavior style are most likely to pursue opportunities in line with their strengths and their purpose. They will be decisive and efficient, and they will achieve the results they desire.

When you are conscious of personality types or behavior styles and can identify them in those around you, you will have an advantage when dealing with people. The better you get at being in the middle, being able to relate and communicate with all the different styles, the more successful you will be in life.

Action: Have you ever taken a personality test? Do one now—they're available online for free!

A Behavioral Matrix

Anything that changes your values changes your behavior.

[GEORGE A. SHEEHAN]

Understanding your own personality style is the best place to start. Then you can begin to understand how to best communicate with others. Obviously human behavior is extremely complicated; hundreds of books have been written on the subject. A simple behavioral matrix designed to quickly pick up a few clues to better understand your style and relate to others can begin your search for awareness.

The process of identifying behavior styles is simple when you become "others"-focused and practice listening to the people you are dealing with. You can contemplate two questions: 1) Is the person *formal* or *informal* in the way he or she dresses, behaves, speaks, and acts? 2) Is the person *dominant* or *easy-going* in his or her style and mannerisms, focus, appearance, expressions, how he or she behaves under stress, etc.? With this information, you can begin to understand how to best relate to this person.

Formal and dominant—Controller/Driver
Formal and easy-going—Promoter/Expressive
Informal and dominant—Analytical/Deliberate
Informal and easy-going—Supporter/Amiable

An interesting study would place one hundred people in a room and simply have them answer the two questions above and then have everyone go into four corners based on their behavior style. You would have almost an equal number in each corner. If you are a Controller/Driver Type and only speak and act in this Controller/Driver style and treat people as if they too are Controller/Drivers, then you will experience communication problems with the other 75 percent of the population! It is well worth your time to get familiar with the different personality styles.

Action: Which style are you? How about your significant other?

The Controller/Driver

> *In the confrontation between the stream and the rock, the stream*
> *always wins, not through strength but by perseverance.*
>
> [H. JACKSON BROWN]

People of the Controller/Driver style tend to be "results oriented" and *appear* to be less concerned about the personal needs of other people. Although they can be very caring, they will tend not to openly show how they feel and are often accused of not caring and being insensitive to the needs of others, caring instead about the job/results. Since the Controller mindset is motivated more by results than feelings, they may appear to be independent, competitive, reserved, and even aloof in their relationships with others.

The Controller/Driver interaction style is characterized by being direct and making things happen. They are interested in getting things done efficiently, and personal and group productivity is of high importance. The Controller will tend to judge others by his or her own personal interactive style and will often expect others to operate in the same style.

Needs:

- To be right and be in control.
- In communicating with controllers, be clear and to the point. Stick to the business at hand and present a well-prepared package.

Fear:

- Loss of control or power

Controllers tend to ask "what" questions.

Action: You can easily identify Controller/Driver personalities in your life. They are Type-A leaders who happily take charge. Usually they're passionate, competitive, organized, efficient, hardworking, and results-oriented people.

The Analyst/Deliberate

Luck is the great stabilizer in baseball.

[TRIS SPEAKER]

The Analyst/Deliberate style may appear uncommunicative, distant, and guarded in relationships. Analysts tend to judge others based on their own need for perfection and need to not be perceived as being wrong. They tend to be sensitive and worry about things being done properly. They want to make the "right" decisions. Therefore, they require detailed explanations, are usually cautious and slow to change, and tend to be low risk takers.

The Analyst makes decisions and judgments based on facts. They also separate emotion from fact and can have difficulty understanding people who are unable to do this. The ability to apply reasoning and logic is one of the Analyst's greatest strengths.

Need:

- Not to be wrong or lose face

Fear:

- Criticism or embarrassment

Analysts tend to ask "Why" questions.

Action: Be prepared to take your time and show the facts as a capable, logical, and accurate presenter when dealing with your Analyst/ Deliberate associates! You know who they are!

Promoter/Expressive

Choose your friends with caution; plan your future with purpose, and frame your life with faith.

[THOMAS S. MONSON]

Promoter/Expressives tend to be warm and approach people in an outgoing and animated way. They will involve people in their thinking and decision-making. They like to work in groups of people and tend to be fast, sometimes making impulsive decisions. Promoters tend to have much consideration for the needs of others, tend to seek social approval, and like to be in the spotlight. Life is a party!

Personal recognition is important, and they are motivated by high visibility. Too many facts or details will often interfere with their process, and they like other people to take an interest in what they think and do.

Needs:

- To be recognized
- To be a part of the "in" group

Fears:

- To experience social disapproval
- To not be seen as unique and special; ignored

Promoters tend to ask "Who" questions.

Action: Who are the excitable, fun-loving and talkative friends in your life? You certainly don't want to bore them with a lot of details, but you do want to recognize their accomplishments!

Supporter/Amiable

> *Talent is God given. Be humble. Fame is man-given. Be grateful.*
> *Conceit is self-given. Be careful.*
>
> [JOHN WOODEN]

The Supporter/Amiable is relationship oriented and works with other people to achieve results. Their friendships and close relationships are the highest priority. They are loyal and seek security and to maintain status quo. The supporter seeks warmth and cooperation in getting things done and will usually seek the recommendations of others. They tend to be slow to change and to be low risk takers except in service to others. The Supporter will build teamwork and will work toward reducing conflict. Belonging to a group is important.

Because of the systematic and thorough approach to both tasks and people, they can be perceived as being too slow or wishy-washy in making decisions. Yet their characteristics of thoroughness, dependability, and loyalty are often the factors that hold an organization together.

Needs:

- To be liked or loved
- To be included

Fears:

- Confrontation
- Lack of harmony

Supporters tend to ask "How" questions.

Action: The most loyal and dedicated people in your life will tend to be Supporter/Amiable. They are your biggest fans and are skilled coaches too! Give your Supporter/Amiable friends a big hug today!

Living Your Dream

> *The higher your energy level, the more efficient your body; the more*
> *efficient your body, the better you feel and the more you will use your*
> *talent to produce outstanding results.*

[ANTHONY ROBBINS]

Dreams Defined

Can you visualize your dreams so clearly that you can see them in your mind's eye? Dreams are the foundation that goals are built on. Dreams are what keep you going when the going gets tough—and it will. Dreams give you hope. Dreams give you a peek into the future you can create for yourself.

Mastering Peak Performance

*Patience and perseverance have a magical effect before which
difficulties disappear and obstacles vanish.*

[JOHN QUINCY ADAMS]

Natural Personality Style: The natural style is how you behave when
you are being most natural. It is your basic style and the one you adopt
when you are being authentic and true to yourself. It is also the style
that you revert to when under stress or pressure. Behaving in this style
reduces your stress and tension and is comforting. When authentic to
this style, you will maximize your true potential more effectively.

Adaptive Personality Style: The adaptive style is how you behave
when you feel you are being observed or how you behave when you
are aware of your behavior. This style is less natural and less authentic
for you or your true tendencies and preferences. When forced to adapt
to this style for too long, you may become stressed and less effective.

*Action: When and where are you most natural? When and where do
you find yourself adapting? Once you understand who you are and
where you are with your behavioral style, you will begin to find ways
to be more effective and motivated in all areas of life.*

Identify Behavioral Styles

The real measure of your wealth is how much you'd be worth if you lost all your money.

[BERNARD MELTZER]

When you are interacting with people, whether in a social setting or business setting, if you can quickly get a feel for the person's personality/behavior style you will then be better equipped to speak their "language." People connect with their own style. So, if you are a Controller/Driver and are chatting with someone you suspect is a Supporter/Amiable, you can slow down, smile, and chit chat about their family and make a connection very quickly!

People want to do business with and interact with people they like, respect, and trust. People tend to trust people who are like-minded and to whom they feel connected. It is in our appearance and our communication where we make our first impression and connections.

Action: What is your most natural style? What style is most difficult for you to be? Think of ways you can make a connection with the other three personality/behavior styles.

How to Identify Behavioral Styles

Do all things with love.

[OG MANDINO]

The first, most important component is to become a good listener. Be "others"-focused. Focusing on the other person's words, body language, and facial expression will give you almost everything you need to know about him or her.

Then you can ask yourself the two questions: Is this person formal or informal and is she dominant or easy-going? Again, listen for how she talks, her orientation and focus:

- Controller/Driver—usually talks about goals, oneself, values, change; about how things could be.
- Promoter/Expressive—usually talks about people, good things, fun, self, the future, and team spirit; about how things could be as well.
- Analyst/Deliberate—usually talks about facts, analyses, rules, details, and instructions; about how things are.
- Supporter/Amiable—usually talks about friends, the team, principles, the past, and serving; about how things are as well.

Action: Name a key personal relationship and the person's style. With your new awareness, how will you interact and communicate with them?

Appearances

> *Focus your message on the results you expect, not on the methods for doing the job.*
>
> [MARTY BROUNSTEIN]

Controllers will appear to be in a hurry, will be direct and say what they think, and may even be blunt. Most of a Controller's opinions are stated as facts, and they interrupt others and may talk to many people at the same time. They may appear to be aggressive and demanding with one question on their mind: "What's the bottom line?"

Promoters appear open and friendly and may talk a lot, mainly about people they know. They are very animated as they get excited very easily but don't focus much on details. You better hurry to get your point across, because most promoters will not listen for long.

Analyticals appear to be reserved and timid because they are quiet. They focus on details as they study specifications and information. They will ask many questions but don't easily express disagreeing views.

Supporters appear calm and thoughtful. They are great listeners and are easygoing. They will ask questions and inquire about specifics. They seem to have strong opinions but don't express them vocally.

Action: Name key business relationships and the people's styles. How will you change your approach when communicating with them?

Be Aware

If you talk to a man in a language he understands, that goes to his head. If you talk to him in his language, that goes to his heart.

[NELSON MANDELA]

Controllers can be impatient and irritated easily. It may be difficult for them to understand others' viewpoints and feelings as they are wondering, "How does this benefit *me*?" Their focus is on the big picture, and they can make decisions quickly. When there is a party, they are in charge!

Promoters may not pay close attention and may ask the same question several times. They tend to jump from subject to subject and stay away from hard facts. Not the most organized people, they tend to make decisions spontaneously. They are very comfortable with physical contact. Promoters are the ones who throw the party.

Analyticals may be very critical and do all of their research before making a decision. They're not comfortable with physical contact. They are the ones who will set the budget for the party.

Supporters can be uncomfortable with new ideas or things. They will ponder alternatives and are slow at making decisions. "Let me think about it" is a common line. They're usually the ones cleaning up after the party.

Action: Study the people you interact with daily. Which personality is most challenging for you to relate to? Do you think it will it help to speak their natural "language"?

Be Proactive

Always be yourself, express yourself, have faith in yourself; do not go out and look for a successful personality and duplicate it.

[BRUCE LEE]

Because people live in society and because they are bound together by the bonds of competition and cooperation, it has always been important for us to understand each other's personalities. You might imagine when our hunter-gatherer ancestors finally cornered a beast they had been pursuing, it would have been important to know which hunter would remain brave when the animal tried to break out and which would flee. The competitive side of human nature requires people to size each other up, look for weaknesses in a rival, and search for the opportunity to come out on top. The number of situations where humans need to understand each other's motives, instincts, and likely reactions is almost limitless.

Most humans seem to be just plain curious about each other. Many of us spend hours chatting with our friends fascinated about the motives, quirks, and relationships of others and ourselves. Even gossip could be considered a study of the personalities of each other and of our own personality.

Life presents us with a series of choices that stretches from the cradle (teddy bear or fuzzy rabbit) to the grave (buried or cremated). Our whole lives are governed by the choices we make, and those choices will be affected fundamentally by our personality. Which career, whom to marry, how many children? Knowing your own personality will help you make good choices. Understanding other people's personality traits will help you relate better with others.

Action: Self-discovery is a lifelong commitment. Have fun and enjoy the journey.

Living Your Dream

> *When I stand before God at the end of my life, I would hope that I would not have a single bit of talent left, and could say, "I used everything you gave me."*
>
> [ERMA BOMBECK]

Goals Defined

Goals are not wishes or resolutions, and they are not vague. Goals are not random or magic or mysterious. Plain and simple, a goal is something very specific that you can identify, you desire to achieve, you plan to achieve, and you put forth effort to achieve.

Goals require concentrated thought, have a specific objective, should be worded positively, and require a commitment. Goals are the steppingstones that lead you to the life of your dreams.

Patience

A man who is a master of patience is master of everything else.

[GEORGE SAVILE]

When you are pursuing your Big Dream, sometimes you will feel like giving up. You will experience setbacks and problems. It may be taking way longer than you like. Doubt begins to creep in; people close to you (often people who never pursued a dream of their own) are telling you it can't be done, you're crazy, and that it wasn't meant to be.

If you are discouraged and feel as though your dream is dying, don't give up! Don't give up too soon on your dream. It's *always* too soon to quit. Keep going! Keep dreaming the dream God has put into your heart. If it were easy, anyone could do it.

It can be the same with you and your life. We can misread the message of circumstances and thereby miss our destiny. When you dream, you can rise above your limitations; you move from where you are to where you are supposed to be. The question is not if you can dream but if you have the courage to follow through and pursue those dreams!

Action: When your initial excitement wears off and everything seems to have stalled, don't be surprised. This is normal. Every person goes through this. When it comes (it may happen more than once), don't give up, and don't throw in the towel. Believe that you can—you have to be tenacious about your vision.

The Purpose of Life

All human wisdom is summed up in two words—wait and hope.
[ALEXANDRE DUMAS PERE]

The purpose of life is to live a life of purpose. What is your assignment in life? Your feelings, ideas, visions, and dreams are the ways God nudges you along toward His perfect plan for your life. When you first respond by recognizing you do have a dream, you are bringing about the birth of your vision.

As explained by Jentezen Franklin in his book *Believe That You Can,* every vision and dream will go through the process of birth, death, and resurrection. You have not really realized a dream unless you've carried a burden, gotten all excited because you have given birth to a newborn vision, and then, sadly, watched what appears to be a death. The vision "dies"—people leave; the money goes away; the situation goes haywire; you just can't figure out what to do about it.

Then, and only then, God will come through with a resurrection. He uses that process to sanctify that dream so that when it really does come to pass, it will not be an egotistical thing for you. Instead, you can declare, "I almost gave up on my dream. I doubted the vision, but the Lord did it anyway!" You will know beyond a shadow of a doubt that God did it, because it used to look so hopeless. See, it really was bigger than you were. You really could not have brought that thing back to life like that. God broke the limits off. He raised it back up. He finished what He started.

Action: If you are in the middle of that process right now, don't give up! Seek encouragement and a new supply of faith. Hold on; help is coming.

Patience Wins the Race

He that can have Patience, can have what he will.

[BENJAMIN FRANKLIN]

You have to endure patiently. It might take a long time, but victory is achievable. It's like the torch race in the ancient Greek Olympics that was different from other races. In the other races, the winner was the one who crossed the finish line first. But in the torch race, they lit a bunch of torches and handed them out to every runner. They started the race with the fires burning, and the only way you could win the torch race was to finish with your fire still burning. Just because you made it first didn't count until they checked to see if your fire was still lit.

The race was not for the swift. Sometimes the winner would be the one who looked like he was barely making it. Only by patient persistence and by letting others pass him could the victor claim his prize. Everyone else might seem to outrun him and outdo him, but they wouldn't win if they lost their fire.

Action: Do you want to be a winning torch racer? Keep moving as fast as you can, but don't lose your fire. The important thing is not how quickly can you make it—it is whether or not you still have your purpose burning in you when you cross the finish line. Only by persistence did the snail make it onto the ark, but he made it, and that's all that counted!

Stages to Every Dream

Patience is the greatest of all virtues.
[CATO THE ELDER]

There is a sequence of how your dream or vision will unfold; you need to grab hold of each step as it occurs.

Imagine Your Dream. The first stage may be just a thought, something that may not mean much to the people around you but is like a revelation to you. It simply won't let you go. You think about it all the time, saying to yourself, "Wow, could I really do that? Yes, I could do that! I can definitely see myself doing that. It could really happen."

Take Action. You can't keep thinking about it forever. In fact, if you turn it around in your mind enough, it's almost inevitable that you will catch hold of the vision and begin to talk to other people about it. It may not be clear; you're just kind of throwing the idea out there to explore the possibility of it. Now it begins to be more than just a thought.

You're talking about it, so you have "caught" it. You are looking into it. You've gone beyond just thinking about it. Many people get this far then let the vision die before taking the next step.

Ownership. Now you have to pay the price. Talk is free, but in the next step you must put it on the line. You need to buy into the dream and take a little risk. You decide to make a change and take a risk. Now you feel uncomfortable *not* moving forward with your dream.

Action: Begin to pay the price in terms of education, making sacrifices to equip yourself for fulfilling your dream. Do whatever you have to do. You have circled the mountain long enough, and now you go in to conquer it. You must sow to reap!

More Stages to Every Dream

> *Learn the art of patience. Apply discipline to your thoughts when they become anxious over the outcome of a goal. Impatience breeds anxiety, fear, discouragement, and failure. Patience creates confidence, decisiveness, and a rational outlook which eventually leads to success.*
>
> [BRIAN ADAMS]

Laser Focus. Now there's no stopping you—you are really committed. You are focused with laser intensity. There may be negativity out there, but you don't hear or see it. You are like a maniac on a mission. You have that look in your eyes; you have the eye of the tiger on the hunt. You persevere through the obstacles, no matter what!

Live Your Dream. You did it—you're *there*! You can grab hold of the prize! You've walked the walk and paid the price. And you are happy you did.

Mentor. There is no success without a successor. Who is mentoring you and who are you mentoring? We are all blessed because of the sacrifices of the Big Dreamers that paved the path for us. They not only believed in their own dreams, but they also taught us that we can believe in our dreams too!

Action: As a person who pursues goals and dreams, you will happily live a life of no regrets. You will not look back on your life and see lost dreams. You will be able to say, "I did it!"—this one, and that one, and that other one too!

Patience Is a Virtue

It is very strange that the years teach us patience—that the shorter our time, the greater our capacity for waiting.

[ELIZABETH TAYLOR]

It has never been easy to be patient, but it's probably even harder now than at any time in history. In a world where messages can be sent across the world instantly, seemingly everything is available with a few clicks of the mouse, and a swift movement of your thumbs can take you into a fantasy game world, it's very hard *not* to expect instant satisfaction.

But patience remains a valuable tool in life. We don't always get instant gratification, and some of the best things in life require years of hard work and waiting. Fortunately, patience is a virtue that can be cultivated and nurtured. It does take time to fulfill this goal, but once this has grown into an ordinary skill for you, you certainly won't be disappointed at what life can offer you with some spare time. You will be surprised by how once boring, restless, and lagging hours can evolve into a passing time of relaxation and peace of mind.

Action: Do you consider yourself a patient person? Do other people consider you a person with patience?

Living Your Dream

Endurance is the crowning quality, And patience all the passion of great hearts.

[JAMES RUSSELL LOWELL]

Dreams vs. Goals

Dreams are not the same as goals. Dreams are essentially passive—anyone can do it, anytime, anywhere. Goals, on the other hand, are active. They require action, and they require effort. Goals require you take initiative and *do something*.

If your dreams are "heaven," then goals are the "stairway to heaven." Goals are the steps that can take you to the realization of your dreams.

How to Be Patient

A hand full of patience is worth more than a bushel of brains.

[DUTCH PROVERB]

Journal. Get a notepad or a piece of paper and a pen or pencil. For one to two weeks, whenever you get that "rushed" feeling and the sense of impatience, write down whatever it is that feeling is associated with (Example: October 1—doctor's appointment). Make sure you take note consistently and consecutively each time the feeling occurs. You will notice that you are more aware of (and subsequently more prepared for) the feeling of impatience. You will also be able to observe the sense of impatience objectively and which events give rise to it. You may come to the conclusion that *circumstances* surrounding the feeling are not causing you angst—the feeling itself is. Being more aware, you will be able to better control impatience when you recognize the trigger that brings it on.

Try to figure out why you are in such a hurry. We tend to lose our patience when we're multitasking or when we're on a tight schedule, expecting the day to pass within (what seems like) only a few short minutes of busyness and chaos. If you're stretching yourself too thin, you should reconsider your to-do list before you attempt to change your natural reaction to an overwhelming situation. Try to be realistic about what you can accomplish in a day. Delegate responsibilities to others if you can; this in itself may be a test of your patience, but you have to learn to share the load.

Action: Create an organizational system for your daily activities. The night before, prepare for the next day by making a list of the six most important tasks you want to accomplish.

Ideas on How to Have Patience

Have patience with all things, but chiefly have patience with yourself. Do not lose courage when considering your own imperfections, but instantly set about remedying them—every day begin the task anew.

[SAINT FRANCIS DE SALES]

Pinpoint the triggers that often influence you to lose your patience. Impatience creeps in insidiously, and if you feel anxious, worried, or unhappy you may not even realize that the underlying cause of these feelings is impatience. To reduce the frequency of impatience, it helps to be aware of it. Which events, people, phrases, or circumstances always seem to influence you to lose your cool? Sit down and make a list of all the things that cause you anxiety, tension, or frustration. At the core of most triggers is a reality that we have a hard time accepting. What are those realities for you?

Overcome bouts of impatience. In the long run, developing patience requires a change in your attitude about life, but you can immediately make progress by learning to relax whenever you feel impatient. Take a few deep breaths and just try to clear your mind. Count to ten slowly before you react to the situation. Remove yourself from the disturbing environment and take a quick walk outside. Close your eyes and take a quick trip to your "happy place." Find what works for you.

Action: Practice your own relaxation techniques. When you feel yourself becoming impatient, use self-control, and practice patience.

Be Aware

Patience serves as a protection against wrongs as clothes do against cold. For as you put on more clothes as the cold increases it will have no power to hurt you. So in like manner you must grow in patience when you meet with great wrongs, then they will be powerless to vex your mind.

[LEONARDO DA VINCI]

Look for patterns. Being aware of your impatience also gives you a chance to learn from it and perhaps uncover a relationship or circumstance that is simply not healthy or constructive and that you may have the power to change. Figure that out, and you can then think logically about the problem issue and decide whether or not your impatience is warranted or helpful. It usually isn't, but when it is you can then figure out ways to fix the root problem rather than simply feeling stressed about it.

Let go if you can't do anything about the impatience trigger. If there isn't anything that you can do to resolve whatever has triggered your impatience, just let it go. Easier said than done, yes, but it's possible, and it's the only healthy thing to do. Initially, you will probably find it difficult to let go if the matter is important to you—waiting to hear back after a job interview, for instance—but you should be able to alleviate impatience that's caused by issues of less consequence (i.e., waiting in line at the grocery store). If you make a concerted effort to be more patient in relatively inconsequential, short-term situations, you'll gradually develop the strength to remain patient in even the most trying and enduring situations.

Action: Determine if an issue is out of your control (i.e., the weather) or something you can manage (i.e., leaving your home earlier for an appointment). Prevent times when you could possibly become impatient.

Good Things Come to Those Who Wait

If I have ever made any valuable discoveries, it has been to owing more to patient attention, than to any other talent.

[SIR ISAAC NEWTON]

Remind yourself that things take time. People who are impatient are people who insist on getting things done *now* and don't like to waste time. However, some things just can't be rushed. Think about your happiest memories. Chances are they were instances when your patience paid off, like when you worked steadily toward a goal that wasn't immediately gratifying or spent a leisurely day with a loved one. Would you have those memories if you had been impatient? Probably not. Almost anything really good in life takes time and dedication, and if you're impatient, you're more likely to give up on relationships, goals, and other things that are important to you. Good things may not always come to those who wait, but most good things that do come don't come right away.

Expect the unexpected. Yes, you have plans, but things don't always work out as planned. Accept the twist and turns in life gracefully. Keep your expectations realistic. This applies not only to circumstances but also the behavior of those around you. If you find yourself blowing up over your child or your spouse accidentally spilling a drink, you're not in touch with the fact that people aren't perfect. Even if the occasion is not an isolated incident but is instead caused by their repeated neglect and carelessness, losing your patience isn't going to make it any better. That's something to be addressed with discussion and self-control.

Action: Compliment someone you know that is a good role model of patience. Ask them for some advice.

Proper Expectations

A high hope for a low heaven: God grant us patience.

[WILLIAM SHAKESPEARE]

Give yourself a break. The meaning of this is twofold. First, take a few minutes to do absolutely nothing. Just sit quietly and think. Don't watch television—don't even read. Do nothing. It may be hard at first, and you may even feel pretty impatient after a minute or two, but by taking some time out you can essentially slow your world down, and that's important for developing the attitude necessary to grow in patience.

Second, stop holding yourself and the world around you to unreachable standards. Sure, we'd all be more patient if babies didn't cry, dishes didn't break, computers didn't crash, and people didn't make mistakes—but *that's never going to happen*. Expecting the world to run smoothly is like beating your head against the wall. Give yourself a break.

Remember what matters. Not focusing on what matters most in this life fuels impatience. Move the world toward peace by being kind, generous in forgiveness of others, being grateful for what is, and taking full advantage of what matters most. When other less important things fuel our impatience, taking time to remember any one of these items reduces our tendency to want something different right now.

Action: Write down your top ten list of most important things to you.

Cherish Patience

Our patience will achieve more than our force.

[EDMUND BURKE]

Always remember that you will eventually get what you want. (This requires maturity and patience to understand and accept!) If you work hard at something, this may be the truth, but most of the time you have to be patient to get what you want.

Just remember, patience is a mental skill that you will never forget, so cherish patience as a major step for you in life. Impatience is something not to be proud of, but something that you should attempt to train yourself out of, before it is something that overthrows your life.

Action: Celebrate success! Congratulate yourself for every bit of progress you make at becoming a person of patience.

Living Your Dream

The Serenity Prayer

*God grant me the serenity
to accept the things I cannot change;
courage to change the things I can;
and wisdom to know the difference.
Living one day at a time;
Enjoying one moment at a time;
Accepting hardships as the pathway to peace;
Taking, as He did, this sinful world
as it is, not as I would have it;
Trusting that He will make all things right
if I surrender to His Will;
That I may be reasonably happy in this life
and supremely happy with Him
Forever in the next.
Amen.*

[REINHOLD NIEBUHR]

SMART FOR ME

Achieving your goals is going to be hard work. Make sure any goal that will require a commitment of your time and energy is worthy of that investment. Ensure your goals are SMART, also ask yourself: "Are these goals SMART FOR ME?"

Specific. Measurable. Attainable. Realistic. Timely. Focused. Optimistic. Ready. Meaningful. Exciting.

Attitude of Gratitude

Gratitude is a vaccine, an antitoxin, and an antiseptic.
[JOHN HENRY JOWETT]

Gratitude is an expression of thanks for gifts we have received. Scientists are finding that an attitude of gratitude is a powerful contributor to a happy life. Some believe that it may be the single most effective way to increase happiness.

According to Dr. Robert Emmons, a professor at the University of California and a leading gratitude researcher and author of the book *Thanks!*, the idea of receiving a gift is central to the concept of gratitude.

While merely appreciating something for its positive qualities does have a positive impact on our lives and emotions, *gratitude* takes the next step beyond. Gratitude happens when we go beyond just appreciating something to acknowledging that we have received a gift that we did nothing to earn or deserve. On some level, the warm emotional rush we feel when we really feel gratitude is very much like the glow we feel from realizing we are unconditionally loved.

The feeling of gratitude is like living in a state of grace. One definition of grace is *unmerited divine assistance given humans for their resurrection and regeneration.* In short, grace is our response to feeling loved unconditionally by God. When we practice an attitude of gratitude, we are practicing feeling loved.

Emmons distinguishes between feeling grateful and being grateful. Feeling grateful is a response to a benefit, while being grateful is a way of life. Gratitude has the power to heal, to energize, and to change lives. Yet often, many of us neither feel grateful, nor are we grateful.

Action: What are you grateful for? Start a list and aim for at least twenty items. Can you get to fifty today? I challenge you to keep going—how many can you think of this week?

The Power of Gratitude

Grace and gratitude go together like heaven and earth.

[KARL BARTH]

Research shows that practicing an attitude of gratitude may be the fastest single pathway to happiness, health, long life, and prosperity. It has been found that people who keep a list or a gratitude journal report great life satisfaction. They exercise more, enjoy life more, and their families and friends notice that they are nicer to be around. People who take the time to notice and appreciate the good things that come their way through grace, luck, or the goodness of others are happier and more peaceful. Grateful people typically do better on cognitive tests and have great problem-solving skills. They practice healthier habits, have better relationships, are more optimistic, and live longer. Gratitude is a powerful basic human emotion.

Think about this: we are wearing clothes others made for us, eating food others grew and prepared for us, using tools others designed and fabricated and taught us how to use, and are even speaking words others defined and explained. The list goes on and on. Any verb we can think of—sleep, play, drive, work, watch, bathe—can be followed by a phrase attributing the action to some supporting role by others. There is nothing we do that is thanks to our own efforts alone.

Action: Smiling, giving compliments, and saying "thank you" are just a few simple ways to show people your gratitude. Develop the habit of being more grateful and see the world in a more positive way!

Becoming Aware

> *Develop an attitude of gratitude, and give thanks for everything that happens to you, knowing that every step forward is a step toward achieving something bigger and better than your current situation.*
>
> [Brian Tracy]

Why do most of us fail to notice the efforts of others? Could it be that we are caught up in our own suffering? We tend to focus on what *life is denying us* and fail to notice what *life is offering us*. When we focus on what life is denying, we see the world as amiss and we struggle.

Gratitude is a lesson that is hard to learn for those who look upon the world amiss. The most that they can do is see themselves as better off than others. And they try to be content because others seem to suffer more than they do. How sad and deprecating are these thoughts!

To live a life of gratitude is to open our eyes to the countless ways in which we are supported by the world around us. Such a life provides less space for our own suffering because our attention is more balanced. We are more often occupied with noticing what we are given, thanking those who have helped us, and repaying the world in some concrete way for what we are receiving and have received in the past.

Action: Having the attitude of gratitude will empower us to be thankful and willing to help others less fortunate than us. We should resist the concept that we are too sick to help those who are more sick or to think we are too poor to help those who have even less than we do.

Being Grateful

When you are grateful, fear disappears and abundance appears
[ANTHONY ROBBINS]

The previous practices may help us feel more grateful, but how about gratitude as a way of life? In other words, being grateful is something that must be cultivated; simply knowing about gratitude is not enough.

Being grateful is no different from being loving or being compassionate. We are naturally grateful, loving, and compassionate when we remove our own internal barriers to being so. And how do we remove these barriers? We become aware and look at all our thoughts that are not grateful, not loving, and not compassionate. By becoming aware, we look without justifying, without resistance, and without judging our lack of gratitude.

Looking without justification, resistance, or judgment requires that we begin to loosen our identification with our thinking. We can have unloving, ungrateful thoughts, but we can become aware of our thoughts without grabbing hold of them and creating a story around them. In that way, we can let them go instead of cementing our identity around them.

In the lesson "Love Is the Way I Walk in Gratitude," *A Course in Miracles* encourages us to be grateful for our place in the unity of life: "We thank our Father for one thing alone; that we are separate from no living thing, and therefore one with Him. And we rejoice that no exceptions ever can be made which would reduce our wholeness. . . . We give thanks for every living thing, for otherwise we offer thanks for nothing, and we fail to recognize the gifts of God to us."

Action: As we first become aware of and then let go of our dysfunctional thinking, gratitude rushes in to fill the space available. We not only feel grateful, we are *grateful.*

How to Be More Grateful

Be thankful for what you have; you'll end up having more. If you concentrate on what you don't have, you will never, ever have enough.

[OPRAH WINFREY]

So how do we develop an attitude of gratitude? If you are worried that such a powerhouse of happiness and success must come with a high price, fear not. It turns out that developing gratitude is surprisingly easy. Here are five proven methods:

- Keep a gratitude journal. Every day or so, write about the good things that happened to you that day. You do not need a special format or to keep to any special schedule, although the people with the most success and results use the journal daily.

- Write a letter of appreciation. Express your gratitude to people who have helped you, particularly those who have helped you without special reward like teachers and nurses. We are touched by others every day.

- Make a gratitude visit. You can express your gratitude in person even more powerfully than in a letter. Gratitude is such a powerful emotion for both the giver and receiver. You may find writing the letter first helps you get your thoughts in order to deliver your message more effectively.

Action: In a minute you can put a smile on someone's face (including your own) by genuinely expressing your gratitude.

More Ways to Be Grateful

*When you arise in the morning, give thanks for the morning light, for
your life and strength. Give thanks for your food, and the joy of living.
If you see no reason for giving thanks, the fault lies with yourself.*

[TECUMSEH, SHAWNEE CHIEF]

- Make a gratitude list. This can often be a quick pick-me-up. Set a goal of listing one hundred things you have to be grateful for, and then keep adding to your list until you reach that number. Some days it is hard to get started, but persistence pays off, as a longer list pushes us to examine our blessings more deeply.

- Take a gratitude walk. This method works a little like the list in that you have a set time period—your walk—to focus on deepening your gratitude. Many people find the movement and variety of walking help their brains and hearts to work better.

*Action: Whatever method you choose, there are quick and easy ways
to develop more gratitude. How fortunate for us that this powerhouse
of happiness and success is so easy to get. So take the time to develop
an attitude of gratitude and you can enjoy a happier life now.*

Living Your Dream

Gratitude helps you to grow and expand; gratitude brings joy and laughter into your life and into the lives of all those around you.

[EILEEN CADDY]

Focus

Setting and achieving goals requires a lot of work—and an investment of resources—like your time, energy, and money, just to name a few. It's important that you focus your efforts toward the completion of the goal to use those resources wisely. If you can't focus your resources toward a particular goal at this time, it's better to wait to pursue that goal until you can.

How to Win Friends & Influence People

> *A friend should be one in whose understanding and virtue we can equally confide, and whose opinion we can value at once for its justness and its sincerity.*
>
> [ROBERT HALL]

How to Win Friends and Influence People is one of the first self-help books ever published. Written by Dale Carnegie and first published in 1936, it has sold fifteen million copies worldwide. This week we will highlight some key tips from this essential book for achievers.

Fundamental Techniques in Handling People

1. Be Nice, or Else
   Here is an important principle in relationships: don't criticize, condemn, or complain. People rarely blame themselves for anything, so if you criticize them, not only are they unlikely to change, but also they may resent you for your comments. Think of more ways to expand our minds around positivity.

2. The Big Secret of Dealing with People
   People will go a long way—sometimes even become insane—just to get the appreciation they need. So be a person who gives honest and sincere appreciation to others. That's the big secret of dealing with people. If you do that, you can't keep people from liking you.

Action: How good are you at making friends? Please read or reread How to Win Friends and Influence People *by Dale Carnegie.*

Make People Like You

You can make more friends in two months by becoming interested in other people than you can in two years by trying to get other people interested in you.

[DALE CARNEGIE]

Six Ways to Make People Like You

1. Do This and You'll Be Welcome Anywhere
    Are you interested in others? Do you want to know about them, do you admire their work, and do you eagerly want to help them? If you do, they will also be interested in you.

2. A Simple Way to Make a Good First Impression
    The easiest way to make a good first impression is so simple that we sometimes forget it: smile. When you smile, people will feel that you are glad to meet them. They will feel accepted and will have a good first impression of you.

3. If You Don't Do This, You Are Headed for Trouble
    People put tremendous importance on their names. Therefore it will be much easier for you to win their hearts if you approach them by using their names. Visualization is a good technique for remembering names.

Action: Smile, give compliments, and call people by name everywhere you go today and every day.

People Will Like You

But friendship is precious, not only in the shade, but in the sunshine of life, and thanks to a benevolent arrangement the greater part of life is sunshine.

[THOMAS JEFFERSON]

4. An Easy Way to Become a Good Conversationalist
    It may seem counterintuitive, but being a good conversationalist is not about how well you speak. It's about how well you listen. Encourage others to talk about themselves, and be a good listener. People will feel appreciated, and they will regard you as a nice person to talk with.

5. Talk in Terms of the Other Person's Interest
    Most people rarely remember specific details about someone they meet—when they think about someone they've met, they remember that person as either good or not good. They also remember how you made them feel.

6. How to Make People Like You Instantly
    The fastest way to make people like you is to make them feel important . . . and do it sincerely. The desire to feel important is perhaps the deepest need someone has, so if you can accomplish this with a smile on your face and love in your heart, they will trust and like you.

Action: Are you a good listener? There is a very good reason we all have one mouth and two ears—we should listen twice as much as we speak!

Win People

> *It is not so much our friends' help that helps us, as the confidence of their help.*
>
> [EPICURUS]

How to Influence People

1. **You Can't Win an Argument**
   You can only lose if you argue, because—no matter what the outcome of the argument is—you won't win someone's heart. So the way to get the best of an argument is to avoid it.

2. **A Sure Way of Making Enemies—And How to Avoid It**
   A sure way of making enemies is by saying that someone is wrong. People don't like that, regardless of whether or not they are actually wrong. Such statements hurt their self-esteem. So learn to respect other people's opinions, even when you disagree.

3. **The Secret of Yes**
   If you want to win other people to your way of thinking, it's important to make them agree with you from the beginning. The way to do that is by asking questions that they will inevitably answer with yes. Every time they say yes, they will become more receptive toward you.

4. **A Formula That Will Work Wonders for You**
   There must be a reason why people say or act the way they do. Find that reason and talk from their point of view. If you understand them, they will in turn be open to understanding you.

Action: Practice the Golden Rule: Treat others as you want to be treated.

Be a Leader

Let us be grateful to people who make us happy, they are the charming gardeners who make our souls blossom.

Be a Leader: How to Influence People Without Giving Offense or Arousing Resentment

1. If You Must Find Fault, This Is the Way to Begin
   As a leader, we sometimes need to correct the people we lead. But how can we do that without offending them? The answer is by praising and giving honest appreciation first. When we do that, they will become much more receptive to the correction we give.

2. How to Spur People On to Success
   The best way to develop good traits in others is not by punishing them for incorrect behavior but by rewarding them for their good behavior. Praise every improvement they make, even the slightest one, and they will continue on in the right direction.

3. People Will Live Up to Their Reputation
   A simple way to influence others is to give them positive expectations to live up to. For instance, if you want someone to be diligent, then treat her as a diligent person and say so to her. Most likely she won't disappoint you.

Action: A simple philosophy: Be a friend to make a friend. Start the process of making a new friend today.

Conclusion

In everyone's life, at some time, our inner fire goes out. It is then burst into flame by an encounter with another human being. We should all be thankful for those people who rekindle the inner spirit.

[ALBERT SCHWEITZER]

Conclusion

How to Win Friends and Influence People contains excellent principles for human relations. The principles are universal and cover practically every important aspect of relationships. The stories in each chapter make it easy to grasp those principles.

The problem, of course, is in putting the principles into practice. Knowing the principles is one thing, but applying them is another. Since most of us have the tendency to be self-centered, we need conscious and serious effort to apply the principles in the book. That's why Dale Carnegie positioned *How to Win Friends and Influence People* as a workbook that we should refer to from time to time.

Action: This is a must-have book for every library. Read it, highlight it, take notes. Truly make the serious effort to practice the principles on a daily basis.

Living Your Dream

We need to give each other the space to grow, to be ourselves, to exercise our diversity. We need to give each other space so that we may both give and receive such beautiful things as ideas, openness, dignity, joy, healing, and inclusion.

[Max de Pree]

Ready or Not?

Many of us aspire to achieve certain things in our life, but we may not be ready to devote our time, energy, and other resources to achieving those goals at this point in our life. There is a time and a season for every purpose—but it is important to recognize your readiness level before committing yourself to a large goal. Carefully consider the price you are willing to pay when you are ready to embark on the process.

The People We Associate With

Fear less, hope more; eat less, chew more; whine less, breathe more; talk less, say more; love more, and all good things will be yours.

[SWEDISH PROVERB]

Where could you be right now—or even better, where could you be tomorrow—if you surrounded yourself with a network of positive support to assist you on your journey?

There's a saying that goes, "We are like the five people that we associate with the most, and our income is an average of those five people."

If you don't like the path you're on, take a look around you to see whom you're associating with. After all, water truly does seek its own level.

It is definitely worth thinking about. The people you associate with have a profound affect on how you feel and what you'll ultimately achieve.

This is one of those areas where there is a large gap between theory and practice. In other words, we often know it's important to limit involvement with negative people, yet we continue to hang around with them.

Action: Take a close look at the five people you hang out with the most. Are they mostly positive or mostly negative?

Nourishing & Toxic People

> *A pessimist sees the difficulty in every opportunity; an optimist sees the opportunity in every difficulty.*
>
> [WINSTON CHURCHILL]

As you might expect, toxic people are the ones who always dwell on the negative. The dictionary defines *toxic* as "poisonous," and toxic people continually spew their verbal poison. In contrast, the dictionary definition of *nourishing* is "to nurture or promote the growth of." Nourishing people are positive and supportive. They lift your spirits and are a joy to be around.

Negative people will always drag you down to their level. They hammer away at you with all of the things you can't do and all of the things that are impossible. They barrage you with gloomy statements about the lousy economy, the problems in their lives, the problems soon to be in your life, and the terrible prospects for the future. If you're lucky, they might even throw in a few words about their aches and pains and recent illnesses.

After listening to toxic people, you feel listless, depressed, and drained. Jack Canfield describes them as "energy vampires"—they suck all the positive energy out of you. One thing is certain: these vampires will wear you down and kill your dreams.

On the other hand, how do you feel when you are around people who are positive, enthusiastic, and supportive? You are encouraged and inspired. You start to pick up their attitude, and you feel as if you have added strength to vigorously pursue your own goals.

Action: Identify the toxic people in your life. Make a point to spend less time with them and more time with the positive influences.

Pick Nourishment

Once you replace negative thoughts with positive ones, you'll start having positive results.

[WILLIE NELSON]

If you had a choice, wouldn't you rather hang out with nourishing people? Well, in fact, you *do* have a choice. It's up to you to determine with whom you spend your time. If toxic people surround you in your daily life, you can do something about it.

To begin with, develop friendships and associations with people who are positive and supportive. In addition, seek out people who are action-oriented and service-oriented. As you spend more and more time in the company of people who have these traits, you, too, will develop the same successful characteristics and put them to use in your life.

Consider with whom you have been spending your time. Examine your friendships and relationships at work and during your leisure hours. Those who occupy your time have a significant impact on your most priceless possession— your *mind*! It is your responsibility to regulate what you allow into your mind.

Action: To refine your mindset fully and skillfully, it is important to associate with the right people. Who you associate with determines how you think, and the outlook you have on life.

Tips

There is little difference in people, but that little difference makes a big difference. The little difference is attitude. The big difference is whether it is positive or negative.

[W. CLEMENT STONE]

Here are some steps you can take to be more responsible about the people you surround yourself with:

- If you regularly have lunch with toxic people at work, stop it. You should be able to find a diplomatic way of extricating yourself from this "poisonous" group.

- If you have a toxic relative (which could be your mother, father, uncle, sister, etc.), it is important to put some limits on your relationship. This does not mean that you abandon this relative and never speak to him or her. However, you should not go out of your way to call that person several times each day if he or she is going to put you down or fill the conversation with negative remarks.

- Form your own positive group with friends or colleagues. Make a commitment to meet with these people on a regular basis (e.g., once a week or once a month) to discuss goals, exchange ideas, and offer support. These should be people who accept you as you are and yet challenge you to be the best that you can be.

Action: Make a list of the people you would like to include in your positive group. Invite them for a cup of coffee to chat.

Like Attracts Like

I don't want to get to the end of my life and find that I have just lived the length of it. I want to have lived the width of it as well.

[DIANE ACKERMAN]

We can be a positive influence on the negative people. It is worth making an effort to steer them in a more positive direction. But if we've been trying for the last nine years and the person insists on being negative, maybe it's time to severely limit the amount of time we spend with that person—or to stop spending time with that individual completely.

As you increase your associations with nourishing people, you will feel better about yourself and about your ability to achieve your goals. You'll become a more positive, upbeat person—the kind of person others want to be around. It may be essential to your success and happiness to associate with positive people more and to limit involvement with negative people.

By the way, as you continue to associate with positive people, the law of attraction starts to kick in. That law states that *like attracts like*. When you are positive, you'll attract more positive people into your life. Of course, if you are *negative*, you'll attract negative people.

Action: Surround yourself with positive, nourishing people at home, at work, at play, at church, at all times—they will lift you up the ladder of success and happiness. Do the same for them!

Get Rich Quick

Attitudes are contagious. Are yours worth catching?
[DENNIS AND WENDY MANNERING]

Positive successful people look at other positive successful people as a means to motivate themselves. They see other successful people as models to learn from. They say to themselves, "If they can do it, I can do it." Modeling is one of the primary ways that people learn.

Positive, motivated people are grateful that others have succeeded before them so that they now have a blueprint to follow that will make it easier to attain their own success. Why reinvent the wheel? There are proven methods for success that work for virtually everyone who applies them.

The fastest and easiest way to create success and wealth is to learn from someone who has already done it. The goal is to simply model their inner and outer strategies. It just makes sense: if you take the exact same actions and have the exact same mind-set, chances are good you will get the exact same results.

When negative/broke people hear about other people's success, they tend to judge them, criticize them, mock them, and try to pull them down to their own level. Do you know people like this? Do you know family members like this? The question is, how can you possibly learn from or be inspired by someone you put down?

Action: Take a look at your friends and associates—if you think it's wrong to prefer to be friends with positive, successful, wealthy people, perhaps you'd rather pick friends who are broke. Remember, energy is contagious—so which type would you like to be subjected to?

Living Your Dream

I have not failed. I've just found 10,000 ways that won't work.

[THOMAS ALVA EDISON]

Be Optimistic

Maintaining a positive attitude and an optimistic outlook are critical to the successful achievement of your goals. A "can-do" attitude will take you a lot farther than focusing on the negative. Be sure your goals are always worded positively, and reach for your dreams! Make it easy; select a goal that will bring you great pleasure, satisfaction, and joy.

Take Ownership of Your Life

Watch, listen, and learn. You can't know it all yourself. Anyone who thinks they do is destined for mediocrity.

[DONALD TRUMP]

Did you ever stop to think that everything you are or ever will be is completely up to you? Just imagine . . .

You are where you are because of *who* you are. Everything that exists in your life exists because of you—because of your behavior, words, and actions.

Because you have freedom of choice and because you have chosen each and every circumstance of your life, you are completely responsible for all of your success and failure, your happiness and unhappiness, your present and future.

Taking ownership of your life is like a parachute jump: It's scary and exhilarating at the same time. It's one of the biggest and most important ideas that can ever occur to you or anyone else.

You are totally responsible for your life. This is the foundation principle you must embrace if you plan for happiness and success in life and work. You most likely know someone who, every time you meet, strikes you by his or her failure to take responsibility for what is happening in his or her work and life. Everything is someone else's fault to some people. They explain away every problem with reasons about why he or she can't affect the situation or the outcome.

Action: Do you take complete responsibility for your life? Start today. This is your year, this is your life, LIVE it!

Blame & Excuses Are the Hallmarks of an Unsuccessful Life

The buck stops here.

[PRESIDENT HARRY TRUMAN]

In interviews with Parole Boards, many jailed individuals who are seeking parole relate a similar pattern in their reasoning and approach to life—nothing was their fault, including the incidents that landed each of them in jail. Do you think this would be a common pattern among incarcerated individuals? Would we find a pattern of "not my fault"?

That is why taking responsibility for choices, actions, and direction is so powerfully important. Without taking responsibility, you'll likely look at your life as a failure because you allowed yourself to be blown hither and yon by any passing wind. And you blamed the wind for how things turned out!

People who take complete responsibility for their lives experience joy and control of circumstances. They are able to make choices because they understand that they are responsible for their choices. Indeed, even when events that are not under your control go awry, you can at least determine how you will react to the event. You can make an event a disaster—or you can use it as an opportunity to learn, to grow, to cherish your faith, and to hold loved ones close.

Action: Which will you choose? To make excuses—or to seize opportunity?

How to Take Responsibility

If it is to be, it's up to me.

[William H. Johnsen]

The most important aspect of taking responsibility for your life is to *acknowledge that your life is your responsibility*. No one can live your life for you. You are in charge. No matter how hard you try to blame others for the events of your life, each event is the result of choices you made and are making. Listen to your heart. Observe yourself talking with coworkers, family members, and friends. Do you hear yourself taking responsibility . . . or placing blame?

Listen to the voice in your head. Eliminate blame; eliminate excuses. If the blame track or the excuse track plays repeatedly in your mind, you are shifting responsibility for your decisions and life to others.

Second, listen to yourself when you speak. In your conversation, do you hear yourself blame others for things that don't go exactly as you want? Do you find yourself pointing fingers at your coworkers or your upbringing, your parents' influence, the amount of money that you make, or your spouse? Are you making excuses for unmet goals or tasks that missed their deadlines? If you can hear your blaming patterns . . . you can stop them.

Third, if an individual you respect supplies feedback that you make excuses and blame others for your woes, take the feedback seriously. Control your defensive reaction, explore examples, and deepen your understanding with the coworker or friend.

Action: Congratulations on making it this far! You are on your way to living the life of your dreams!

Silence the Negative

The first step toward success is taken when you refuse to be a captive of the environment in which you first find yourself.

[MARK CAINE]

Excuses for failure, excuses about your choices in life, and excuses about what you feel you have accomplished fuel dysfunctional thinking—and consequently, undesirable actions and behaviors. Making excuses is the hallmark of people who fail to succeed. Instead, take 100 percent responsibility for your actions, your thoughts, and your goals!

Part of the power of taking responsibility for your actions is that you silence the negative, unhelpful voice in your head. When you spend your thinking time on success and goal accomplishment, instead of on making excuses, you free up the emotional space formerly inhabited by negativity.

The next time you catch yourself making an excuse, whether for the late project, the unmet goal, or the job you work, gently remind yourself—*no excuses.* Spend your thought time planning your next successful venture. Positive thinking becomes a helpful habit. Excuses fuel failure.

You can't accept responsibility for a situation and be angry at the same time. You can't accept responsibility and be unhappy or upset. The acceptance of responsibility negates negative emotions and short-circuits any tendencies toward unhappiness.

Action: The very act of accepting responsibility calms your mind and clarifies your vision. It soothes your emotions and enables you to think more positively and constructively. In fact, the acceptance of responsibility often gives you insight into what you should do to resolve the situation.

Sardines

Make each day your masterpiece.

[JOHN WOODEN]

You may have heard the story of the construction worker who opens up his lunch box at the noon break and unwraps his sandwich to find that it contains sardines. He gets really upset and complains loudly to everyone around him about how much he hates sardines.

The next day, the same thing happens: a sardine sandwich. Again, the construction worker shouts and complains about how much he hates sardines for lunch.

The third day it happens again. By this time, his fellow workers are getting fed up with his loud complaining. One of them leans over and says to him, "If you hate sardines so much, why don't you tell your wife to make you some other kind of sandwich?"

The construction worker turns to the fellow and says, "Oh, I'm not married. I make my own lunches!"

Many of us get into the same situation as the construction worker's and complain about circumstances that are almost entirely of our own making.

Action: Is this true for you? Look over your relationships and ask where this might be true in your life. Are you happy with your job? Are you happy with the amount of money you're earning? Are you happy with your level of responsibility and your activities each day?

Do Something Different

Choose a job that you like and you will never have to work a day in your life.

[CONFUCIUS]

You took your job, you assumed the responsibilities, and you accepted the wage. If you're not happy with any of them, for any reason, then it's up to you to do something different.

You're earning today exactly what you're worth—not a penny more, not a penny less. In life, we tend to get exactly what we deserve.

If you're not satisfied with the amount you're getting, look around you at people who are doing the kind of work you would like to do and earning the kind of money you would like to earn. Ask them what they're doing differently from what you're doing.

What are the causes of the effects they're getting? Once you know what they are, accept complete responsibility for your situation, apply your wonderful mind and abilities, back them with willpower and self-discipline, and get busy making the changes you need to make to enjoy the life you want to enjoy.

Your great aim in life is to develop character. Character is composed of self-esteem, self-discipline, the ability to delay gratification, and the willingness to accept full responsibility for your life and everything in it.

Action: The more you say to yourself, "I am responsible," the stronger, better, and finer a person you become. And every part of your life will improve at the same time!

Living Your Dream

I like nonsense, it wakes up the brain cells. Fantasy is a necessary ingredient in living; it's a way of looking at life through the wrong end of a telescope. Which is what I do, and that enables you to laugh at life's realities.

[DR. SEUSS]

Make It Meaningful

Achieving each of your goals should advance you at least a little bit closer to the life of your dreams. Your goals should also be in harmony with your purpose and mission in life. If you're going to invest your time and energy into realizing a goal, make sure it's a meaningful goal that will serve you well.

Get Motivated

When you confront a problem, you begin to solve it.

[RUDOLPH GIULIANI]

Why do successful people succeed? Achievers have different talents, personalities and skills. But they have one thing in common: successful people are highly motivated. In fact, the more motivated a person is, the more success he or she experiences. Motivated people advance farther and faster in their careers, earn more money, are more productive, experience more satisfying relationships, and are happier than the less-motivated people around them.

Motivation is one of the greatest keys to success in every area of our lives. Education, talent, and your network of people are all valuable, but your personal motivation trumps all of these things.

Motivation is the power that creates action. It's like the gas in your car that makes it go. Motivation is the fuel of success. Is it possible to harness the power of motivation to motivate yourself and others to live to their true potential?

Motivation is not one-size-fits-all. In her book, *Get Motivated*, Tamara Lowe reveals her findings from an eight-year study on what motivates people. She determined that we all have our very own "Motivational DNA." Understanding the strategies that motivate you and others are the keys to success. But first we must understand motivation, which we'll be covering this week.

Action: What motivates you to get out of bed in the morning? Make a list.

Everyone Is Motivated Differently

They say time changes things, but you actually have to change them yourself.

[ANDY WARHOL]

Zig Ziglar has said, "There are no unmotivated people." Everyone is motivated. Bank robbers are motivated to rob banks and drug addicts are motivated to do drugs. They are motivated, but by the wrong things.

Everyone is motivated differently. You will sometimes hear parents say, "After my first child, I thought I had parenting figured out. Then my second child came along and all the rules changed!" What worked well with the first child may not work at all with the second. Even in childhood, we each have our own unique motivational code.

Why do you suppose managers have such a difficult time energizing departments or igniting team morale? It is because every single team member is motivated differently. Managers usually try to increase productivity by using strategies that they themselves find motivational. When those tactics aren't effective with some, instead of concluding that most people are not motivated, it would be wise to learn the technique that does motivate the others. Everyone is motivated, but the same drivers that motivate the manager may not motivate all.

Action: What motivates you? Get a handle on that and harness it, and you can see dramatic differences.

Everyone Has a Unique Motivational Type

The happiest times in my life were when my relationships were going well—when I was in love with someone and someone was loving me.

[BILLY JOEL]

Every person has a unique achievement pattern or Motivational DNA. Just as your genetic DNA determines your physical attributes, your Motivational DNA dictates how you are best motivated. It is composed of the drives, needs, and awards that motivate you. This pattern is unique to you; it is a part of who you are.

The quality of your life is largely determined by your motivation. Every one of us is hard-wired with a precise motivational matrix that determines exactly what motivates us and what doesn't. What works for someone else may not work for you. Why? It's in the DNA. You were made to be motivated in a specific way. There are certain motivators that excite and inspire you, and other de-motivators that you dislike and don't work.

According to Tamara Lowe's research, the success and failures of your relationships, finances, health, personal goals, and professional endeavors are all shaped by Motivational DNA. Not only that, your ability to energize and motivate those around you is directly connected to your skill in decoding *their* motivational types.

Action: Exceptional leaders intuitively recognize and respond to the motivational styles of those around them. They instinctively sense how to inspire themselves and others—so understand your own type, and then learn how to reach others!

What Motivates One Person Can De-Motivate Another

Some people like chaos and others like structure. I like the latter.
[CHRISTY TURLINGTON]

It's easy to be mystified by the seemingly arbitrary nature of success. How can one person with extraordinary talent, passion, and commitment succeed, while someone else with an equal amount of talent, passion, and commitment fails?

Is motivation internal or external? Influenced most by the environment or genetics? Can motivation alone change undesirable behavior? Is it possible to motivate someone to do something they truly don't want to do? What type of incentives motivate people best?

Parents with more than one child will readily agree that each child is unique. They are surprised how each child, though raised in the same house by the same parents at the same time, is so different—how can this be? Being able to "crack the code" to your child's motivational DNA will help to determine what will motivate them to take out the trash or even get good grades in school.

It is easy to understand how one person can be motivated and another de-motivated when we consider all the different factors that could motivate a person—everything from love to money, from curiosity to contribution, from feeling valued to the fear of failure.

Action: If you know what motivates you, you will also understand what de-motivates you. Learn this for those who depend on you for their motivation, and you can really create great change.

No One Is "Better" Than Any Other

Winning the prize wasn't half as exciting as doing the work itself.
[Maria Goeppert-Mayer]

There is no "best" Motivational DNA, just as there is no "best" blood type. You may have type A while your friend may have type B, but neither is better than the other. They are equally good—until one of you needs a blood transfusion. Then it is *crucial* to have a donor with a compatible type. Giving someone the wrong type of blood can be fatal.

In the same way, if you try to motivate someone using strategies that are effective for motivating *you*, it can absolutely kill your friend's motivation.

An example to describe how this works is a keyless electronic safe in a home. The safe has a digital keypad that is programmed to unlock the vault when a six-digit code is entered in a specific sequence. When the right numbers are pressed in the correct sequence, the door opens. If the wrong numbers are pressed, a beeping noise indicates that the incorrect code was entered—try again. If the correct code is not entered within three tries, the system will shut down. Then the safe will not accept any more codes—even the correct code.

Sadly, a similar process takes place with people. If you keep attempting to motivate them in the wrong way, they eventually shut down. They lock up. It is essential to understand, decipher, and apply the code-cracking skills of Motivational DNA.

Action: How serious are you about pursuing and achieving your goals and dreams?

Drives, Needs, Awards

Change is never easy.

[SALLY FIELD]

Motivational DNA is made up of drives, needs, and awards. The drives for *connection* and/or *production* are the internal forces that mobilize a person to act. The needs for *stability* and/or *variety* are core requirements that a person must have in order to feel fulfilled. *Internal* and/or *external awards* are the type of compensation or remuneration a person desires to reward achievement and encourage performance.

All six of the motivators (connection, production, stability, variety, internal awards, and external awards) inspire everyone. To different degrees, all of us desire connection with other people, and we like to be productive. Everyone wants to experience some measure of both stability and variety. We all crave internal awards (like appreciation) as well as external awards (like financial compensation). Each of us has a definite preference for three of these motivators.

Action: Ask yourself the following three questions to give yourself a simple assessment of your basic motivational makeup.

Do you tend to be more competitive or cooperative? Competitive people have a production *drive. Cooperative people tend to be more people-oriented, or have a* connection *drive.*

Do you prefer constancy or change? People who prefer constancy have a stability *need—they like order and routine. In contrast, people who prefer change have a* variety *need.*

Which would make you feel more valued at work: sincere appreciation without a financial bonus, or a bonus without appreciation? If you prefer appreciation, you are motivated by internal awards, *and if you prefer money, then* external awards *motivate you.*

Living Your Dream

> *I know the price of success: dedication, hard work and an unremitting devotion to the things you want to see happen.*
>
> [FRANK LLOYD WRIGHT]

Get Excited!

Excitement and enthusiasm are powerful forces. They can keep you going when you run into obstacles or things don't go quite as you planned. When your goal is big enough to excite you and scare you at the same time, you are on the right track!

Remember, your level of desire to achieve a particular goal—to realize the fulfillment of a particular dream—is directly proportionate to your ability to achieve it. When you're excited about something, fired up just thinking about it, and you want that something in a powerful way, your subconscious will figure out how and what to do to get it!

How to Get Motivated

People without information cannot act responsibly.

[KEN BLANCHARD]

Increased motivation can improve the quality of our lives, financially, physically, and emotionally. When people are inspired to live to their full potential, they excel. Motivated people are more fulfilled and productive. They enjoy life more.

When you have an idea of your motivational profile, you can adopt characteristics from all six motivators to better relate to people, achieve goals and to motivate yourself to get through a difficult situation.

Become familiar with the six motivators (drive—producer, connector; need—variable, stability; and awards—internal, external) your own Motivational DNA, and the three questions to help you identify others' motivational styles.

Let's put the motivational profile into action. Select your most challenging short-term goal (something you can realistically accomplish within ninety days). Write it down.

The following days are designed to help you create a personal plan of action. Answer the questions for each of your three primary motivational factors. Include as much detail as possible for each of your answers.

The questions address the obstacles you will encounter, the people and organizations that can assist you, and ways to sustain focus, make the process more enjoyable, organize your plan, and provide inspiration for times when willpower is not enough.

Action: After you answer these questions, you will have strategies and inspirational ideas to help you achieve your goal!

Intentional Focus

Not only do I knock 'em out, I pick the round.

[MUHAMMAD ALI]

Connectors

- What organizations can I connect with to help me achieve my goal?
- Who has successfully accomplished the same (or similar) goal and can help me strategize to overcome the obstacles I will encounter?
- What groups can I join to support me and fuel my motivation?
- Who can encourage me to stay on track and help make me accountable?

Producers

- How can I turn this goal into a competition?
- What obstacles and distractions will I need to navigate in order to achieve my goal?
- How will I overcome those obstacles?
- Which people, groups, and organizations can I employ to help me do the heavy lifting?

Action: You can apply this technique to every goal you wish to achieve.

Stabilizers & Variables

> *I feel very adventurous. There are so many doors to be opened, and I'm
> not afraid to look behind them.*
>
> [ELIZABETH TAYLOR]

Stabilizers

- What existing systems and structures can I utilize to help me reach my goal?
- What can I do now to research and create a methodology that will help me succeed?
- How can I eliminate distractions and focus on doing something every day that will cause me to make progress toward accomplishing my goal?
- How will achieving my goal add balance and stability to my life?

Variables

- What can I do to add fun to the equation and at the same time advance me toward my goal?
- What are the most creative and interesting ways to accomplish my goal?
- If Plan A doesn't work, what will I do for Plans B through Z?
- How will I add variety, joy, and excitement to the process so that I don't get bored?

Action: Have you identified the actions that motivate you the most?

Internals & Externals

Just play. Have fun. Enjoy the game.
[MICHAEL JORDAN]

Internals

- Why is this goal meaningful to me?
- How will it make a positive difference to others?
- What are the things that will keep me from quitting when the going gets tough or the pace becomes tedious?
- What inner resources will I utilize to take actions daily toward my goal?

Externals

- How will I personally benefit by achieving this goal?
- What incremental rewards can I build into the process to help me accomplish my goal?
- How does realizing this goal set me up for even greater success?
- What big reward will I give myself when I cross the finish line?
- Most of us don't attempt anything challenging until we are motivated to do it. But the dilemma is that we usually don't know how to create the motivation we desire. Don't wait to get inspired—intentionally motivate yourself.

Action: If you are serious about achieving your goal, write your answers to the above questions and those from the days before. Invest the time to give thoughtful, detailed answers in writing.

Motivating Others

Watching women achieve their dreams is the thing that keeps me inspired.

[MARY KAY ASH]

Is there a secret to motivating, inspiring, and energizing others? The real key to motivating people and teams is to find out what they love and what they're good at. This is critical information that sparks motivation. Knowing what people love and where they excel is essential to understanding how to motivate them.

At some point in our lives, we have all been inspired by someone else. You can probably remember your favorite teachers and coaches from school. Great teachers and coaches will use many different motivational techniques to appeal to their students' style of motivation. You excelled in the class or sport because those educators appealed to your motivational style of learning.

In order to get motivated and stay motivated, a person has to 1) like the activity, and 2) be able to do it well. When you are motivating yourself, it is essential that you understand your own motivational type. But when you are motivating someone else, *your* type is irrelevant. When dealing with others, all that matters is their type. You must modify how you interact with them based on their type to get the best results.

Action: When you are familiar with the types of motivators, you can easily identify someone else's motivational style and communicate better. What is your spouse's motivator? How can you communicate better? Review the last few weeks if you need to.

Creating Rapport

Try not to become a person of success, but rather a person of value.

[ALBERT EINSTEIN]

Rapport is the experience of being in agreement with someone you trust. When a person is in rapport with you, he or she is inclined to concur, cooperate, and collaborate with you.

In order to effectively communicate with and motivate others, it helps to create a space where people feel understood, appreciated, and safe.

The next time you want to inspire someone to take action, match their body language, tonality, and pacing. If they are fast-paced, pick up your pace when you speak with them. If they are seated with their hands folded, have a seat and do the same. You can create unity when conforming your posture and communication style to that of the person you are speaking with.

Action: Remember you are matching their style, not mocking. Your voice, gestures, and body language ought to be similar, not identical. Pay attention to and try to harmonize with: posture, body language, gestures, facial expressions, eye contact, pitch of voice, tonality, pacing (rhythm and speed), volume, words, and phraseology.

Living Your Dream

Performance, and performance alone, dictates the predator in any food chain.

[SEAL TEAM]

Enlist the Help of Other People

While there are some goals you can complete on your own, it's infinitely easier to have the advice and support of others who have already completed similar goals or who can simply encourage you. Reach out to other like-minded people to help you with your goals or to become a part of your support system.

An interesting thing happens when you enlist the help of other people. Often, they will know someone who can directly help you achieve one or more of your goals in some small or even more significant way. Having planted the seed of your idea in their subconscious minds, those people will also unconsciously begin looking for ways to help you. Why work alone when you can have a team on your side?

What Do You Really Want Out of Life?

All that is necessary to break the spell of inertia and frustration is this: act as if it were impossible to fail. That is the talisman, the formula, the command of right-about-face which turns us from failure towards success.

[DORTHEA BRAGG]

At this point, you should have some idea of what you really want out of life. Think about it. You can live the life of your dreams—it is possible. It doesn't matter where you came from. Your past does not determine your future. It doesn't matter what you know or who you know. We all have the opportunity to improve our quality of life. But it starts with this question: What do you really, really, really, want?

In order to be set up for success in life, you need to be very clear about what you want. What do you wish to have in your life that you don't have now? Who would you like to be? What do you want to do with your life that you are not already doing? How would you like to contribute to society? What dreams totally light you up? What makes your heart smile just thinking about it? How do you want to be remembered? What would you like your legacy to be?

If you take the time to dig deep and answer the questions for yourself, what you really want becomes your life's compass. Knowing what you really want creates a benchmark that will guide you in goal achievement.

Action: We learn and grow through repetition. Even if you have determined several of your goals and dreams, continue to participate in this week's activities, you may be inspired to dream more dreams!

Begin at the End

The man is a success who has lived well, laughed often, and loved much; who has gained the respect of intelligent men and the love of children; who has filled his niche and accomplished his task; who leaves the world better than he found it, whether by an improved poppy, a perfect poem, or a rescued soul; who never lacked appreciation of earth's beauty or failed to express it; who looked for the best in others and gave the best he had.

[BESSIE ANDERSON STANLEY]

God loves dreamers (and doers) with big dreams. There is an element of both faith and hope in every dream. Yet there is a huge difference between dreams and goals. Anyone can dream. But the process of achievement will begin when you create a goal, write it down, and actively initiate and implement the steps necessary to get to that goal.

It wasn't raining when Noah built the ark. You can't control the future, but you *can* plan for it. Create a clearly defined picture of what you really want in life. This picture should be so vivid that seeing it in your imagination energizes you right now. Visualize the end at the beginning.

Take an inventory of your gifts, talents, and skills. You already have most of what you need. List all of the personal resources that you can use to achieve your goal. Include natural talents, developed skills, financial resources, and organizational tools that will help you attain your goal.

Action: You must also identify your constraints. If you are willing to admit your faults, you have one less fault to admit. List every obstacle that you are likely to encounter and every challenge that you will need to overcome in order to achieve your goal. Next, come up with at least three ways to overcome each of those obstacles.

Be Prepared

> *People of mediocre ability sometimes achieve outstanding success because they don't know when to quit. Most men succeed because they are determined to.*
>
> [GEORGE HERBERT ALLEN]

You should plan for incremental success. Never test the depth of a river with both feet. Think big, but start small. Look for reproducible strategies. Even if you hit a home run once, you won't win the game unless you can do it again and again and again. Don't make the amateur mistake of over-leveraging yourself.

Count the cost. Incoming fire has the right of way. Brace yourself for unexpected adversity. Attaining your goal is going to cost you—count on it. Decide in advance if you are willing and able to pay the price. Do you have what it takes to hold on financially and emotionally? Don't invent if you can reinvent.

The early bird may get the worm, but the second mouse gets the cheese. It takes more effort to create than to re-create. Identify a successful individual or organization and model what they are doing. If you do exactly what they do, you should get similar results. But if you do it better, faster, smarter, and more cost-effectively, you will get even *better* results.

Action: Make sure you are working smarter, not harder. Write down three areas where you could work smarter.

Don't Become Discouraged

*I've missed more than 9,000 shots in my career. I've lost almost 300
games. Twenty-six times, I've been trusted to take the game winning
shot and missed. I've failed over and over and over again in my life.
And that is why I succeed.*

[MICHAEL JORDAN]

In the pursuit of any significant goal, you will get discouraged. You
will feel like giving up. Guaranteed. Every major endeavor comes with
a special bonus: the opportunity to fail publicly. In order to succeed,
you have to be prepared to wrestle with fear, wrangle with doubts, and
slap down the temptation to quit. You will have to sustain your moti-
vation and power past the fear of failure.

When you are tempted to quit, remember that the weight of diffi-
culty is the acid test of leadership. Losers crumble under the load, but
true leaders buck up.

After the initial burst of excitement that propels you when you
start in on a goal, you may experience a slow leak of motivation. The
demands of life will get in your way. You may make some good
progress but then be lulled into a state of contentment and start to
coast. You may slowly cruise to a standstill and quickly lose the
progress you have made. This is why sustained energy and momentum
is important.

How can you sustain momentum? You must appeal to your moti-
vational patterns. Sometimes you may need to push yourself to get
results. It may be helpful to surround yourself with a support network
to assist you. Stay focused. But be ready to make adjustments as
needed.

*Action: Remember to keep your eye on the prize—your dream.
Always take advantage of opportunities to create positive momentum
toward the pursuit of your goals and dreams.*

Big Goals Take Time

Our goals can only be reached through a vehicle of a plan, in which we must fervently believe, and upon which we must vigorously act. There is no other route to success.

[STEPHEN A. BRENNAN]

Be patient. Life is not a sprint. It's an endurance sport. Big goals take time. There will be huge, looming obstacles to overcome. Sometimes life is unfair and bad things do happen to good people. If you are feeling a little discouraged, the good news is . . . the past is *in the past*. It is over and done. Yesterday does not determine your tomorrow. What you do today determines your future. Stick with your success system. Don't worry about setbacks. Failure is not final unless you quit.

Success and failure are like Siamese twins. You can't have one without the other. Everyone makes mistakes. The secret of highly successful people is they do one thing right—they keep going.

When you want to quit, keep going. When the naysayers and doomsayers are predicting your demise, keep going. When your dream appears so dim it is barely a flicker, stick with it.

Action: Even when you get countless "no"s and rejection; remember you only need one "yes"! With every "no," you are that much closer to your "YES"!

Gain the Competitive Advantage

*Apply yourself. Get all the education you can, but then, by God, do
something. Don't just stand there, make something happen.*

[LEE IACOCCA]

In business and in life, competition is a bittersweet reality. Unfortu-
nately, hard work and a dream are not enough for anyone to become a
standout success. To get ahead of the pack and finish first, you need a
toolbox loaded with the tools to help you maneuver life.

How can you outpace, outmaneuver, and outlast your competi-
tion? No matter what your business, profession, or service, this is your
ticket to the top. The secret to being number one . . . is being number
one! The real key to being the best . . . is *being the best*!

You must motivate yourself to learn more, do more, and be more
than everyone around you. You must strive for excellence in every-
thing you do to finish first. You've got to work longer, smarter, faster.
You need to be knowledgeable, articulate, energetic, confident, compe-
tent, and courageous. You have to be *the best*.

"Good enough" is *not* good enough to succeed at the highest lev-
els. You've go to be the best if you want to enjoy all of the rewards of
success.

You will have to make some sacrifices and pay the price to be on
top of your game. That means investing the time, effort, and money
that it takes to develop superior skill. Be committed to keep growing
and constantly improving yourself.

*Action: Be the one to set the standard. Never be satisfied with "good
enough"; always strive for excellence! What is the one thing that will
set you apart from the pack?*

Living Your Dream

Be fanatics. When it comes to being and doing and dreaming the best, be maniacs.

[A. M. Rosenthal]

Talk to People Who've Done What You Want to Do

If possible, talk with someone who's already attained the goal or dream you aspire to. Find out what it's really like when the goal is completed and the dream comes true. How did it feel? Was it everything they thought it would be? Ask them how they did it. Was it worth all the effort? Would they do it all over again? Why or why not? Learn from their experience.

Business Building Tips

The most successful men in the end are those whose success is the result of steady accretion. . . . It is the man who carefully advances step by step, with his mind becoming wider and wider—and progressively better able to grasp any theme or situation—persevering in what he knows to be practical, and concentrating his thought upon it, who is bound to succeed in the greatest degree.

[ALEXANDER GRAHAM BELL]

Balance in life is important. The highest-priority areas for most people are career, finances, making a contribution, their relationships, and health. To finish first in all of these areas in life requires *effort*. You really can have it all—balance in every area of your life—but it takes diligence and commitment. Achieving success in one area and failing in another is not enough. If your business is thriving and you're making lots of money but your teenager is on drugs and your marriage is falling apart . . . you've failed. Likewise, if you are fit and healthy and have great relationships but your career is awful and your bank account is empty . . . you are certainly not winning at life. The good news is that you can make adjustments to create balance in your life.

Why not begin today?

Achieving success in life is not simple or easy. If it were easy, everyone would be happy, healthy, rich, making a positive contribution in the world, involved in gratifying relationships, and living a spiritually fulfilling life.

Action: This week we will review some fundamental tips for creating success in your career. Evaluate yourself on the job. How are you doing? Name three areas where you feel you can improve.

Be Enthusiastic

> *Nothing in the world can take the place of persistence. Talent will not;*
> *nothing is more common than unsuccessful men with talent. Genius*
> *will not; unrewarded genius is almost a proverb. Education will not;*
> *the world is full of educated derelicts. Persistence and determination*
> *are omnipotent. The slogan "press on" has solved and always will solve*
> *the problems of the human race. No person was ever honored for what*
> *he received. Honor has been the reward for what he gave.*
>
> [CALVIN COOLIDGE]

Be enthusiastic about every task—yes, even the unpleasant ones! This quality alone will set you apart from 99 percent of people in the workplace. It will practically guarantee a promotion. It could secure your job and speed up your advancement. It will make you more money.

When you are given an assignment, always say, "Yes! I would be happy to do that! I'll get right to it!" You must be enthusiastic about your job and yourself. You must be convinced that your efforts make a difference and that even the less desirable tasks will receive your best performance.

Cultivate the attitude of the super achiever. How do you do this? Be cheerful, upbeat, and positive *every single day*. You commit to be a ray of sunshine everywhere you go. Oh, and be punctual—early is best—to all of the places you go!

Action: Do you light up a room when you enter—or when you leave?

Say Something Worthwhile

The great successful men of the world have used their imagination . . .
they think ahead and create their mental picture and all it details,
filling in here, adding a little there, altering this a bit and that a bit, but
steadily building—steadily building.

[ROBERT J. COLLIER]

Learn to communicate skillfully. A rich, powerful vocabulary will give you the extra edge you need to express your ideas effectively, communicate with greater precision, and demonstrate your intellectual acumen.

At work, be friendly to people, but don't chitchat or gossip. Keep your conversations brief and to the point. Do not get caught up in social conversations during company time. It's not responsible and is wasteful. Rather than getting results, if you idly talk too much you'll simply be wasting everyone's most precious resource—time.

Your written communications must always be exceptional. Avoid dashing off sloppy emails when you are in a hurry. Your words should be clear, incisive, and free from spelling and grammatical mistakes. Well-composed correspondence is an attribute of excellence. Make sure you take the extra moment to spell-check everything you send out. Practice writing persuasively and passionately, so that your reader will feel inspired to implement your recommendations.

Action: When you say something, do people listen—or do they wish you would stop talking? What are you talking about that might make people shut down?

Your Appearance

> *Life is made up of small pleasures. Happiness is made up of those tiny*
> *successes. The big ones come too infrequently. And if you don't collect*
> *all these tiny successes, the big ones don't really mean anything.*
>
> [NORMAN LEAR]

Generally, you should look good and be well groomed, at work and in
every professional capacity. Your hair should be styled, your nails
trimmed and nice, your clothing ironed and neat. Wear good shoes,
and always have fresh breath. Your self-esteem and confidence will
escalate when you take a few simple steps to put your best self out
there.

Go to a dermatologist for treatment if you have problem skin.
Make an appointment with your dentist right away if you need to have
your teeth fixed. You will not want to hide your smile and enthusiasm
because you are embarrassed about your teeth. The time and money
you spend to maintain and improve your appearance will return expo-
nentially with better jobs, raises, bonuses, and improved self-
confidence.

Make sure your work area is organized and tidy. Be efficient. When
you accumulate piles of paper around your office, it does not make
you look busy; it makes you look disorganized, frazzled, and over-
whelmed. Take action and file everything. Invest the time to be organ-
ized. Then stay organized.

Action: Do you take healthy pride in your appearance—or do you try
to avoid being noticed?

Focus on Your Strengths

We must have the courage to bet on our ideas, to take the calculated risk, and to act. Everyday living requires courage if life is to be effective and bring happiness.

[MAXWELL MALTZ]

Understand your own strengths and your weaknesses. Accept your weaknesses and look for people to fill in the gaps caused by them. Do more of what you are good at. Be more of who you *really* are. If you have a natural ability for something, develop those gifts. It will make you that much more successful. Focusing on your strengths will always make you better at what you do.

It is imperative that you connect with and cater to your customers. Always be impeccable with your word. Do what you say you are going to do, when you say you are going to do it. It is a good idea to under-promise and over-deliver. If it takes more time than you expected on a project, work late to finish the job.

Action: You are wise to be aware of and work on improving your weaknesses, but show the world your strengths! What are your top five strengths?

Be an Owner

The supreme quality for leadership is unquestionably integrity. Without it, no real success is possible, no matter whether it is on a section gang, a football field, in an army, or in an office.

[LUCILLE BALL]

Treat your company's money as if it were your own. Ultimately, it *is*. When you have the reputation for being fiscally responsible, you will advance in your career and end up making more money. Purchase only what is needed to create success. Do not spend one cent of the company's money wastefully. Do your best to come in under budget. Don't inflate budget projections. Learn to get more done with less money, without neglecting what's best for the customer. Never let cost cutting cause you to produce inferior products or give subpar service—that is a gigantic career killer. It will not improve your business; on the contrary, it will ultimately harm it.

***Action:** If you show that you are able to handle small amounts of money within your company, you'll be entrusted with more—and will begin to earn more to take more home, too.*

Living Your Dream

And while the law of competition may be sometimes hard for the individual, it is best for the race, because it ensures the survival of the fittest in every department.

[ANDREW CARNEGIE]

Congratulations!

You are in the home stretch! Celebrate! Do something to reward yourself for your perseverance! You are on your way to living the life of your dreams!

Build Your Fortune

Money isn't the most important thing in life, but it's reasonably close to oxygen on the "gotta have it" scale.

[ZIG ZIGLAR]

As we continue to explore ways to achieve balance in our life, we must get clear on our beliefs about money. Money is not the root of all evil—the *love* and disrespect of money will cause problems.

Many people grow up hearing things such as, "Money doesn't grow on trees," "No, you can't have that, it's too expensive, and we don't have enough money," etc. Listening to this sort of talk, we form the belief that there is not enough money to go around—this is a *lack* mentality. And those rich people, we might think, have taken more than their fair share, so they are bad.

How motivated are you to ensure that you are making wise financial decisions? Taking care of yourself and your family with a solid financial strategy safeguards and improves your standard of living.

Money can't buy love and happiness. However, creating *financial freedom* will allow you the personal freedom to relax and focus on what truly makes you happy.

Action: Make a list of some lack mentality beliefs you grew up with. Do you now believe in abundance?

Multiple Streams of Income

There is only one class in the community that thinks more about money than the rich, and that is the poor. The poor can think of nothing else.

[OSCAR WILDE]

If you only have one form of income—the salary from your day job—you live in danger that something could happen to reduce or eliminate that income. If you get injured or lose your job, you will lose your weekly paycheck, and you'll be left scrambling for a solution.

Sadly, way too many people must live paycheck to paycheck. On the other hand, wealthy people tend to invest their money in a wide range of income-producing vehicles, including other businesses, real estate, tax shelters, stocks, and other investments that generate dividends. If one source of their income slows down or goes away, they can still rely on income from the others.

It is wise to try to develop multiple streams of income. You can do this by developing a marketable skill that can be sold freelance, working part-time to accumulate savings, starting a home-based or Web-based business, and consulting a financial advisor to create a long-term investment strategy.

Action: If you somehow lost your primary source of revenue, do you have a Plan B?

Invest for the Future

The use of money is all the advantage there is in having it.

[BENJAMIN FRANKLIN]

You can earn money legally two ways in the United States: with people at work and with money at work. People at work make a living; money at work can make a *fortune*. The rich get richer when they have their money at work.

We grow up with the belief that you need to go to school to get a good education, get a job, work hard for forty years, and retire comfortably. The average person thinks he will get rich by winning the lottery or receiving an inheritance. In most cases, a job will make you a living, but it will *not* make you rich. Your job may allow you to live in a big house or drive a nice car, but it will not make you wealthy. But your job *can* give you the initial capital you need to invest in your future.

Are you motivated by earning money to buy the good things in life? Take a moment to envision what your life could be like five, ten, and fifty years down the road if you sacrifice a little today by investing wisely on a regular basis. Maybe you are motivated by how you can make a contribution to your family's security or make a difference in the world and leave a legacy. Becoming a wise investor will allow you to do this too.

Don't let your lack of knowledge keep you from starting to invest. Without the proper motivation, it could be intimidating to investigate in the virtually endless array of investment opportunities to choose from. Each type will carry a certain amount of risk.

Action: So instead of being intimidated into inaction, take a class, read a book, study online, ask a trusted advisor who will teach you how to invest your money confidently and competently.

Live Below Your Means

> *My favorite things in life don't cost any money. It's really clear that the most precious resource we all have is time.*
>
> [STEVE JOBS]

Living below your means does not mean you should suffer. Living below your means is about reducing nonessential expenses and cutting costs in a way that doesn't make you feel deprived of the things you need. It is the best way to avoid unnecessary debt. No one wants to live their life dictated by the whim of a company cutting back or the erratic forces of the economy. Will you still have a job next week? Will you be able to pay the mortgage and buy gas in an economic downturn? Living below your means is a great way to obtain some control and help you achieve financial freedom.

Funding your education and purchasing a home are two circumstances in which it is recommended that you borrow money. Most experts suggest that your mortgage should not exceed more than 28 percent of your gross monthly income. It is also recommended that you keep all of your debt—including mortgage, auto payments, and credit cards—at less than 37 percent of your gross monthly earnings. If it is more than that, find a way to bring down your monthly debt obligation.

Avoid using credit cards for impulse and depreciating purchases. Make saving a requirement and put away 10 percent or more of your pretax income each month. It is a good idea to set aside money in an emergency fund so that you won't have to use a credit card when you need household or auto repairs.

Action: Question every purchase. Do you really need to splurge on eating out again this week? Set a budget for your weekly spending and then be conscious of ways to save money when making purchases. Incorporate financial discipline into your life.

Improve Your Credit Score

> *Of the billionaires I have known, money just brings out the basic traits in them. If they were jerks before they had money, they are simply jerks with a billion dollars.*
>
> [WARREN BUFFETT]

Most types of loans are approved or denied based on your credit score. A poor credit score can cost you money. The lower your score, typically the higher the interest rate you will be charged. You will pay more in interest. Your credit score will also be a determining factor for how much you will be qualified to borrow for a car or home.

Paying your bills on time and reducing your debt load will improve your score. Check your score with a major credit bureau to fix obvious mistakes on your credit report. Your balance-to-credit-limit ratio—how much money you owe on your credit cards relative to your credit card limit—also plays a significant part in determining your score. Try to keep your balances below 25 percent of your credit card limit. It is not a good idea to open new credit card accounts, or close old ones, near the time you are going to apply for a loan.

Action: You can strive to achieve great results with fewer resources. The person who can do this will always be in demand. Don't continue to throw money at all problems—throw creativity and brainpower instead.

Embrace Lifelong Learning

I'd say it's been my biggest problem all my life . . . it's money. It takes a lot of money to make these dreams come true.

[WALT DISNEY]

Successful people are lifelong learners. And *learners are earners!* High achievers will go out of their way to pursue educational opportunities. The investment you make in yourself and your education will pay off, both financially and in your quality of life.

Brian Tracy is an expert on corporate and personal performance and the author of more than forty books. Here are some thoughts he shares in his newsletters and his blog about lifelong education:

All skills are learnable. All business skills are learnable. All sales skills are learnable. All investment skills are learnable. And you can master all of these skills. You are so smart you could learn multiple languages. You can learn anything you need to learn to achieve any goal you have in life. Ask yourself, what is the one skill that, if I mastered it, would improve my life the most? Identify your weakest skill and work on it every day until you've mastered it. Make the rest of your life into a do-it-to-yourself project. In other words, your whole life becomes a series of taking your weakest skill and leapfrogging it forward. If you commit to strengthening your weakest skill and leapfrogging it forward. . . . If you commit to strengthening your weakest and most needed skills—and if you do that for the rest of your life—I am convinced that you'll become one of the most competent, intelligent, sought-after, and highest-paid people in the country.

Action: Do you make time to read daily? Is your car a moving university? Do you participate in educational events? Is your personal growth a priority?

Living Your Dream

> *There are two things people want more than sex and money—*
> *recognition and praise.*
>
> [MARY KAY ASH]

Identify the Personal Benefits

What's in it for you? What is your prize for completing your goals? Identify the tangible and intangible benefits you will realize when you complete your goals. This could be a simple feeling of self-satisfaction, less stress, or status in the community. There are no right or wrong answers—only the achievement of some tangible or intangible reward that has meaning for you personally.

In reviewing some of the dreams you've written down, what do you think your primary motivations are for completing your goals? What makes you tick? What provides your greatest motivation?

Making a Contribution to Society

Every goal, every action, every thought, every feeling one experiences, whether it be consciously or unconsciously known, is an attempt to increase one's level of peace of mind.

[SYDNEY MADWED]

Our purpose in life is absolutely designed to make a contribution to God's master plan. You will know you are on the right track when you experience a sense of spiritual fulfillment as you achieve your goals and advance toward your big dream.

It is a challenge to jump out of bed in the morning when you feel hollow or unsatisfied inside. Knowing you are pursuing your goals and dreams and touching the lives of others will keep you energized and eager to take on new challenges and tackle more in life. That sense of purpose and a feeling of spiritual fulfillment are fundamental to fueling your passion for pursuing your dream life.

Action: We know it takes a village to raise a child. Don't take it all on by yourself. We all need strong connections with other people to inspire great achievement. When we feel fulfilled in our personal relationships—with our family, friends, and those around us—we have more energy to take on more challenges.

Never Compromise Your Integrity

A life lived with integrity—even if it lacks the trappings of fame and fortune—is a shinning star in whose light others may follow in the years to come.

[DENIS WAITLEY]

If you are going to talk the talk, then you must walk the walk! Always be impeccable with your word and do what you say you are going to do. It is essential to always be honest and do what you know is right. Never compromise on your values or principles—they are truly what will sustain you in challenging times.

When you know who you are and what you believe, then it will be simple to take a stand and hold your ground. We don't all know exactly what we believe in spiritually. That is OK. But now is the time to seek answers. Investigate spiritual truths. Become biblically literate. Seek wise counsel. It is important to your success to find out what you believe . . . and why.

If you don't live out your beliefs, then you don't *really* believe them. A God-talk walk without virtuous action is hypocrisy. Live strong. We've got to walk the talk and be people of spotless integrity!

Action: Everybody has a story to share. Schedule a meeting with someone whose commitment to integrity you admire. Listen to and learn from the wisdom of their experiences.

Benefits of Community

*As your faith is strengthened you will find that there is no longer the
need to have a sense of control, that things will flow as they will, and
that you will flow with them, to your great delight and benefit.*

[EMMANUEL TENEY]

Studies have shown that a person can have better health, make more
money, enjoy more gratifying relationships, live longer, have higher
self-esteem, a stronger marriage, and significantly better relationships
with their children by making one simple decision—attending the
church of your faith on a regular basis.

Worshipping with a community of like-minded people can pro-
duce significant physical, financial, and social advantages, with the
benefit of spiritual enrichment. Check out the numerous studies done
on people who attend worship services at least once a week. The find-
ings are amazing. They tend to have lower incidence of heart disease,
have lower blood pressure, have better overall physical and mental
health, experience less depression, are hospitalized less, have lower
mortality rates, have less stress, experience less substance abuse, enjoy
better social support, are less lonely, live longer, have more stable mar-
riages, and enjoy a higher level of income. Now that is a phenomenal
return on investment!

*Action: Find a place of worship where you can be fed and grow your
spirituality as well as serve and share your gifts.*

Family First

> *Once you agree upon the price you and your family must pay for*
> *success, it enables you to ignore the minor hurts, the opponent's*
> *pressure, and the temporary failures.*
>
> [Vince Lombardi]

We have all heard that no one on their deathbed has ever asked to see the trophies and plaques and to see a reminder of their accomplishments. No, most of us will want the people we love around us when we leave this earth.

So no matter how much you accomplish in your life, how many promotions you receive, or how much wealth you accumulate, if your relationship with your family suffers, it will diminish the joy of your other achievements. Life is way too short to spend it disconnected from your family.

When you look back on your life and define success, if you have the love and respect of your family and they enjoy spending time with you, then you have succeeded. It will be worth whatever sacrifices are necessary to strengthen your marriage, build friendships with your children, and improve your relationships with all of your family members.

Action: Who do you need to call today to begin restoring and/or nurturing a significant relationship?

Remember, It's Not About You

When you are immune to the opinions and actions of others, you won't be the victim of needless suffering.

[MIGUEL RUIZ]

Do your very best to treat everyone with respect. Be nice to everyone you come in contact with—even those who don't deserve it. And do it with a smile on your face and love in your heart!

Keeping your emotions in check is a practice in self-control. Nobody likes to be around a complainer; whiners are not winners! Try to remain calm when others become irate. Never raise your voice in anger—no matter the circumstance. Be known as someone who responds to situations with grace and humility.

You can remain calm even when someone corrects you regarding a mistake you have made—and we all make mistakes. You can actually welcome and embrace correction! Try this—thank the other person for pointing out your mistake. Tell them, "I am absolutely committed to change. I appreciate that you took the time to bring this to my attention." How refreshing this will be. Own your mistakes and strive to correct them.

Action: You can be an inspiration to others. If you constantly look for ways to encourage people around you, everyone will feel more motivated to live their best life. You can simply do this by living your life as an example. As you strive to help others become better personally and professionally, you will have a wonderful sense of fulfillment.

Make a Point to Get to Know People

*A friendship can weather most things and thrive in thin soil; but it
needs a little mulch of letters and phone calls and small, silly presents
every so often—just to save it from drying out completely.*

[PAM BROWN]

Do your best to remember people's names and recall details about their
lives. When you meet someone, repeat their name several times in
your first conversation with them. This has a twofold purpose: 1) peo-
ple love to hear their names, and 2) it helps you carve the name into
your memory.

Don't be lazy by not remembering important details about your
colleagues, clients, and customers. You can make notes about people
you meet shortly after you meet them. Make a note of their spouse's
name and children's names, their hobbies, what is happening in their
lives, and so on. Store it in your contact list or database.

Showing people you care about them by expressing interest in
their lives is building a bridge to a relationship. Then, when you meet
them again, ask about their family members by name—it is like sweet
music to anyone's ears!

*Action: Take the time to write a handwritten note, make a phone call,
and schedule a coffee date with the people most important to you. You
will be glad you did!*

Living Your Dream

> *If instead of a gem, or even a flower, we should cast the gift of a loving thought into the heart of a friend, that would be giving as the angels give.*
>
> [GEORGE MacDONALD]

Celebrate Success

Working toward your goals is hard work. To keep your motivation high, build in the little rewards at critical points in your plan. Self-motivation is the key to success, and there's nothing like positive reinforcement to keep self-motivation high. The rewards do not need to be elaborate—tickets to see a show or movie, lunch with a friend, or buying a little something for yourself. Recognizing your progress and accomplishment is vital.

Pillars of Good Health

Some people are willing to pay the price, and it's the same with staying healthy or eating healthy. There's some discipline involved. There are some sacrifices.

[MIKE DITKA]

For a healthier, happier, more prosperous life, the importance of good health cannot be overstated. An inappropriate attitude to health can make us vulnerable to the invasion of germs and diseases that can result in a shortened life span. The great news is that good health is achievable. It will require determination, drive, and a willingness to make small changes in your lifestyle. To make the transition to a healthier lifestyle as painless as possible, it is best to start off slowly and implement small changes in phases.

Moderation is the key to success. Excessive smoking or drinking can certainly be detrimental to your good health. It may be okay to occasionally enjoy a few alcoholic drinks, and some may say small amounts of red wine are actually good for you, but there is no such exception for smoking. If you smoke, please talk to your doctor to discuss a smoking cessation program. Smoking endangers your health and the health of those around you. The sooner you quit smoking, the faster your body can begin to repair the damage.

Good health is easy to achieve, but you need to make changes in your diet and lifestyle now. Start by walking up the stairs at work instead of taking the elevator. Or swap that hamburger and fries you were going to have for lunch for a healthy wrap or salad. Small changes are the best way to start making an investment in your good health for the future.

Action: Pick one unhealthy habit and cut it out for a week. It could be diet soda or fast food—anything you think isn't good for you. It can be any bad habit, like bailing on the gym after work or forgetting to call a family member. Start strengthening your will power in small increments to help the goal be more manageable and attainable in the long run. Make a change for a week, and if it's going well, try it for a month!

Become Energized with Exercise

Physical fitness is not only one of the most important keys to a healthy body, it is the basis of dynamic and creative intellectual activity.

[JOHN F. KENNEDY]

One of the most important facets of good health is adequate exercise. Exercise can help us achieve good health by strengthening our cardio-vascular system, strengthening our muscle mass, and reducing the effects of stress on the body. To ensure that exercise does not appear to be a chore to you, it is best to find a variety of exercises that you enjoy doing. For those who prefer to be outdoors, walking, biking, hiking, jogging, or running may be a good form of exercise to take up. On the other hand, for those who enjoy swimming, a membership to a local pool may be the answer.

There are many alternative forms of exercise that you may find beneficial. Yoga, Pilates, and Zumba are wonderful forms of exercise that help to strengthen your body and promote flexibility and can be great stress relievers. You may enjoy recreational sports like tennis, golf, or soccer. No matter what your interests are, you are sure to find an exercise that will keep you moving!

Action: 24 hours x 7 days a week = 168 total hours. Pick four days of the week to spend one hour of that day participating in an exercise that gets your heart rate up, builds strength, builds endurance, and burns fat. Your future eighty-year-old self will thank you! Just do it!

Count on Your ZZZZZs

A man is not rightly conditioned until he is a happy, healthy, and prosperous being; and happiness, health, and prosperity are the result of a harmonious adjustment of the inner with the outer of the man with his surroundings.

[JAMES ALLEN]

On average, most people need around eight hours sleep a night (although this can vary between three hours and eleven hours, depending on the person and his or her age).

If we are regularly short of sleep, then our concentration and our effectiveness suffer and our energy levels decline. We have all seen and experienced this.

This diminishes our effectiveness in our job and can therefore increase stress: As our concentration wanders, we start to make mistakes. As our energy declines, we become less proactive in what we do, reducing our control over events. This means that a situation that is already difficult and stressful can become worse, needing even more sacrifice to bring it back under control.

Make sure you get enough sleep. If you have become used to being tired all the time, you will be amazed by how sharp and energetic you will feel once you start giving your body and brain adequate sleep.

Action: Having trouble sleeping? Become an early riser by setting your alarm for the same time each morning and getting up when it goes off every day—no matter what! Then go to bed when you are tired and ready to fall asleep. It may take a few days to create your body's new sleep rhythm, but it works.

You Are What You Eat

A healthy attitude is contagious but don't wait to catch it from others.
Be a carrier.

[TOM STOPPARD]

Another essential part of achieving and maintaining good health is making healthy choices at meal times. Improving poor eating habits may seem like an especially daunting task for some people. Instead of a radical change, try starting off slowly with something simple like adding more raw whole fruits and vegetables to your daily intake of food, or try a piece of fruit or cheese for dessert rather than ice cream. Drinking eight to ten glasses of water per day is an important key to good health.

Simply be aware of the choices you are making. If you make an effort to eat sweets and salt in moderation and make sure the bulk of what you consume is nutritious and full of vitamins and minerals, you'll move a long way toward healthy eating.

One thing to work toward eliminating in your diet is processed foods. Some people rely upon the convenience of pre-packaged frozen foods that they can just pop in the microwave for a few minutes and create a "complete" meal.

A healthier approach would be to do a little planning and preparation by making a menu for the week and even cooking several nutritious meals on the weekend and freezing individual portions. This way you will maintain the convenience of fast meals but you also know what ingredients are used in the preparation. With a little planning and preparation, you can be eating healthier in no time.

Action: Have plenty of healthy snacks and water bottles on hand for a "quick fix." Nuts, dried fruit, hummus and pita chips, carrot and celery sticks, snack bars, protein shakes, yogurt, granola, and jerky are all great "grab and go" energy restorers.

Rest & Relaxation

It's better to be healthy alone than sick with someone else.

[PHIL MCGRAW]

Rest is what we do to allow stress to subside. Rest at the end of a day, and at the end of a week, helps us to calm down and rejuvenate.

Doing fun things that we enjoy in our leisure time compensates us for the stress we experience at work, bringing some balance back into life. This is particularly important if we routinely experience unpleasant levels of stress.

A good way of getting rest and relaxation is to take up an enjoyable, non-rushed sport or hobby. If you spend all your working day competing, then it can be very pleasant to completely unwind for some of your free time. Slow physical activities such as sailing or walking are good for this, as are others where there is little or no pressure for performance. Reading novels, family activities, or socializing can also be very restful. Simply put, do what you love to do and what will make you happy.

Action: Vacations are particularly important, and you really do need to take them. Just looking at your vacation destination on your dream board will inspire you to relax! Take your vacation and spend time relaxing to recharge your batteries—this will allow you to keep on enjoying life to its fullest.

Finish Well

I'm concentrating on staying healthy, having peace, being happy, remembering what is important, taking in nature and animals, spending time reading, trying to understand the universe, where science and the spiritual meet.

[JOAN JETT]

Here's some good news—the score doesn't count at halftime! Live strong and finish well.

In golf, players strive for a full swing with complete follow-through. Pro golfers say, "You have to finish well to play well." In life, it is the other way around. You have to play well to finish well. It is never too late to make adjustments.

Who you are is far more valuable than what you do. Be wise, be kind, and do right. Starting strong in all your goals and dreams to live a healthier, happier, more prosperous life is important; sustaining the action is crucial. How you finish will become your legacy.

Action: Your investment of a little time, energy, and effort into the health of the CEO of You, Inc. (your body) will certainly pay huge dividends and eliminate the threat of a hostile take over! A measure of prevention could eradicate the need for a cure.

Living Your Dream

> *Learning is the beginning of wealth. Learning is the beginning of health. Learning is the beginning of spirituality. Searching and learning is where the miracle process all begins.*
>
> [JIM ROHN]

Get Happy

Smile at everyone you meet or come in contact with—even if you don't feel like it and they don't deserve it! Make your smile the first thing someone sees. You will be amazed at how this gesture disarms people and sets the tone for a positive encounter. The world can be a hostile and frustrating place at times, but when we make these small efforts, it makes a big difference in bringing warmth and positivity into our daily lives.

Leadership

The most successful people in life are those who have the best information.

[BENJAMIN DISRAELI]

Why is leadership important to living the life of your dreams? Leaders help themselves and others to do the right things. They set direction, build an inspiring vision, and create something new. Leadership is about mapping out where you need to go to "win." Leadership is dynamic, vibrant, and inspiring.

Leaders work hard to live the life they want. They focus on living their dreams. That's why leaders are so inspiring.

If you are unhappy with any area of your life, ask yourself why— why aren't you living your dream? Some responses might include:

- I don't have enough money.
- I don't have enough education.
- I can't take that type of risk.
- I don't have that type of talent.
- I don't have the time to pursue it.

If any of those reasons "explain" why you aren't living the life you want to lead, then the real reason you aren't living the life of your choice is YOU. The thoughts above are limiting thoughts. Many people will tell you that you can't do something; you have to be the one who tells yourself you *can*. Leaders don't hold themselves back; instead, they seek ways to overcome adversity and challenge. Remember that at one point Bill Gates was broke, Albert Einstein had no advanced degrees, Martin Luther King contemplated playing it safe, and Michael Jordan failed to make his high school basketball team.

Action: What excuses have you been making that are holding you back from creating results? List three.

What Is Leadership?

The man who succeeds above his fellows is the one who early in life clearly discerns his object, and towards that object habitually directs his power.

[EARL NIGHTINGALE]

For some people, leadership is intuitive. It comes fairly easily. They act on instinct; what they do works, and they can't easily explain it. To other people, leadership is a mystery. They have no idea what dynamics are at play. All they know is that sometimes people listen to what they have to say and work with them, and other times they're alone scratching their heads.

Leadership is dynamic. It's fluid. It changes from person to person, from moment to moment. But that doesn't mean it doesn't follow a pattern. And it doesn't mean you can't develop a level of mastery, even if you don't possess abundant natural leadership gifts.

Let's take a look at leadership expert John Maxwell's book, *The Five Levels of Leadership*. Here's how it works. We gain influence with people in levels—five levels to be exact. Every person who leads others has to start at the bottom level with another person and work his or her way up to higher levels one at a time.

Action: So what level do you think you are on? Well, it's time to take your life and leadership skills to another level!

Positional Leaders

Four short words sum up what has lifted most successful individuals above the crowd: a little bit more. They did all that was expected of them and a little bit more.

[A. LOU VICKERY]

According to John Maxwell, position is the lowest level of leadership—the entry level. The only influence a positional leader has is that which comes with the job title. People follow because they have to. Positional leadership is based on the rights granted by the position and title. Nothing is wrong with having a leadership position. But everything is wrong with using position to get people to follow. Position is a poor substitute for influence.

People who make it only to Level 1 may be bosses, but they are never *leaders*. They have subordinates, not team members. They rely on rules, regulations, policies, and organizational charts to control their people. Their people will only follow them within the stated boundaries of their authority. And their people will usually do only what is required of them. When positional leaders ask for extra effort or time, they rarely get it.

Positional leaders usually have difficulty working with volunteers, younger people, and the highly educated. Why? Because positional leaders have no influence, and these types of people tend to be more independent.

Position is the only level that does not require ability and effort to achieve. Anyone can be appointed to a position.

Action: Leadership can be defined as one's ability to get others to willingly follow. Every organization needs leaders at every level. What level are you at? What level do you want to achieve?

Permission & Production Leaders

I trust that everything happens for a reason, even when we're not wise enough to see it.

[OPRAH WINFREY]

According to John Maxwell, Level 2 is based entirely on relationships. On the permission level, people follow because they want to. When you like people and treat them like individuals who have value, you begin to develop influence with them. You develop trust. The environment becomes much more positive—whether at home, on the job, at play, or while volunteering.

The agenda for leaders on Level 2 isn't preserving their position. It's getting to know their people and figuring out how to get along with them. Leaders learn who their people are. Followers learn who their leaders are. People build solid, lasting relationships. You can like people without leading them, but you cannot lead people well without liking them. That's what Level 2 is about.

One of the dangers of getting to the permission level is that a leader can stop there. But good leaders don't just create a pleasant working environment. They get things done! That's why they must move up to Level 3, which is based on results. On the production level, leaders gain influence and credibility, and people begin to follow them because of what they have done for the organization.

Many positive things begin happening when leaders get to Level 3. Work gets done, morale improves, profits go up, turnover goes down, and goals are achieved. It is also on Level 3 that momentum kicks in.

Action: Leading and influencing others becomes fun on this level. Success and productivity have been known to solve a lot of problems. What people skills can you work on to excel at this level of leadership?

Empower Others

> *Opportunity is missed by most people because it's dressed in overalls and looks like work.*
>
> [THOMAS EDISON]

Leaders become great not because of their power, but because of their ability to empower others. That is what John Maxwell says leaders do on Level 4. They use their position, relationships, and productivity to invest in their followers and develop them until those followers become leaders in their own right. The result is reproduction; Level 4 leaders reproduce themselves.

Production may win games, but people development wins championships. Two things always happen on Level 4. First, teamwork goes to a very high level. Why? Because the high investment in people deepens relationships, helps people to know one another better, and strengthens loyalty. Second, performance increases. Why? Because there are more leaders on the team, and they help to improve everybody's performance.

Level 4 leaders change the lives of the people they lead. Accordingly, their people follow them because of what their leaders have done for them personally. And their relationships are often lifelong.

Action: Do you have a clear vision? Do you have a vivid picture of where you want to go, as well as a firm grasp on what success looks like and how to achieve it? But it's not enough to have a vision; leaders must also share it and act upon it. Take action!

Pinnacle Leadership

Quality is never an accident. It is always the result of intelligent effort.
[JOHN RUSKIN]

The highest and most difficult level of leadership is the pinnacle. While most people can learn to climb to Levels 1 through 4, Level 5 requires effort, skill, and intentionality, but also a high level of talent. Only naturally gifted leaders ever make it to this highest level. What do leaders do on Level 5? They develop people to become Level 4 leaders.

Developing leaders to the point where they are able and willing to develop other leaders is the most difficult leadership task of all. But here are the payoffs: Level 5 leaders develop Level 5 organizations. They create opportunities that other leaders don't. They create legacy in what they do. People follow them because of who they are and what they represent. In other words, their leadership gains a positive reputation. As a result, Level 5 leaders often transcend their position, their organization, and sometimes their industry.

Action: Integrity is considered a leader's most important character trait. A person of integrity is the same on the outside and on the inside. Such an individual can be trusted because he or she never veers from inner values, even when it might be expeditious to do so. A leader must have the trust of followers and therefore must display integrity.

Living Your Dream

> *Men make history and not the other way around. In periods where there is no leadership, society stands still. Progress occurs when courageous, skillful leaders seize the opportunity to change things for the better.*

[HARRY S. TRUMAN]

Leadership Qualities

Vision is having a clear vivid picture of where to go. *Integrity* is the integration of outward actions and inner values. *Dedication* means spending whatever time or energy is necessary to accomplish the task at hand. *Magnanimity* means giving credit where it is due. Leaders with *humility* recognize that they are no better or worse than other members of the team. *Openness* means being able to listen to new ideas, even if they do not conform to the usual way of thinking. *Creativity* is the ability to think differently, to get outside of the box that constrains solutions. *Fairness* means dealing with others consistently and justly. *Assertiveness* is the ability to clearly state what one expects so that there will be no misunderstandings. A *sense of humor* is vital to relieve tension and boredom, as well as to defuse hostility.

Leadership Skills

At the age of seven, a young boy and his family were forced out of their home. The boy had to work to support his family. At the age of nine, his mother passed away. When he grew up, the young man was keen to go to law school but had no education.

At twenty-two, he lost his job as a store clerk. At twenty-three, he ran for state legislature and lost. The same year, he went into business. It failed, leaving him with a debt that took him seventeen years to repay. At twenty-seven, he had a nervous breakdown.

Two years later, he tried for the post of speaker in his state legislature. He lost. At thirty-one, he was defeated in his attempt to become an elector. By thirty-five, he had been defeated twice while running for Congress. Finally, he did manage to secure a brief term in Congress, but at thirty-nine he lost his re-election bid.

At forty-one, his four-year-old son died. At forty-two, he was rejected as a prospective land officer. At forty-five, he ran for the Senate and lost. Two years later, he lost the vice presidential nomination. At forty-nine, he ran for Senate and lost again.

At fifty-one, he was elected the President of the United States of America.

The man in question: Abraham Lincoln.

[AUTHOR UNKNOWN]

Action: What were some of your biggest setbacks in life? How did you overcome them?

Born or Made

Leaders must be close enough to relate to others, but far enough ahead to motivate them.

[JOHN C. MAXWELL]

Many of us are acquainted with Abraham Lincoln's eloquent example of persistence and determination in achieving victory. We read his story, stop for a moment, and then sigh and say: "Wow! That's the stuff real leaders are made of."

And in saying this, it's all too easy for us to think about leaders like Lincoln almost as mythological creatures, separate from the rest of humanity and empowered by some mysterious quality that smooths their path toward inevitable success. This is the view of leadership that many people have traditionally taken: that leaders are marked out for leadership from early on in their lives, and that if you're not a leader, there's little you can do to become one.

But the truth is that you *can* develop great leadership skills. With patience, persistence, and hard work, you can become a highly effective leader.

Action: There are many leadership skills and competencies that, when combined and applied, go toward making you an effective leader. You have the ability to develop each of these skills within yourself. Who are you following? And who is following you?

Personal Characteristics

Integrity has no need of rules.

[ALBERT CAMUS]

Successful leaders tend to have an abundance of certain personality traits. Two key areas of personal growth and development are fundamental to leadership success: confidence and a positive mental attitude.

Confident people are usually inspiring, and people like to be around individuals who believe in themselves and what they're doing. Likewise, if you're a positive and optimistic person who tries to make the best of any situation, you'll find it much easier to motivate people to do their best.

You build confidence by mastering significant skills and situations and by knowing that you can add real value by the work you do. One of the best ways to improve your confidence is to acknowledge all of the things you've already accomplished.

A positive mindset is also associated with strong leadership. However, being positive is much more than presenting a happy face to the world. You need to develop a strong sense of balance and recognize that setbacks and problems do happen—it's how you deal with those problems that makes the difference.

Positive people approach situations realistically, prepared to make the changes necessary to overcome a problem. Negative people, on the other hand, often give in to the stress and pressure of the situation. This can lead to fear, worry, distress, anger, and failure.

Action: Understanding your thinking patterns and developing good stress management techniques will allow you to eliminate negative thoughts and feelings.

Decision-Making

The task of the leader is to get his people from where they are to where they have not been.

[HENRY KISSINGER]

Successful people know the power of being able to make decisions. Actions produce results, but the first step is *deciding to act*.

We all make decisions each and every day, but many people do not make bold, purposeful decisions. By not making conscious decisions, they allow life to simply "happen" to them. They end up reacting to their circumstances instead of being proactive and creating the life that will fulfill their purpose.

Decision-making is an integral part of leadership. You are not going to get the results you desire by living a passive life. You have to decide exactly what you desire so you can make the appropriate choices to achieve your goals.

Do you love your life? You get to decide what your life looks like. You can make the decision to be grateful for everything that is good in your life. You can make the decision to act in a loving and compassionate manner in all of your relationships. You can make the decision to create abundance so you can contribute to the organizations that share your passions.

If you always keep your goals in focus, it makes it much easier to determine the choices that you need to make to achieve them. Be consciously aware of the decisions you are making so you can determine if they will best serve your purpose.

Action: Ask yourself this: "What is it that I want to achieve, and what decisions do I need to make right now, in this moment, to help me reach my goals?" Be bold and make the decision to make the choices and take the actions that will move you forward today.

Qualities of a Leader

Good business leaders create a vision, articulate the vision,
passionately own the vision and relentlessly drive it to completion.

[JACK WELSH]

Good leadership is essential for achieving an extraordinary life. The need for examples of leadership has never been clearer than now. If you have made the decision to take on the leadership role of your life, you will need these three qualities:

- **Compassion** Do you have it? It is a deep awareness of the suffering of another coupled with the wish to relieve it. Leadership isn't *using* others to build your kingdom; it's loving and serving them in order to build God's!

- **Creativity** Tap into yours. The true leader looks for a creative solution in every problem and then acts on it.

- **Commitment** Real Leaders don't quit—they couldn't even if they wanted to. There is always a price to be paid for success, so ask yourself, "Do I have what it takes?"

Action: A leader must be able to communicate his or her vision in terms that cause followers to buy into it. He or she must communicate clearly and passionately, as passion is contagious. What is your contagious passion?

Leadership Questions

The task of leadership is not to put greatness into humanity, but to elicit it, for the greatness is already there.

[JOHN BUCHAN]

We all have chinks in our armor. The important thing is to discover your flaws and deal with them.

Are you thinking about what you are thinking about? Remember, we become what we think about.

Are your priorities in order? Are you paying attention to what is most important in your life? Too many become "successful" at the cost of lost health or a broken home.

Are you accountable to anybody? We need people in our lives with 20/20 vision to cover our blind spots and keep us in balance. Authority without accountability equals disaster.

Why are you doing this? How should it be done? When should I do it?

Action: A good leader must have the discipline to work toward his or her vision single-mindedly, as well as to direct his or her actions and those of the team toward the goal. Action is the mark of a leader—so ask yourself if you are acting.

Living Your Dream

> *The supreme quality for leadership is unquestionably integrity.*
> *Without it, no real success is possible, no matter whether it is on a*
> *section gang, a football field, in an army, or in an office.*
>
> [DWIGHT D. EISENHOWER]

John Wooden's Success Principles

Competitive greatness. Poise. Confidence. Condition. Skill. Team Spirit. Self-control. Alertness. Initiative. Intentness. Industriousness. Friendship. Loyalty. Cooperation. Enthusiasm.

Emotional Intelligence

A sense of humor . . . is needed armor. Joy in one's heart and some laughter on one's lips is a sign that the person down deep has a pretty good grasp of life.

[HUGH SIDEY]

Emotional intelligence (EQ) is a different type of intelligence. It's about being "heart smart," not just "book smart." The evidence shows that emotional intelligence matters just as much as intellectual ability, if not more so, when it comes to happiness and success in life. Emotional intelligence helps you build strong relationships, succeed at work, and achieve your goals.

The skills of emotional intelligence can be developed throughout life. You can boost your own EQ by learning how to rapidly reduce stress, connect to your emotions, communicate nonverbally, use humor and play to deal with challenges, and defuse conflicts with confidence and self-assurance.

Emotional intelligence is the ability to identify, use, understand, and manage your emotions in positive and constructive ways. It's about recognizing your own emotional state and the emotional states of others. Emotional intelligence is also about engaging with others in ways that draw people to you.

Action: Observe how you react to people. Do you rush to judgment before you know all of the facts? Do you stereotype? Look honestly at how you think and interact with other people. Try to put yourself in their place, and be more open and accepting of their perspectives and needs.

Core Abilities

Anger and jealousy can no more bear to lose sight of their objects than love.

[GEORGE ELIOT]

Emotional intelligence consist of four core abilities:

- **Self-awareness** The ability to recognize your own emotions and how they affect your thoughts and behavior, know your strengths and weaknesses, and have self-confidence.
- **Self-management** The ability to control impulsive feelings and behaviors, manage your emotions in healthy ways, take initiative, follow through on commitments, and adapt to changing circumstances.
- **Social awareness** The ability to understand the emotions, needs, and concerns of other people, pick up on emotional cues, feel comfortable socially, and recognize the power dynamics in a group or organization.
- **Relationship management** The ability to develop and maintain good relationships, communicate clearly, inspire and influence others, work well in a team, and manage conflict.

Most of us know that there is a world of difference between knowledge and behavior—our behavior is applying that knowledge to make changes in our lives. There are many things we may know and want to do but don't do or can't do when we're under pressure. This is especially true when it comes to emotional intelligence.

Action: Do you seek attention for your accomplishments? Humility can be a wonderful quality. When you practice humility, you can be quietly confident about your actions without seeking praise for yourself. This gives others a chance to shine.

EQ vs. IQ

An effort made for the happiness of others lifts above ourselves.

[LYDIA M. CHILD]

Most of us have learned not to trust our emotions. We've been told emotions distort the more "accurate" information our intellect supplies. Even the term *emotional* has come to mean weak, out of control, and even childish. "Don't be a baby!" we say to the little boy who is crying on the playground. "Leave him alone! Let him work it out!" we admonish the little girl who runs to help the little boy.

On the other hand, our abilities to memorize and problem-solve, to spell words and do mathematical calculations, are easily measured on written tests and slapped as grades on report cards. Ultimately, these intellectual abilities dictate which college will accept us and which career paths we're advised to follow.

However, intellectual intelligence (IQ) is usually less important in determining how successful we are than emotional intelligence (EQ). We all know people who are academically brilliant and yet are socially inept and unsuccessful. What they are missing is emotional intelligence.

Emotional intelligence is not learned in the standard intellectual way; it must be learned and understood on an emotional level. We can't simply read about emotional intelligence or master it through memorization. In order to learn about emotional intelligence in a way that produces change, we need to engage the emotional parts of the brain in ways that connect us to others. This kind of learning is based on what we see, hear, and feel. Intellectual understanding is an important first step, but the development of emotional intelligence depends on sensory, nonverbal learning and real-life practice.

Action: We tend to respond emotionally to things that capture our attention. Write in your journal how you feel about and what you think about the events of your day.

Developing Emotional Intelligence

All human beings are also dream beings. Dreaming ties all mankind together.

[JACK KEROUAC]

Emotional intelligence consists of five key skills, each building on the last:

1. The ability to quickly reduce stress.
2. The ability to recognize and manage your emotions.
3. The ability to connect with others using nonverbal communication.
4. The ability to use humor and play to deal with challenges.
5. The ability to resolve conflicts positively and with confidence.

Anyone can learn the five skills of emotional intelligence at anytime. But there is a difference between learning about emotional intelligence and applying that knowledge to your life. Just because you know you should do something doesn't mean you will—especially when you're feeling stressed. This is especially true when it comes to the skills of emotional intelligence.

When you become overwhelmed by stress, the emotional parts of your brain override the rational parts—hijacking your best-laid plans, intentions, and strategies. In order to permanently change behavior in ways that stand up under pressure, you need to learn how to take advantage of the powerful emotional parts of the brain that remain active and accessible even in times of stress. This means that you can't simply read about emotional intelligence in order to master it.

Action: You have to learn the skills on a deeper, emotional level—experiencing and practicing them in your everyday life.

Rapidly Reduce Stress

As knowledge increases, wonder deepens.
[CHARLES MORGAN]

When we're under high levels of stress, rational thinking and decision-making go out the window. Runaway stress overwhelms the mind and body, getting in the way of our ability to accurately "read" a situation, hear what someone else is saying, be aware of our own feelings and needs, and communicate clearly.

The first key skill of emotional intelligence is the ability to quickly calm yourself down when you're feeling overwhelmed. Being able to manage stress in the moment is the key to resilience. This EQ skill helps you stay balanced, focused, and in control—no matter what challenges you face.

Stress Busting: Functioning Well in the Heat of the Moment

Develop your stress-busting skills by working through the following three steps:

- Realize when you're stressed—The first step to reducing stress is recognizing what stress feels like. Many of us spend so much time in an unbalanced state that we've forgotten what it feels like to be calm and relaxed.

- Identify your stress response—Everyone reacts differently to stress. Do you tend to space out and get depressed? Become angry and agitated? Freeze with anxiety? The best way to quickly calm yourself depends on your specific stress response.

- Discover the stress-busting techniques that work for you—The best way to reduce stress quickly is through the senses: sight, sound, smell, taste, and touch. But each person responds differently to sensory input, so you need to find things that are soothing to you.

Action: Make a list of your best stress-busting techniques: Taking a walk, listening to music, a nice candlelight bath, reading by a cozy fire, an aromatherapy message or facial . . . mmmm, nice!

Connect to Your Emotions

Eagles come in all shapes and sizes, but you will recognize them chiefly by their attitudes.

[E. F. SCHUMACHER]

The second key skill of emotional intelligence is having a moment-to-moment awareness of your emotions and how they influence your thoughts and actions. Emotional awareness is the key to understanding yourself and others.

Many people are disconnected from their emotions—especially strong core emotions such as anger, sadness, fear, and joy. But although we can distort, deny, or numb our feelings, we can't eliminate them. They're still there, whether we're aware of them or not. Unfortunately, without emotional awareness, we are unable to fully understand our own motivations and needs or to communicate effectively with others.

What Kind of a Relationship Do You Have with Your Emotions?

- Do you experience feelings that flow, encountering one emotion after another as your experiences change from moment to moment?

- Are your emotions accompanied by physical sensations that you experience in places like your stomach or chest?

- Do you experience discrete feelings and emotions, such as anger, sadness, fear, joy, each of which is evident in subtle facial expressions?

- Can you experience intense feelings that are strong enough to capture both your attention and that of others?

- Do you pay attention to your emotions? Do they factor into your decision-making?

Action: If any of these experiences are unfamiliar, your emotions may be turned down or turned off. In order to be emotionally healthy and emotionally intelligent, you must reconnect to your core emotions, accept them, and become comfortable with them.

Living Your Dream

There is only one difference between a long life and a good dinner: that, in the dinner, the sweets come last.

[ROBERT LOUIS STEVENSON]

Expect the BEST, and Be Prepared for Everything Else

Decide now what you will do if the worst happens. Obstacles to your goal can come in one or more of several forms. You will run into negative people and negative comments and even negative self-talk. So what action steps will you take to overcome?

Other obstacles may be external or internal—shortage of time, energy, or money may be external obstacles to come up. Decide now how you will handle this. Internal obstacles disguised as well-meaning friends and family who are trying to "help you avoid being disappointed" or "just don't want to see you get your hopes up" may speak up. In reality, though, they may be jealous, insecure, or fearful that if you improve your own life, you will no longer need them.

Whenever possible, identify potential obstacles in advance and create a plan of action to overcome these obstacles. Addressing them in advance is easier and more effective than waiting until the obstacle confronts you.

Emotional Intelligence Skills

*This is what I learned: that everybody is talented, original and has
something important to say.*

[BRENDA UELAND]

Being a good communicator requires more than just verbal skills.
Oftentimes, what we say is less important than how we say it or the
other nonverbal signals we send out. In order to hold the attention of
others and build connection and trust, we need to be aware of and in
control of our nonverbal cues. We also need to be able to accurately
read and respond to the nonverbal cues that other people send us.

Nonverbal communication is the third skill of emotional intelli-
gence. This wordless form of communication is emotionally driven. It
asks the questions: "Are you listening?" and "Do you understand and
care?" We answer these questions in the way we listen, look, move,
and react. Our nonverbal messages will produce a sense of interest,
trust, excitement, and desire for connection…or they will generate
fear, confusion, distrust, and disinterest.

*Action: Part of improving nonverbal communication involves paying
attention to:*

> *Eye contact*
> *Facial expression*
> *Tone of voice*
> *Posture and gesture*
> *Touch*
> *Timing and pace*

Use Humor & Play to Deal with Challenges

The idea is to die young as late as possible.
[ASHLEY MONTAGU]

Humor, laughter, and play are natural antidotes to life's difficulties. They lighten our burdens and help us keep things in perspective. A good hearty laugh reduces stress, elevates mood, and brings our nervous system back into balance.

The ability to deal with challenges using humor and play is the fourth skill of emotional intelligence. Playful communication broadens our emotional intelligence and helps us:

- **Take hardships in stride.** By allowing us to view our frustrations and disappointments from new perspectives, laughter and play enable us to survive annoyances, hard times, and setbacks.

- **Smooth over differences.** Using gentle humor often helps us say things that might be otherwise difficult to express without creating a flap.

- **Simultaneously relax and energize ourselves.** Playful communication relieves fatigue and relaxes our bodies, which allows us to recharge and accomplish more.

- **Become more creative.** When we loosen up, we free ourselves of rigid ways of thinking and being, allowing us to get creative and see things in new ways.

Action: Examine how you react to stressful situations. Do you become upset every time there's a delay or something doesn't happen the way you want? Do you blame others or become angry at them, even when it's not their fault? The ability to stay calm and in control in difficult situations is highly valued—in the business world and outside it. Keep your emotions under control when things go wrong.

Resolve Conflict Positively

Always bear in mind that your own resolution to succeed is more important than any other.

[ABRAHAM LINCOLN]

Conflict and disagreements are inevitable in relationships. Two people can't possibly have the same needs, opinions, and expectations at all times. Resolving conflict in healthy, constructive ways can strengthen trust between people. When conflict isn't perceived as threatening or punishing, it fosters freedom, creativity, and safety in relationships.

The ability to manage conflicts in a positive, trust-building way is the fifth key skill of emotional intelligence. Successfully resolving differences is supported by the previous four skills of emotional intelligence. Once you know how to manage stress, stay emotionally present and aware, communicate nonverbally, and use humor and play, you'll be better equipped to handle emotionally charged situations and catch and defuse many issues before they escalate.

Action: Tips for resolving conflict in a trust-building way:

Stay focused in the present. When we are not holding on to old hurts and resentments, we can recognize the reality of a current situation and view it as a new opportunity for resolving old feelings about conflicts.

Choose your battles. Arguments take time and energy, especially if you want to resolve them in a positive way. Consider what is worth arguing about and what is not.

Forgive. If someone else's hurtful behavior is in the past, remember that conflict resolution involves giving up the urge to punish.

End conflicts that can't be resolved. It takes two people to keep an argument going. You can choose to disengage from a conflict, even if you still disagree. Take responsibility for your actions, and try to make things right for your part.

Emotional Honesty

Openly revealing our feelings establishes credibility.

[GERRY SPENCE]

Emotional honesty means expressing your true feelings. To be emotionally honest we must first be emotionally aware. This emotional awareness is related to our emotional intelligence. It is our emotional intelligence, combined with the necessary learning, practice, and experience, which gives us the ability to accurately identify our feelings.

Emotional intelligence may also give us the ability to decide when it is in our best interest to be emotionally honest by sharing our real feelings. There may be times when it is not healthy or safe for us to be emotionally honest. In general, though, we would be better off individually and as a society if we would be more emotionally honest.

If we are more emotionally honest with ourselves, we will get to know our "true selves" on a deeper level. This could help us become more self-accepting. It could also help us make better choices about how to spend our time and who to spend it with.

If we are emotionally honest with others, it may encourage them to be more emotionally honest too. When we are open and honest, we are more likely not to be asked or pressured to do things which we do not want to do.

Action: Examine how your actions will affect others—before you take those actions. If your decision will impact others, put yourself in their place. How will they feel if you do this? Would you want that experience? If you must take the action, how can you help others deal with the effects?

Society and Emotional Honesty

A man sooner or later discovers that he is the master-gardener of his soul, the director of his life.

[JAMES ALLEN]

It takes emotional awareness, self-confidence, even courage to be emotionally honest.

This is because, in many ways, society teaches us to ignore, repress, deny, and lie about our feelings. For example, when asked how we feel, most of us will reply "fine" or "good," even if that is not true.

Children start out emotionally honest. They express their true feelings freely and spontaneously. But the training to be emotionally dishonest begins at an early age. Parents and teachers frequently encourage or even demand that children speak or act in ways that are inconsistent with the child's true feelings. The child is told to smile when actually she is sad. She is told to apologize when she feels no regret. She is told to say "thank you" when she feels no appreciation. She is told to stop complaining when she feels mistreated. She may be told it is rude and selfish to protest being forced to act in ways that go against her feelings.

As children become adolescents, they begin to think more for themselves. They begin to speak out more, talk back more, and challenge the adults around them. If these adults feel threatened, they are likely to defend themselves by invalidating the adolescent's feelings and perceptions. There is also peer pressure to conform to the group norms.

Through all of this, children and adolescents learn they can't be honest with their feelings. They gradually stop being emotionally honest with their parents, their teachers, their friends . . . and even themselves. They learn it just doesn't pay to express one's true feelings.

Action: Children and adults will feel valued when you listen to their wants and needs and are able to empathize or identify with them on many different levels.

Emotionally Honest Parents

It is time for parents to teach young people early on that in diversity there is beauty and there is strength.

[MAYA ANGELOU]

Parents can create an emotionally safe environment where the child or adolescent are free to be emotionally honest . . . or they can create just the opposite. The way we were parented is probably the main factor in how emotionally honest we are later in life.

The primary way to create an emotionally safe environment is through emotional validation. When we are accepted and validated emotionally, we aren't afraid of being rejected or punished for expressing the feelings, thoughts, questions, or perceptions we might have. We are free to be ourselves, and our parents get to know us as we really are. When we are accepted as we really are—and not just as the image we believe we need to portray—we feel a strong sense of inner security. We can be more emotionally honest with others because we are not as afraid of their rejection. Since we feel secure within ourselves, others' acceptance or rejection is simply not as important to us. We are freer to be ourselves with everyone. This quality attracts other people who are also secure and can be themselves. Therefore, we are likely to be surrounded by secure, self-confident, emotionally honest people as the years go by.

Action: Do a self-evaluation. What are your weaknesses? Are you willing to accept that you're not perfect and that you could work on some areas to make yourself a better person? Write down three areas where you'd like to improve. Have the courage to look at yourself honestly—it can change your life.

Living Your Dream

> *If communication is to be successful, if love is to be successful, if relationships are to be successful, we must give up the absurd notion that there is something "heroic" or "strong" about lying, about faking what we feel, about misrepresenting, by commission or omission, the reality of our experience or the truth of our being. We must learn that if heroism and strength mean anything, it is the willingness to face reality, to face truth, to respect facts, to accept that which is, is.*
>
> [NATHANIEL BRANDEN]

Know Your Limits

Your time is limited. Your money is limited. Your energy level is limited. All resources have some kind of limit to them. Review your goals and revisit the resources necessary objectively. Ask yourself, "Is it realistic to pursue that particular goal now?" Recognize your limits and then set your goals within those limits to keep them achievable. Or maybe your desire is strong enough to push the limits to do whatever it takes to realize your dreams!

Procrastination

> *The wise man does not lay up his treasures. The more he gives to others, the more he has found his own.*
>
> [LAO TZU]

Procrastination, the habit of putting tasks off to the last possible minute, can be a major problem in both your career and your personal life. Side effects include missed opportunities, frenzied work hours, stress, a feeling of being overwhelmed, resentment, and guilt. Let's explore the root causes of procrastination and give you several practical tools to overcome it.

The behavior pattern of procrastination can be triggered in many different ways, so you won't always procrastinate for the same reason. Sometimes you'll procrastinate because you're overwhelmed with too much on your plate and procrastination gives you an escape. Other times you'll feel tired and lazy, and you just can't get going.

There are various causes of procrastination, and we will consider several intelligent ways to respond to and overcome this bad habit during this week.

Action: Is fear of rejection, fear of failure, or fear of what other people think causing you to procrastinate? As we have learned, taking action is the key to overcoming any fear. So, consider this—what other people think of you is really none of your business. Just do it!

Stress

> *It is an undoubted truth, that the less one has to do, the less time one finds to do it in.*
>
> [EARL OF CHESTERFIELD]

When you feel stressed, worried, or anxious, it's hard to work productively. In certain situations procrastination works as a coping mechanism to keep your stress levels under control. A wise solution is to reduce the amount of stress in your life when possible, so that you can spend more time working because you *want* to, not because you *have* to. One of the simplest ways to reduce stress is to take more time for play.

Making time for guaranteed fun can be an effective way to overcome procrastination. Decide in advance what blocks of time you'll allocate each week to family time, entertainment, exercise, social activities, and personal hobbies. Then schedule your work hours using whatever time is left. This can reduce the urge to procrastinate because your work will not encroach on your leisure time, so you don't have to procrastinate on work in order to relax and enjoy life. Realize that your work should be enjoyable enough that you're motivated to do it. If you aren't inspired by your daily work, it might be time to admit that you made a mistake in choosing the wrong career path and seek out a new direction that does inspire you.

Benjamin Franklin advised that the optimal strategy for high productivity is to split your days into one-third work, one-third play, and one-third rest. Once again the suggestion is to guarantee your leisure time. Hold your work time and your playtime as equally important, so one doesn't encroach upon the other.

Action: Making your work environment a happy, peaceful, and relaxing place will help to reduce stress levels. Get started today at your home or office.

Overwhelm

There are a million ways to lose a work day, but not even a single way to get one back.

[TOM DEMARCO]

Sometimes you may have more items on your to-do list than you can reasonably complete. This can quickly lead to feeling overwhelmed, and ironically you may be more likely to procrastinate when you can least afford it. Think of it as your brain refusing to cooperate with a schedule that you know is unreasonable. In this case the message is that you need to stop, reassess your true priorities, and simplify.

Options for reducing schedule overload include elimination, delegation, and negotiation. First, review your to-dos and cut as much as you can—cut everything that isn't truly important. This should be a no-brainer, but it's amazing how poorly people actually implement it. People cut things like exercise while leaving plenty of time for TV, even though exercise invigorates them and TV drains them. When you cut items, be honest about removing the most worthless ones first, and retain those that provide real value.

Second, delegate tasks to others as much as possible. Ask for extra help if necessary. And third, negotiate with others to free up more time for what's really important. If you happen to have a job that overloads you with more work than you feel is reasonable, it's up to you to decide if it's worthwhile to continue in that situation. Jobs that push people to the point of feeling overwhelmed are counterproductive for both the employer and the employees.

Action: We shoot ourselves in the foot, to begin with, by telling ourselves how horrible a particular project is. Changing our attitude toward the task, when possible, may go a long way toward keeping us from procrastinating. Tell yourself that the task isn't so bad or difficult, that you either know how to do it or you can learn how while you're doing it. Attitude is everything!

Peak Performance

A year from now you may wish you had started today.

[KAREN LAMB]

Be aware that the peak performers in any field tend to take more vacation time and work shorter hours than the workaholics. Peak performers get *more* done in *less* time by keeping themselves fresh, relaxed, and creative. By treating your working time as a scarce resource rather than an uncontrollable monster that can gobble up every other area of your life, you'll be more balanced, focused, and effective.

It's been shown that the optimal workweek for most people is forty to forty-five hours. Working longer hours than this actually has such an adverse effect on productivity and motivation that less real work gets done. This is especially true for creative, information-age work.

Action: Try a simple experiment to test this concept for yourself. You can measure your efficiency ratio as the number of hours you spend doing important work divided by the number of hours you spend in your office each week. You may be shocked to find how very few hours of real work you accomplish while spending long extra hours in your office. If you focus your efforts and create massive action in fewer hours at work, you will be more relaxed and get more free time!

Laziness

The best way to get something done is to begin.

[UNKNOWN]

Often we procrastinate because we feel too physically and/or emotionally drained to work. Once we fall into this pattern, it's easy to get stuck due to inertia because an object at rest tends to remain at rest. When you feel lazy, even simple tasks seem like too much work because your energy is too low compared to the energy required by the task. If you blame the task for being too difficult or tedious, you'll procrastinate to conserve energy. But the longer you do this, the more your resolve will weaken, and your procrastination habit may begin spiraling toward *depression*. Feeling weak and unmotivated shouldn't be your norm, so it's important to disrupt this pattern as soon as you become aware of it.

The solution is straightforward: get up and physically move your body. Exercise helps to raise your energy levels. When your energy is high, tasks will seem to get easier, and you'll be less resistant to taking action. A fit person can handle more activity than an unfit person, even though the difficulty of the tasks remains the same.

Diet and exercise are critical in keeping your energy levels consistently high. A healthy diet that includes a balance of protein, fat, and carbs with plenty of fresh fruits and vegetables is key to giving your body good "fuel." When you exercise regularly, your metabolism stays high throughout the day. You will find you will have the energy and mental clarity to tackle whatever comes your way.

Action: Tasks seem easier to complete when you have a healthy diet and plenty of exercise. The tasks will be the same, but you will have grown stronger.

Lack of Motivation

I'd be more frightened by not using whatever abilities I'd been given. I'd be more frightened by procrastination and laziness.

[DENZEL WASHINGTON]

We all experience temporary laziness at times, but if you suffer from chronically low motivation and just can't seem to get anything going, then it's time for you to let go of immature thought patterns, to embrace life as a mature adult, and to discover your true purpose in life. Until you identify an inspiring purpose, you'll never come close to achieving your potential, and your motivation will always remain weak.

Sometimes our passion for our jobs or careers simply begins to fade. We may be competent at what we do, and we may even do well financially. Maybe you are just not interested in what you are doing. Consequently, you find yourself procrastinating on some projects. You may have tried to boost your motivation by using a variety of techniques to no avail. It could be that you need to find a more inspiring career path.

Center your work around an *inspiring purpose*, and you'll greatly reduce your tendency to procrastinate. Finding your purpose is a powerful way to defeat procrastination problems because you won't procrastinate on what you *love* to do. Chronic procrastination is actually a big warning sign that tells us, "You're going the wrong way. Take a different path!"

Action: This is a good time to review your dreams and goals. Are you doing something every day toward living your dream life? Knowing you are working toward a worthwhile goal or dream will motivate you to jump out of bed in the morning!

Living Your Dream

You have powers you never dreamed of. You can do things you never thought you could do. There are no limitations in what you can do except the limitations of your own mind.

[DARWIN P. KINGSLEYS]

Goals That Stretch You—But Not Too Far

To get what you've never had, you must do what you've never done. The best goals require you to stretch and grow—to become a little bit better person or accomplish a little more than you have to date. At the same time, goals must be attainable—not so far out of reach that failure is assured. Set your goal just outside of your comfort zone to see what it will make of you to stretch and achieve that goal. As you have success and set new goals, continually up the ante to continue to challenge yourself.

Only you are able to determine just how important your dreams are to you and how much you are willing to stretch to get them. If you are determined to realize your dream, you'll be amazed at how you can stretch to meet your goals. What are you willing to do to achieve your goals and realize your dreams? Strive for excellence in achieving your dreams—you deserve it!

Self-Discipline

> *Know the true value of time; snatch, seize, and enjoy every moment of it. No idleness, no laziness, no procrastination: never put off till tomorrow what you can do today.*
>
> [LORD CHESTERFIELD]

Self-discipline is the ability to get yourself to take action regardless of your emotional state.

Even when motivation is high, you may still encounter tasks you don't want to do. In these situations, self-discipline works like a motivational backup system. When you feel motivated, you don't need much discipline, but it sure comes in handy when you need to get something done but really don't want to do the work. If your self-discipline is weak, however, procrastinating will be too tempting to resist.

Imagine what you could accomplish if you could simply get yourself to follow through on your best intentions—no matter what. We can only know a person's true intentions based on the results we see.

If you really want to overcome procrastination, you must release any attachment to the fantasy of a quick fix and commit to making real progress. You need to recognize that you won't solve your procrastination problems overnight, just as a single visit to the gym won't make you an athlete.

Action: Sometimes it helps to change your environment—shake it up! The key is to create an environment that fits the success you're going to create. A fresh coat of paint works wonders along with new personal photos. Surround yourself with things that make you happy! Get organized and clear your mind—spend a day de-cluttering, create a system for organization, and then stick with it!

Time Management

It is well to be up before daybreak, for such habits contribute to health, wealth, and wisdom.

[ARISTOTLE]

Do you ever find yourself falling behind because you overslept, because you were too disorganized, or because certain tasks just fell through the cracks? Bad habits like these often lead to procrastination, often unintentionally.

The solution in this case is to diagnose the bad habit that's hurting you and devise a new habit to replace it. For example, if you have a problem oversleeping, take up the challenge of becoming an early riser. If you want to become an early riser (or just exert more control over your sleep patterns), then try this: Go to bed only when you're too sleepy to stay up, and get up at a fixed time every morning.

If you are overwhelmed by all there is to do, focus on your top three priorities and break down the action steps to reach each goal. If feeling overwhelmed tends to lead to procrastination, get in the daily habit of making a list every night of the two key things you must accomplish the next day; put the most challenging and difficult task first.

Action: If being disorganized is causing you to get behind on important projects, make more decisions. *Clutter and disorganization is often the result of* failing to decide *what to do about or with something. Touch every paper and email once! Try it today!*

Time Blocking

Procrastination is opportunity's assassin.
[Victor Kiam]

For tasks you've been putting off for a while, try using the time-blocking method to get started. Here's how it works: First, select a small piece of the task you can work on for just thirty minutes. Then choose a reward you will give yourself immediately afterwards. The reward (anything you find pleasurable) is guaranteed if you simply put in the time; it doesn't depend on any meaningful accomplishment. Because the amount of time you'll be working on the task is so short, your focus will shift to the impending pleasure of the reward instead of the difficulty of the task. No matter how unpleasant the task, there's virtually nothing you can't endure for just thirty minutes if you have a big enough reward waiting for you.

When you time-block your tasks, you may discover that something very interesting happens. You will probably find that you continue working much longer than thirty minutes. You will often get so involved in a task, even a difficult one, that you actually *want* to keep working on it. Before you know it, you've put in an hour or even several hours. The certainty of your reward is still there, so you know you can enjoy it whenever you're ready to stop. Once you begin taking action, your focus shifts away from worrying about the difficulty of the task and toward finishing the current piece of the task which now has your full attention.

When you do decide to stop working, claim and enjoy your reward. Then schedule another thirty-minute period to work on the task with another reward. This will help you associate more and more pleasure to the task, knowing that you will always be immediately rewarded for your efforts. Working toward distant and uncertain long-term rewards is not nearly as motivating as immediate short-term rewards. By rewarding yourself for simply putting in the time, instead of for any specific achievements, you'll be eager to return to work on your task again and again, and you'll ultimately finish it.

Action: You can do anything for thirty minutes! Try it today!

Sufficient Skills

> *Procrastination is the bad habit of putting off until the day after*
> *tomorrow what should have been done the day before yesterday.*
> [NAPOLEON HILL]

If you lack sufficient skill to complete a task at a reasonable level of quality, you may procrastinate to avoid a failure experience. You then have three viable options to overcome this type of pattern: educate, delegate, or eliminate.

First, you can acquire the skill level you need by training up. Just because you can't do something *today* doesn't mean you'll *never* be able to do it. Someday you may even master that skill. You can continue to apply and upgrade that skill. If you can't do something, don't whine about it—educate yourself to gain skill until you become proficient.

A second option is to delegate tasks you lack the skill to do. There are far too many interesting skills for you to master, so you must rely on others for help. You may not realize it, but you're already a master at delegation. Do you grow all your own food? Did you sew your own clothes? Did you build your own house? Chances are that you depend on others for your very survival. If you want a certain result but don't want to acquire the skills to get that result, you can recruit others to help you. This frees you to spend more time working from your strengths.

Thirdly, you may conclude that a result isn't needed badly enough to justify the effort of either education or delegation. In that case the smart choice is to eliminate the task. Sometimes procrastination is a sign that a task needn't be done at all.

Action: Pick a task you have been putting off—do you need to educate, delegate, or eliminate?

319

Perfectionism

Procrastination is the thief of time.

[EDWARD YOUNG]

Perfectionism is a common form of erroneous thinking that leads to procrastination. Believing that you must do something *perfectly* is a recipe for stress, and you'll associate that stress with the task and condition yourself to avoid it. So you put the task off to the last possible minute until you finally have a way out of this trap—now there isn't enough time to do the job perfectly, so you're off the hook because you can tell yourself that you could have been perfect if you only had more time. But if you have no specific deadline for a task, perfectionism can cause you to delay indefinitely.

The solution to perfectionism is to give yourself permission to be human. Have you ever used a piece of software that you consider to be perfect in every way? No way. Realize that an imperfect job completed today is always superior to the perfect job delayed indefinitely.

Perfectionism also arises when you think of a project as one gigantic whole. Replace that one big "must be perfect" project in your mind with one small imperfect first step. Your first draft can be very, very rough. You're always free to revise it later.

Action: Are you a perfectionist? Do you allow your expectations of perfection for yourself and those around you to generate procrastination? ("If I don't have the time and energy to do it perfectly, I don't do it at all!") Perfection is hardly ever achievable; instead strive for excellence. Perfectionists get nothing done!

Get a Grip & Just Do It!

> *Nothing separates the generations more than music. By the time a child is eight or nine, he has developed a passion for his own music that is even stronger than his passions for procrastination and weird clothes.*
>
> [BILL COSBY]

Some of these solutions are challenging to implement, but they're effective. If you really want to tame the procrastination beast, you'll need something stronger than quick-fix motivational *rah-rah*.

This problem isn't going away on its own. You must take the initiative. The upside is that tackling this problem yields tremendous personal growth. You'll become stronger, braver, more disciplined, more driven, and more focused. These benefits will become hugely significant over your lifetime, so recognize that the challenge of overcoming procrastination is truly a blessing in disguise. The whole point is to grow stronger.

Action: Get a grip and just do it. At the end of the day, it boils down to taking action. You can do all the strategizing, planning, and evaluating, but if you don't take action, nothing's going to happen. You probably know people who keep complaining about their situations but still refuse to take action. Reality check: no one procrastinates her way to success, and that's not going to change. Whatever it is you are procrastinating on, if you want to get it done, you need to get a grip on yourself and do it.

Living Your Dream

The significant problems we face cannot be solved by the same level of thinking that created them.

[ALBERT EINSTEIN]

Identify Factors Within Your Control

Whenever possible, create goals that are within your control. For example, having an article accepted in a national magazine is beyond your control. You could write the best article ever, but if the editor doesn't accept it for whatever reason, you have no control over that. So if you set a goal to have an article published in a national magazine, your goal could fail—through no fault of your own.

It's better to set goals over which you *do* have control. For example, set a goal to send out five articles this month to national magazines. You may or may not be published in a national magazine, but the achievement of your goal won't be contingent on someone else's actions. Writing and sending out the five articles is within your control and can be achieved.

Remember, even "impossible" dreams contain the seeds of goals you can set for yourself that are well within your control. Ask yourself what you can do to take a step closer to achieving that impossible dream—and then set yourself a goal to do it!

Innovation

> *Innovation is the specific tool of entrepreneurs, the means by which they exploit change as an opportunity for a different business or a different service. It is capable of being presented as a discipline, capable of being learned, capable of being practiced. Entrepreneurs need to search purposefully for the sources of innovation, the changes and their symptoms that indicate opportunities for successful innovation. And they need to know and to apply the principles of successful innovation.*
>
> [PETER DRUCKER]

What does it mean to be innovative? The term *innovation*, along with its shopworn adjective, *innovative*, and its breathless verb, *innovate!* has become every product manager's rallying cry, every design consultant's pursuit, and every press release writer's staple. The word's been wrapped around everything from the latest Apple i-something to a new scooter. So how can one term be used to describe such vastly different things? In essence, what does *innovation* really mean?

Technically, *innovation* is defined merely as "introducing something new." There are no qualifiers of how groundbreaking or world-shattering that something needs to be—only that it needs to be better than what was there before. And that's where the trouble starts when an organization requests "innovation services" from a consulting firm. Exactly what are they really requesting? The fact is, innovation means different things to different people.

Action: What does innovation mean to you?

Creative Ideas

Creativity is thinking up new things. Innovation is doing new things.

[THEODORE LEVITT]

Everything begins with a thought. An inspiration. An idea that you can do something that has never been done, improve something, change something, or do it cheaper or better than it has been done before.

Creating a paradigm shift that will add value to the lives of others is considered innovative. This is a unique ability to see the unfolding patterns of the future and recognize the emergence of fresh ways to interpret our surroundings. When the paradigm shift occurs, the new system eliminates old ways of doing things and gives rise to innovative opportunities.

Most ideas come from a desire to fill a need or a gap or expand upon an existing way of doing things. My friend Rick Goren invented the Qube, a cotton swab dispenser. He came up with the idea when a glass container with a lid fell off his bathroom counter and shattered. He knew there must be a better way to store and dispense cotton swabs. In one afternoon, he sat down and designed the new, more practical container. He shared the idea with a few friends (market research), and then within a year, Qubes were being ordered and shipped to major retailers all over!

Action: We all have ideas; even if it is simply your closet isn't big enough to hold all of your clothes, so you have the idea to build a bigger closet. The innovator takes ACTION on his or her ideas—that is what makes the difference!

Presentation

The innovation point is the pivotal moment when talented and motivated people seek the opportunity to act on their ideas and dreams.

[W. ARTHUR PORTER]

An innovative visionary mind will look at a situation and see future improvements, while most people look at the same situation and only see the present and complain about it!

Successful innovators develop the ability to clearly define and articulate their vision, clearly define their plan for strategic action, and rapidly gain support for their initiatives. They will educate and help others understand their vision and come up with a game plan to make it a reality—especially to the people who can affect the success of the idea.

The innovator's view is of the unfamiliar—which represents change. How do you present a view of the future that only you can envision? Your ability to do a good presentation of your idea is the tool you use to influence others and enlist critical support.

You can have a good idea—there are lots of good ideas—but equally as important is marketing those good ideas.

Action: Do you believe strongly enough in your dream to enthusiastically engage others to support your efforts? Name three people you think may support your idea.

Take Action

Creativity requires the courage to let go of certainties.

[ERICH FROMM]

Taking that good idea and making it into a reality will require massive action! Are you focused and equipped to effectively execute your plan of action?

Now the real fun begins! Your innovative idea has gained some interest and possibly established a marketplace audience. You must now tune up and strategically deploy the activity in such a way that results and expectations are coherent and crystal clear. Set your goals and plan to have all working parts continuously monitored for performance, results, and running on all cylinders.

Put together a game plan and a business plan, set time and financial goals, and make the commitment necessary.

In life we have different seasons. In the "spring," we work to organize, plan, and begin the process of sowing our goals and dreams. The "summer" is the time to work hard implementing and tending to our task of building and putting in the massive action with the long days of effort. If we have planted our good seeds in good soil, the "autumn" will see our wonderful harvest of success. Our genuine effort has paid off and we will reap what we have sown. Then comes the "winter" of rest and well-deserved relaxation—a time to prepare for the next springtime.

Action: This IS your year to design and pursue the life of your dreams!

Perseverance

> *Innovation—any new idea—by definition will not be accepted at first. It takes repeated attempts, endless demonstrations, and monotonous rehearsals before innovation can be accepted and internalized by an organization. This requires courageous patience.*
>
> [WARREN BENNIS]

You can count on difficulties and setbacks as an innovator breaking new ground. Be prepared to persevere through difficult times.

The early American pioneers faced unthinkable challenges and even took arrows in the back to pursue the idea of creating a new life for themselves and their families. Trailblazing is not for the weak of heart. An innovative idea will require mental toughness for staying the course long enough to make breakthroughs. Innovation is launching into unfamiliar territory.

Be prepared to fail. You *will* fail! Look forward with excitement to your failures. Consider each failure as one step closer to success. Thomas Edison never considered his ten thousand attempts to invent the iridescent lightbulb failures— he believed in his vision and didn't plan to stop until he had success!

Action: The only way to really fail is to quit! Don't ever quit on your dreams!

Velocity

Imagination is everything. It is the preview of life's coming attractions
[ALBERT EINSTEIN]

Now put it all together and LAUNCH. A good idea without taking action will die quickly or become outdated . . . or worse yet, be marketed by someone else! Don't wait—do your due diligence, research, and take off!

Take your innovative idea and create a game plan to present to people who can assist you in the process. Take the necessary action, but be prepared to persevere through disappointments and failures along the way.

It is important to utilize the networks and resources available to you as you pursue the success of your vision. To be an extraordinary visionary, your best bet is to be connected or get connected. This will allow you to move faster than the average Joe.

Action: Have you ever said, "Wow, I could have thought of that!" Often, people will have a good idea but lack the ability, passion, or perseverance to make it happen. Then along comes a person with the guts, brains, street smarts, and more to make it happen. Which one are you? You have what it takes—you can do it!

Living Your Dream

> *Capital isn't so important in business. Experience isn't so important.*
> *You can get both these things. What are important are ideas. If you*
> *have ideas, you have the main asset you need, and there isn't any limit*
> *to what you can do with your business and your life.*
>
> [HARVEY FIRESTONE]

Take Ownership

"You, Inc." It's your dream. You set the goals. Take full responsibility for your goals. Set out to achieve them because you believe in them and they are what you want in your life. At the same time, remember that you own your goals—they don't own you. When a goal no longer serves its purpose—your purpose—it's time to make adjustments.

Simple Things Do Matter

As long as you're green, you're growing. As soon as you're ripe, you start to rot.

[RAY KROC]

The concept that little things matter is a somewhat basic idea. When you face a choice, you can take a simple positive action. Or you can take a simple negative action. Simple actions, repeated over time, will determine the life you will lead.

Every day, every hour, every moment of your life, you face a choice. People who feel successful and those who don't feel that way do so because of the little choices they make about what they think, say, and do.

The little things that lead to success are easy to do, and easy *not* to do. They can be as simple as being impeccable with your word, having a positive mental attitude, and always doing your best. The steps can be very small—as small as choosing a different response in the moment.

You will find that small actions compound over time. For example, if you exercise for an hour a day, you won't see much difference after a couple days or even a week. But after a couple of months you will notice a big difference. A little effort each day will result in huge rewards over time. If you read just ten pages of a good book every day, it might not seem like a lot. But after one year, you will have read more than two dozen 150-page books. It is the same with learning another language, playing a musical instrument, or improving at a sport. A little practice each day will result in huge rewards over time.

Action: What simple activities can you do today to become the person you want to be a year from now? How many can you list?

Knowing and/or Doing

*Success seems to be connected with action. Successful people keep
moving. They make mistakes, but they don't quit.*

[CONRAD HILTON]

Knowing how to do something and actually doing it are two different
things. Knowing what to do is not the same as doing it, because even
with the talent and intelligence to know the right things to do; we can
still end up making the wrong choices.

Knowing how to do something isn't actually doing the thing. Hav-
ing the answer to a problem isn't the same thing as using the answer to
solve the problem. That's because the little things that are important to
do are also easy *not to do*, so many people don't do them.

You may know this from your own life experiences. What is eas-
ier—trying something you're afraid of, or not even trying in the first
place? Following your own instincts, or trying to please others? Avoid-
ing your feelings because they're too hard or painful to face, or facing
them square on? Getting up early to work out in the morning, or hit-
ting the snooze button?

The answer is pretty obvious—it's often a whole lot easier not to
do the simple things.

*Action: Success can mean going against what other people may think
about you and sacrificing for what you really want. Try to start doing
the little positive things . . . even when you don't feel like it. Believe in
yourself and in what you know is important. To make a better life for
yourself, start acting on what you know is right to do.*

The Ripple Effect

Luck comes to a man who puts himself in the way of it. You went where something might be found and you found something, simple as that.

[LOUIS L'AMOUR]

You have heard the expressions "Timing is everything" or "She was in the right place at the right time." What that means is that by doing the small, positive things, you increase the chances that other positive things will happen to you. It's like tossing a rock into a pond—you'll see a splash and the ripples spreading out, but those ripples can go far beyond what you see. They can go all the way to the opposite shore.

It is the same thing in life, although you often may not see the ripples until something good (or not so good) happens. For better or for worse, even your smallest actions create a ripple effect that has a huge impact on you and the people around you, even when you don't see it or aren't aware of it.

When you take a small, positive step, you never know where it will lead. But if you take that first step, the chances are great that more positive things will happen to you.

Even a miracle sometimes takes action. God had all the power to perform the miracle of parting the Red Sea. But it still took the action of Moses believing enough to take that first step and lift his staff above the water for the miracle to actually happen.

Action: BELIEVE YOU CAN DO IT!

Make the Right Choice at the Right Moment

Anyone can dabble, but once you've made that commitment, your blood has that particular thing in it, and it's very hard for people to stop you.

[BILL COSBY]

Only you can define what success means to you. But however you define it, achieving that slight edge to help you succeed basically means doing the right thing at the right time. That is where it all starts, and that often takes a lot of courage.

Take a moment and think about what does success mean to you. Success is more than finding the right job or making a lot of money. When you have the faith and the courage that you know the right thing to do and *do it*, you will make the right choices.

Little things matter. What makes you do the little things, whether positive or negative? Willpower doesn't determine what you do. Willpower is basically forcing yourself to do something you don't really want to do. You can't force yourself to go to work early or stay late to help a co-worker on a project if you don't really feel like it—not for long. That may work for a while, but it won't work in the long run. You can't keep forcing yourself to do something if you don't really want to do it.

Action: Willpower alone does not drive your actions; it is your attitude. People make decisions based on how they feel, not on what they know. How's your attitude?

Attitude

The greatest discovery of my generation is that human beings can alter their lives by altering their attitude.

[WILLIAM JAMES]

Your attitude shows in everything you do. Your attitude is so powerful that people can sense it before you even say a word. Your body language conveys your attitude—you can sense how someone feels by the way he or she walks down the street, enters a room, or sits on a chair. Your attitude determines both your simplest and most complicated actions—from the way you carry yourself to the way you deal with difficult times.

Does controlling your attitude allow you to control your actions? That doesn't exactly work because you don't have one single attitude. Your attitudes are changeable. You can be happy when you walk into the office, then frustrated within five minutes when you are faced with a pile of unfinished work on your desk. Then you might be sad when you chat with a coworker who tells you her dog died.

Your attitude is changing all the time. As your attitude changes, your feelings also change. Some days you're not going to feel great. It is almost impossible to force yourself to feel happy when you're not. Trying to *control* your attitude and feelings might work temporarily, but not for long.

Action: The key to how your life turns out is your ability to understand the source of your attitude. And the source of your attitude is your philosophy—*the way you see yourself and the way you see the world.*

Your Philosophy

> *Whatever is true, whatever is honorable, whatever is just, whatever is pure, whatever is lovely, whatever is gracious . . . think about these things.*
>
> [PHILIPPIANS 4:8]

In order for you to do the little, positive things, it is important to discover the source of your attitude. Understanding what is at the heart of what you feel and believe is the key to achieving what you want in life. Your life philosophy is the way you see yourself and the way you see the world.

Understand your view of life or how you see things. Your philosophy is what determines your attitude and your actions, whether you realize it or not. This is the secret that lies behind the puzzle of fate and destiny: Two people will grow up in the same difficult family or tough neighborhood. One person will overcome it and the other won't. Why? Because how they view their experiences will determine how they react to them.

You create your destiny with your actions. But your attitudes determine your actions, and your attitudes result from how you see the world—by your philosophy.

Action: One of the quickest paths to success is to get out of the past. It is a good idea to review mistakes and disappointing events because that helps you to make better choices in the future and take responsibility. Then use the past as a tool to do things differently in the present and move on.

Living Your Dream

Everything can be taken from a man or a woman but one thing: the last of human freedoms—to choose one's attitude in any given set of circumstances, to choose one's own way.

[VIKTOR FRANKL]

Break It Down and Take Action

Success can be defined as the progressive realization of a worthwhile goal or dream. Begin with the end in mind—your Big Dream. Achieving your Big Dream requires a plan of action—your goals. Goals require action. Every goal is comprised of specific action steps that will lead to the achievement of that goal. Some goals require a few action steps and others require many. In some cases, a goal can have so many action steps that you should set smaller goals within a goal.

Start With Small Steps

You've gotta dance like there's nobody watching,
Love like you'll never be hurt,
Sing like there's nobody listening,
And live like it's heaven on earth.

[WILLIAM W. PURKEY]

You may not be able to see what is at the top of the stairway, but to climb to the top, you must take that first step. Every achievement, accomplishment, and success starts somewhere. Every task, large or small, begins with a first step. That first step can sometimes be hard to take. Yet one small step can lead to results you never imagined.

On a chilly day in December 1955, Rosa Parks was an unknown forty-two-year-old seamstress in Montgomery, Alabama. On that day she took a small step, because she decided she'd had enough. She was tired after a long day's work. Most of all, she was tired of being treated the way she was—and tired of every other person of her color being treated that way, too. So when she was told to give up her bus seat to a white passenger, she refused, even when the bus driver threatened her with arrest.

It wasn't an empty threat—Rosa Parks was arrested, convicted, and fined for violating a city law that black passengers had to give up their bus seats to white passengers. But the step she took led to the start of a new civil rights organization. Not long after, the newly formed Montgomery Improvement Association elected a young and relatively unknown minister named Dr. Martin Luther King Jr. to be its spokesperson, launching a political movement that over the next decade ended legal segregation in the United States and transformed race relations in our country.

Action: What difference can one step make? Think about Rosa Parks.

It Looks Harder Than It Is

There are only two ways to live your life. One is as though nothing is a miracle. The other is as though everything is a miracle.

[ALBERT EINSTEIN]

Everything does begin with the faith to take that first step. But when you are contemplating something that is new or is outside your comfort zone, taking the first step can seem very difficult. Some people let their fears dominate and never take that first step. The fear is not because the first step *is* difficult; it is the perception that the first step *looks* difficult. Who wants to make a mistake and look ridiculous, right?

Even when you do find the courage to take that first step toward your Big Dream, there is no guarantee you will find success the first time. Sometimes you take the step and don't get what you wanted. But when you do face your fears and take a risk, you will find it easier the next time, and if you learned from your mistakes you may even do it better.

Taking risks and overcoming your fears is the way we program our subconscious—the more you do certain kinds of things (especially challenging and difficult things), the more you become comfortable with them, and the more they become habit.

Action: Step outside your comfort zone today in at least one way!

A Lucky Break

To live is the rarest thing in the world. Most people exist, that is all.

[OSCAR WILDE]

Some people don't start taking small steps toward their goals and dreams because they are waiting for a lucky break. You may know someone who is hoping to make the PGA Tour or become a movie star or a famous author.

The truth is that very few people have the talent to become superstars in sports or the entertainment industry, where the odds of making it big are a million to one. Everyone hoping to become the next Tiger Woods or Julia Roberts will eventually find that out. And since the lucky break didn't turn out the way they hoped, many of these people give up. They are victims of the lucky break syndrome.

A lot of people look up to the wrong role models for success. We see people in sports and entertainment as heroes, but we don't see the years of hard work behind the success. Michael Jordan didn't become *The* Michael Jordan overnight. Any great athlete pays the price: hours and hours and hours of practice with no one watching or cheering. There are no overnight successes!

Lucky breaks do happen. They are slowly grown, like a crop: planted, cultivated, and ultimately harvested. Success is not a random accident. Life is not a lottery ticket.

Action: Waiting for a lucky break puts you at the mercy of the world around you. That's a passive place to live. Over time it creates a victim mentality, and that mentality tends to become a self-fulfilling prophecy. It will keep you from ever taking action and creating breaks for yourself. And the only way to create those breaks is through small steps—the power of simple daily actions, compounded over time.

Itty Bitty Steps

We don't see things as they are, we see them as we are.

[ANAÏS NIN]

How do you eat an elephant? One bite at a time! When you find it difficult to take steps toward a goal, you may build your confidence by breaking the task into the smallest steps possible. For example, if you have a goal to run a marathon, learn a new language, or play a musical instrument, you can start by doing it ten minutes a day. Ten minutes a day of anything can have a huge impact on your life. If you start with small steps, you are more likely to stick with the task than avoid it.

Your life satisfaction will probably be a lot higher if you view your life as a series of many small milestones, instead of one huge milestone that you may or may not ever achieve. That's not to say that you shouldn't have big goals, only that you should also have smaller ones to focus on along the way.

If you want to lose forty pounds, great. But don't just focus on that one huge goal. If you do, then every time you get on the scale, you're only going to notice that you haven't achieved your goal yet, and so you continually reinforce failure in your mind.

Break it down into smaller goals. There are plenty of goals you can try to accomplish even before losing one pound. Maybe you want to start reading a book about weight loss, or find a support group, or learn a new healthy recipe.

Action: A series of small accomplishments will keep you on track and make you feel good about your life, whether or not you eventually go on to accomplish your ultimate goal. If you end up eating the whole elephant, that's wonderful. But don't forget to enjoy the bites along the way.

The Second Step

It does not do to dwell on dreams and forget to live.

[J. K. ROWLING]

The second step is just as important as the first. Many people take the first step, don't see any immediate success . . . and quit. How many people have the strength and courage to take the second step?

Babies make their way around the world by crawling on their hands and knees. Everyone around them is walking, and then one day they get it into their little head that maybe they will give walking a try.

They grab onto something above them like a chair or a big toy and pull themselves upright. They stand up, holding onto something for support—a little wobbly and unsure, but they are on their way, and there is no turning back. These little ones let go and take those first amazing, bold steps—and smack! They usually fall right down on their behinds.

Does the baby think, "I hope nobody saw that. You know, maybe I'm not cut out for walking. And crawling isn't so bad. Lots of people crawl . . ."? No—she gets back up and takes a second step.

The second step is usually no better than the first. But that second step is where babies start to learn how to walk. From that point on, it is only a matter of time before they are really walking—no hands, no holding onto Mom or Dad, all by themselves.

Action: So are you ready to quit crawling and start walking out your dream? I hope so, because you can do it!

Life Is a Journey, Not a Destination

Sometimes the questions are complicated and the answers are simple.

[DR. SEUSS]

Think back to some of your past successes or observe someone you admire that is successful.

Steps to Success

- Adjust the course. If you don't see immediate success, learn from the first step and take the second step.
- Be persistent. Never, ever give up—keep stepping in the direction of your goals and dreams.
- Start somewhere. It is OK to start at the bottom and work your way up to the top of the stairway.
- Welcome the difficulties and failures. Welcome the tough times as learning experiences and chances to make you stronger to persevere.
- Create your own luck. By not giving up and taking action, you will put yourself in the position to take advantage of a better opportunity when it comes along.

When you start something new, you feel excited and full of energy. But soon the excitement wears off or you are faced with a difficult challenge and the new job or new relationship or new project isn't as exciting as it was before. This is the hard part of the journey—the long stretch between a beginner and mastery.

Action: Don't be afraid of failure. Can you imagine if you had been afraid of failure as a baby? "Shoot, I knew I wasn't cut out for that whole walking thing. What was I thinking? I was crazy to even try!" Falling down is the way you learn to fly!

Living Your Dream

The Choice

A wealthy man offered his two sons a choice between two gifts. One gift was a million dollars in cash. The other gift was a single, shiny copper penny.

"You both have the same choice—either one million or one penny. If you choose the million, it will be deposited in your bank account today. If you choose the penny, I will double the pennies you have every day for the next thirty-one days."

The first son took the penny, and the second son took the million dollars.

Over the next weeks, the second son visited his brother every day and listened to him describe how his pennies were piling up, starting with two pennies on day two, and four pennies on day three. A few days into the third week, the first son's pennies had grown to $655.35. On day twenty-eight, the first boy's pennies had passed the million-dollar mark. On day twenty-nine, he passed the two-and-a-half-million mark. On day thirty, his pennies totaled five million. And on day thirty-one, he had $10,737,418.24.

The boy who chose the penny had discovered the extraordinary power of compounding interest—how money, even a very small amount of money—can grow over time.

The true gift was wisdom in knowing how to respect and use money.

The boy who chose the million had his one million. But the boy who chose the penny was worth more than ten million dollars after a month. Because he wasn't greedy, because he was careful with his money, and because he understood how money can grow over time, he achieved true wealth. The choice the wealthy man offered his two sons is the same choice the world offers you every day.

Small actions compound over time into big results. The actions you take today, whether it's about money, friendships, or your health, can have a huge impact on your life over time.

Make Your Dreams Come True

Life is an opportunity, benefit from it.
Life is beauty, admire it.
Life is a dream, realize it.
Life is a challenge, meet it.
Life is a duty, complete it.
Life is a game, play it.
Life is a promise, fulfill it.
Life is sorrow, overcome it.
Life is a song, sing it.
Life is a struggle, accept it.
Life is a tragedy, confront it.
Life is an adventure, dare it.
Life is luck, make it.
Life is too precious, do not destroy it.
Life is life, fight for it.

[MOTHER TERESA]

By now your dream life should be a solid vision. It is time to turn your dreams into reality. Now is the time to plan your future, to reflect on the things you have experienced and how they have affected you.

What have you learned from your past experiences? How have you grown? How do you need to continue to grow? What areas in your life do you need to work on? Have you written down your goals and dreams and put together a plan of action to achieve them?

Success is not an accident. People who achieve what they want in life do it by following a very specific recipe. Perhaps they are not even aware that they've taken specific steps, but everyone who has ever created success in their lives, whether consciously or not, has followed more or less the same process.

Action: Congratulations! You have come a long way in following This Is Your Year! *You are ready to launch into pursuing and fulfilling your Big Dream!*

Know Your "Why"

You don't get in life what you want. You get what you are.

[LES BROWN]

If the *why* is big enough, the *how* is easy. Conversely, if your *why* is not identified or significant, then any level of difficulty in the *how* will be enough to defeat you.

Example: If you were told to walk the length of a twenty-foot steel two-by-four on the ground as a fun challenge, you would do it, no problem. If the two-by-four was placed ten stories high, bridging two buildings, and you were told to do it for fun, no doubt you would say "No way!" Why not? The *how* is too difficult and the risk/reward ratio and the reason for doing it are too small.

Now, if on the roof of the second building was your one-year-old child and the building was on fire, would you do it? Of course! What's different? It's the same two-by-four, the same length spanning the buildings, and the same difficulty. However, the *why* has changed. The reason for doing it has become far greater than the difficulty or risk. Any *how* is possible if the *why* is big enough.

Action: Know your **why** *and the* **how** *will come. Why do you want to pursue your Big Dream?*

Vivid Vision

Everything you can imagine is real.

[PABLO PICASSO]

The most important skill for creating success in anything is the skill of envisioning. This is creating a picture in your mind of something you want that is so vivid it feels real.

Remember your subconscious mind—that part of you that controls 99.9 percent of what unfolds in your life—needs a clear picture of your destination. Once you have a clear, vivid picture imprinted in your mind, your brain goes to work on finding a route to get you there.

Destination has to come first. To create your dream life, you have to start with some sort of vivid picture of where it is you're headed. You start with the end in mind.

Pick a dream you have, any dream—an accomplishment, a dream house, dream job, dream relationship. Write it out on a piece of paper or in a journal.

Write your dream in the present tense, and be very specific. "I will have my own coffee shop business by December," or "I will be successful in writing a book by the end of this year." Say your goal out loud—*every day*. This is where dreams start.

Make your dream vivid. Envisioning isn't simply creating a picture in your mind. That's wishful thinking. Envisioning means making it *real*. You need to make it physical, emotional, and that involves your senses. The more vivid it is, the more it starts to become real.

Action: You are more likely to accomplish a vivid, detailed vision with a specific time frame to accomplish it. Goals are dreams with deadlines.

Every Day

> *I wanted a perfect ending. Now I've learned, the hard way, that some poems don't rhyme, and some stories don't have a clear beginning, middle, and end. Life is about not knowing, having to change, taking the moment and making the best of it, without knowing what's going to happen next. Delicious ambiguity.*
>
> [GILDA RADNER]

Life is a series of adventures that add up to your journey. It is not a matter of the first or second step you take, or even the third. There are thousands of steps to take when you work toward your goals, and each one gives you the opportunity to get off course and lose your way.

Whether you stay on the path you want or get distracted and veer off is a question of how you've programmed your subconscious mind. One of the best ways to program yourself to stay on the path is through repetition—show your subconscious your dreams every day. It is the same reason you want to keep yourself in the company of positive people. You need to avoid the temptations that can lead you astray.

Picturing your dream every day is like feeding your subconscious with a diet rich in *yeses*! Once you've got your picture, wrap it around yourself and immerse yourself in it.

Action: Positive affirmations and declarations about achieving your dream are as important as looking at your dream every day. Write out a list of positive statements and read them aloud every day when you declare your dream!

Your Plan

If you don't know where you are going, any road will get you there.

[LEWIS CARROLL]

Many people get thrown off track when it comes to making a plan of action. How will you know if it will work or not?

Well, you *don't know.* Nobody does. But knowing whether it'll work or not doesn't matter. The point is not to come up with a plan that is a sure thing. The point is to simply come up with a plan that will get you started. Having a specific, realistic, measurable, achievable goal will set your plan up for success.

It is up to you to take the necessary steps to achieve your goals. If you want something, get up and make it happen for yourself. You can do it!

You have to start somewhere. You have to start with a plan. But understand the plan you start with will not be the plan that gets you there. Be prepared to change your plan over and over again. You'll meet obstacles. The unexpected will happen. You'll have to adjust course, because you'll continuously be learning. Your plan gives you a place to begin.

Don't make the mistake of thinking you need a perfect plan. A plan is not the same as getting there—it's only your starting point. If you put too much energy into trying to make your plan perfect, you will take all the life and joy out of doing it!

Action: Don't try to figure it all out. Whatever you can believe and dream, you can achieve. You can do it!

Steady Wins

You cannot find peace by avoiding life.
[Virginia Woolf]

The moral of the story about the tortoise and the hare is that slow and steady wins the race. But in reality, going slow is not always better. Sometimes you can move *too* slowly and miss out. Sometimes fast is better. If you are crossing a street and a car is coming fast, forget the tortoise. Sometimes fast is the best strategy; sometimes slow is. Sometimes it changes.

The key word here is *steady*—steady wins the race. That's the truth of it.

Don't underestimate the power of momentum. We know from physics that a body at rest tends to stay at rest—and a body in motion tends to remain in motion. That's why the small things you do every day are so important. Once you're in motion, it's easy to keep in motion. Once you stop, it's hard to get going again.

If you work every day toward your goals, it takes less energy to get started every day. Once you get started and you're in a rhythm, it is easy to keep yourself going.

Imagine taking a twenty-minute walk every morning and then working out for another twenty minutes in the afternoon. If you did that every day for a week, how would you feel at the end of the week? But what if you decided to do the whole week's worth of exercise on just one day each week. You take a 140-minute walk in the morning and then work out 140 minutes in the afternoon—all in one day—then didn't do anything for the next six days. How well would that work?

Action: Steady wins the race. Think about your goals and dreams. Now, think of small steps you can take each day to begin making them come true.

Living Your Dream

If you can dream it, then you can achieve it. You will get all you want in life if you help enough other people get what they want.

[Zig Ziglar]

Schedule Regular Reviews/Assessments

It is a good idea to periodically check your progress toward your goals. Evaluate your progress and determine whether you have met, exceeded, or fallen short of your goals. If you've met your goals, are you getting measurably closer to achieving your dream? (You should be!) Set new goals and identify new action steps to continue drawing you even closer.

If you fell short of your goals, try to determine what went wrong. Were your expectations too high? Did you run into unforeseen obstacles? Do you need to implement a Plan B?

Continue checking and rechecking your progress toward your goals regularly. When you achieve one goal—remember to celebrate and reward yourself—promptly review your dream for the future and select a new goal. Then start right in again—identifying the benefits of achieving it, creating action steps, marking target dates and checkpoints on your calendar, etc.

Enjoy the Journey

> *Happiness is not something you postpone for the future; it is something you design for the present.*
>
> [JIM ROHN]

If you work really hard to achieve your goals but don't enjoy the journey, you're delaying the essence of life. Committing to your goals doesn't mean you slave away at work you dislike, celebrating only the destination. A real abiding commitment means that you love what you do each day. You are at least as passionate about the path as you are about the results. If you love the path you're on, your passion motivates you to keep taking the next step.

But passion alone isn't enough. Passion requires focused direction, and that direction must come from three other areas: your purpose, your talents, and your needs.

First, purpose and passion go hand in hand. If you don't know your life purpose, your passion won't be guided by conscience. Many criminals go this route—they are very passionate about certain actions, but those actions aren't motivated by a higher purpose.

When your passion and purpose point in the same direction, it means you fall in love with the path of service. You love what you do, and it also contributes positively to the world. This creates a synergy, which increases your passion manifold. This is a natural consequence of doing something you love to do that you know is making a difference.

Action: Dream your life, then live your dream.

Passion + Talent + Need

Sometimes our light goes out, but is blown again into instant flame by an encounter with another human being.

[ALBERT SCHWEITZER]

Passion isn't enough—it must be blended with talent. Passion can get you pretty far, but there are plenty of people who are passionate and incompetent, and their passion isn't sufficient to save them.

Have you ever known anyone who got really excited about an idea but couldn't follow through? The good news is that you can develop your talent—you can educate yourself to learn new knowledge and skills. But the ultimate goal here is to discover where your greatest talents lie.

What talents, if you were to fully develop them, could be extremely strong for you? You may come up with several answers, but which ones overlap with your passion? When you do what you love to do *and* you become really good at doing it, your passion will increase, and your results will be amplified.

Thirdly, passion must be blended with need. At the very least, you have to direct your passion in such a way that you'll be able to feed yourself. But if you master the blending of passion, purpose, and talent, it will not be too difficult to satisfy your needs . . . or even to achieve financial abundance.

Action: What do you really, really, really feel passionate about for your life? What are you waiting for—go for it!

Key to Fulfillment

That it will never come again is what makes life so sweet.

[EMILY DICKINSON]

The key to fulfillment is to work from your greatest strengths, with passion, in the service of purpose.

Doing what you're best at ensures that you're working efficiently. Being passionate about what you do means that you'll work hard at it. And serving a purpose means that you're contributing and making a real difference in others' lives. When you do all three, you're contributing the maximum value you possibly can. And if you can't generate a fantastic income doing that, you won't be able to generate a better one doing anything else. This is the very definition of value. It is precisely what people will be eager to pay you for.

Everyone can find an area where their circles of passion, purpose, talent, and need overlap. The best place to start is with purpose, by listening to that still-small voice inside of you. Once you know you are on the path toward your purpose in life, then move on to passion and talent—each of these will likely contain many possibilities. There are probably several things you love to do and several things you can become really good at. List them out for each category. Then take time to reflect on possible areas of overlap between purpose, passion, and talent. Remember that the talent circle can be moved with additional education and skill building.

Action: When you decide to live a life of purpose on purpose and then begin to take action toward your goals and dreams, you will discover a more meaningful life.

Balance

The most wasted of all days is one without laughter.

[E. E. CUMMINGS]

When you find the area of overlap between purpose, passion, and talent, the need area tends to be fairly easy to fulfill. The first three areas will suggest potential careers. Here's another way of thinking about it:

Need = what you must do
Talent = what you can do
Passion = what you love to do
Purpose = what you should do

Many people see these four areas as inherently in conflict. How many times have you heard people spout limiting beliefs such as, "You can't make money (need) doing what you love (passion)"?

Nonsense. You can find a path on which all four of these areas are in harmony. You can find a way to work from your greatest strengths while doing what you love to do in the service of purpose. This will take care of all your basic needs—even achieving abundance.

But the first step is to simply decide to do it. Decide that your life is worth enough to you to get all four of these areas working together. You don't have to go broke doing what you love. You don't have to work at a job you hate. You don't have to see meaningful contribution as something out of sync with your everyday reality.

Action: Take some time to reflect on what kind of career, what kind of life, would allow you to put these four areas in harmony—all of them pointing in the same direction. No conflict. It can be done.

Daily Disciplines

Now and then it's good to pause in our pursuit of happiness and just be happy.

[GUILLAUME APOLLINAIRE]

To create the desired balance in your life, you must focus on the important areas of living a happy, healthy, and prosperous lifestyle. Ultimate success in life is being healthy physically, emotionally, socially, intellectually, and spiritually. Achieving balance in life and then being faithful, diligent, and obedient to God's perfect plan for your life will bring you peace, joy, and prosperity.

Physical Health entails taking care of your body with proper nutrition, wellness, and fitness. Exercising daily and eating whole, naturally grown foods is a discipline that will inspire and give you the energy to live a long, healthy life.

Emotional Health is a lifelong exercise in personal growth. Reading daily from a positive personal development book will give you the positive attitude and a lifelong love of learning and growing.

Social Health includes building meaningful relationships with family and friends, as well as making a positive contribution to the lives of others. And, in the end, this is what life is all about. Nurturing these relationships takes a concerted effort of time and energy.

Intellectual Health is pursuing your desired level of personal and financial success in life.

Spiritual Health is living an attitude of gratitude and faith. Believe that God has a perfect plan for your life, and then plan to live a life of purpose.

Action: 4DBC—Daily Disciplines Done Daily Build Character. Create the habit of focusing your energy on living a healthier, happier, more prosperous life! See what happens.

Celebrate Success

> *The more you praise and celebrate your life, the more there is in life to celebrate.*
>
> [OPRAH WINFREY]

Success breeds success. Each night before you go to bed, think about your successes of the day.

This idea comes from a story about Olympic gymnast Bart Connor. Nine months before the 1984 Olympics, he tore his bicep muscle.

They said he would never make it back in time to compete in the Olympics. But not only did he make it back, he won two gold medals! When Bart was asked how he did it, Bart thanked his parents.

He said, "Every night before bed, my parents would ask me what my success was. So I went to bed a success every night of my life. I woke up every morning a success. When I was injured before the Olympics, I knew I was going to make it back because I was a success every day of my life." Talk about a confidence booster!

It works for children, and it works for adults in businesses, schools, and organizations because when we focus on what people are doing right, they do more things right. Teams and organizations that focus on and celebrate success create more success. Success becomes ingrained in the culture, and people naturally look for it, focus on it, and expect it.

Action: We will see more of what we focus on in our life. If we look for and celebrate success, we'll see more of it. It works for Olympic athletes, children, and all the rest of us.

Living Your Dream

I dream of painting and then I paint my dream.

[Vincent Van Gogh]

Making a Dream into Reality

This is your year to become a dream achiever! Keep your dream in front of you at all times. Be clear on why this dream is important to you. Visualize yourself living this dream often.

Identify the pros of realizing this dream and the cons of not pursuing your dream. How *BIG* a game of life do you want to play? How badly do you want to see this dream become reality in your life? How *hard* are you willing to *work* to achieve this dream?

How can you realize your dream? Identify the goals that, when accomplished, will lead you to the realization of your dream. Put each goal in writing. Use positive words and make sure they meet SMART FOR ME criteria. Now, TAKE ACTION! You can do it!

Believe That You Can

> *We can never judge the lives of others, because each person knows only*
> *their own pain and renunciation. It's one thing to feel that you are on*
> *the right path, but it's another to think that yours is the only path.*
>
> [PAULO COELHO]

The purpose of life . . . is living a life of purpose. God is the giver of dreams. He is looking for people to whom He can transfer His passion and dream—people to whom He can give a vision and a dream. He uses dreams to help us discover our purpose in life. Successful people are dreamers. Your dreams will carry you through the hard times in life. You must believe that you can accomplish your dreams!

Average people can only see the immediate surroundings and complain. Successful dreamers can see beyond the current situation. They know, "Where I am right now is not where I am going." They create a vision in their minds of what will be. Make sure you write your dream down and keep it in front of you.

Please know that every successful person has gone through a period of setbacks and discouragement. With your dream in front of you, it is important to surround yourself with other positive dreamers so you can all encourage one another.

Action: Important people do important things. Believe that you can.
Build that business, get that degree, launch that ministry, birth that
dream. If you can believe it, you can be it!

Take Hold of Your Destiny

> *The race is not to the swift, Nor the battle to the strong, Nor the bread to the wise, Nor riches to men of understanding, Nor favor to men of skill; But time and chance happen to them all. For man also does not know his time: Like fish taken in a cruel net, Like birds caught in a snare, So the sons of men are snared in an evil time, When it falls suddenly upon them.*
>
> [ECCLESIASTES 9:11–12]

"Time and chance happen to them all." We could also understand this as: God gives everybody a shot at destiny. He created you for something. *Chance* in this context means, "to collide with your destiny." You are headed for a collision with God's will for your life.

At the moment of your conception, one little sperm among millions of them were all racing to become *you*. YOU are one in a million—a winner! Every single life has a destiny. God wants us to know why we were born.

Now, there is a promise and a warning in the words above. The promise is that every one of us has a God-ordained destiny. The warning is that you can miss your destiny when the right moment comes if you are entangled in something you have no business being involved in.

Spending some quiet time with God to discover your destiny is time well spent, and it all begins with a thought. Once you've grabbed hold of your dream, hang on to it in spite of the doubts and difficulties that attack you. Disentangle yourself from whatever holds you back.

Action: Trust and have faith all the way. Keep your focus on God. He will make a way for your dreams to come true.

Desire, Passion & Power

> *Yesterday is but a vision, and tomorrow is only a dream. But today well lived makes every yesterday a dream of happiness, and every tomorrow a dream of hope.*
>
> [ANONYMOUS]

It begins with desire. You must first have a desire to be motivated to do anything. When you have the desire to pursue your God-given assignment, you will find your highest fulfillment. Your desire will unlock your compassion and creativity. Make no excuses!

Your desire to pursue your dream will create the passion necessary to make it happen. Passion is the one quality, the distinguishing characteristic that can excite God more than any other. Passion is the one thing that can make one person succeed where another fails. Passion will take you from mediocrity to excellence. What fires you up? What is your passion? When you desire to follow your purpose, you will come alive with a consuming passion.

When God sees passion in people, He releases His power through them. When you have an emotional, boundless enthusiasm for God's perfect plan for your life, you will find that He has already equipped you with the talents and skills necessary to fulfill this plan.

How passionate will your effort be? How badly do you want to achieve success? Badly enough to pursue your dream with all that is in you? Your passion produces faith, and faith produces power. You must have a passionate determination to release the power to see your dreams come true.

Action: You are being called to change the world through the passion and purpose within you. Get hold of that passion and nothing will be impossible.

Enthusiasm

> *Vision without action is merely a dream. Action without vision just passes the time. Vision with action can change the world.*
>
> [JOEL BARKER]

Have you realized that if anything is going to change concerning your future, you will have to do something about it personally? You can start where you are with what you have *right now* and do what you can to pursue your dream.

"Be ready in season and out of season" (2 Timothy 4:2). We're supposed to be prepared and ready for whatever happens. The word *season* in Greek has to do with opportunity. We need to be prepared, because the season will change and the opportunity to act will appear. You may only get one shot at your dream.

When you go confidently in the direction of your dream with enthusiasm and the perseverance to finish what you start—that is when the miracle happens.

We should be turbocharged about our lives. Being fired up is a key ingredient to living the life of your dreams! Did you know that the word *enthusiasm* comes from a Greek root, *entheos*, which means "*in God*," or "*possessed by God*"?

Action: When an opportunity comes along, it is God's gift to you. What you do with that opportunity is your gift to God.

Hold on to Your Dream

I focus on turning negatives into positives. If you want it and you dream about it, there's nothing that's going to stop you.

[Chris Witty]

Reaching your dream is a process—it will take time, persistence, and patience. You can discover how to enjoy the process, even if it takes a long time and leads you through an uncharted course that requires your total faith and commitment. Hold on!

Ecclesiastes 9:10 says, "Whatever your hand finds to do, do it with your might." That means giving yourself diligently to the task at hand. It involves passion, determination, and excellence. It's the opposite of just getting by or doing the minimum requirement.

The secret to discovering your destiny is finding something you enjoy doing so much that you would be willing to do it for free. Then, become so good at it that people are willing to pay you to do it. And then do *more*!

One of the greatest life lessons that you can ever grab hold of is this: don't just do what's expected. Don't just do what your job description says, what people expect you to do. Do what's expected . . . and then some. Go that extra mile. Have the work ethic of a champion. Go in early and stay late, go above and beyond what is expected of you. Always do your best, and strive for excellence. You'll increase your value tremendously when you do that!

Action: Believe in your dream, and believe in yourself. Have the faith that God is on your side. Have a servant's heart. If you help somebody with their dream, God will reveal yours to you.

Live the Life of Your Dreams

Keep your dreams alive. Understand to achieve anything requires faith and belief in yourself, vision, hard work, determination, and dedication. Remember all things are possible for those who believe.

[GAIL DEVERS]

It is time to unlock your vision and for you to embrace it. God has a plan for you, and it's already in action right now. As time goes on, your vision will become clearer and clearer to you. You will realize that your dream has become your passion and begin to almost carry you.

However, that doesn't mean that the journey is going to be smooth. You will face hindrances and obstacles and all kinds of hassles. Your character will be shaped and formed in the process, and you will grow in your faith. One of the ways you will know that you have taken hold of the right vision is that it will be bigger than you are.

Focus on your dream. You will have to take every step by faith. Faith steps are the only kinds of steps that will get you anywhere. Keep your eyes on God and on the dream He has given you. It will be very special.

Last but not least, it is a good idea to write down your vision and keep it in front of you. Then, when life gets hectic, you won't lose track of it. When you hit a fork in the road, you'll know which way to turn. And when you need to draw on your patience and even your perseverance, you will have something to refer to.

Action: God will not let you down. Believe that you can because you believe that He can. You can depend on Him! His power is limitless!

Living Your Dream

Nothing is impossible, the word itself says "I'm possible!"

[AUDREY HEPBURN]

Believe That You Can!

Living your dreams isn't easy. It takes persistence and tenacity, along with faith in yourself, in God, and in the vision He has given you. You already have everything you need to fulfill your purpose. You receive the power when you have the courage to live the life of your unforgettable dreams.

You are never more like God than when you're dreaming, because God is a dreamer. His nature is in you, and that's why you can look at something that appears to be nothing and believe in it.

Believe that you can realize your dreams. Grab hold of your dreams and trust in the Dream Giver—"For with God nothing shall be impossible" (Luke 1:37)!

Become a Dream Life Mentor

*When the heart is set right, then the personal life is cultivated; when
the personal life is cultivated, then the family life is regulated; when the
family life is regulated, then the national life is orderly; and when the
national life is orderly; then there is peace in the world.*

[CONFUCIUS]

YOU did it—you have arrived! You should now be well on your way to
living the life of your dreams! Recall the person you were when you
started this year-long journey. How have you grown? My hope for you
is that you were encouraged, challenged, and empowered through this
year and that you gained an abundance of ideas to reshape your life for
the better. Who you are is way more valuable than what you do.

Remember that your positive thoughts will create miracles in your
life. Consciously choose to think the thoughts that will create the posi-
tive results you dream of. Every thought you think counts—so keep
your affirmations positive and very specific! "I am beautiful, success-
ful, healthy, happy, friendly . . ."

Now it is your turn. Become an example and a mentor for the peo-
ple around you. People will ask what is different about you. Share this
book and the ideas with someone you love, a young person, a gradu-
ate, a stay-at-home mom, someone looking for something more out of
life—OK, share it with everyone! Very few people are pursuing their
dreams; show them it is possible. You can decide to make a difference
in the world!

When is knowledge power? Power is when you apply the knowl-
edge and take action. Its up to you—will you implement the informa-
tion you have read? Will you really pursue the dreams in your heart?
Will you share your passion, talents, and gifts with the world? Please
start strong, sustain the action, and finish victorious!

*Action: Be thankful that you have today, the first day of the rest of
your life . . . live it like it is your last day on earth. AND make it so
beautiful that it will be worth remembering!*

Thought Leaders

I encourage you to continue your lifelong learning by reading books from the great thought leaders who inspired me to pursue my dream life.

Bible

James Allen

Jack Canfield

Dale Carnegie

Arron Chambers

Gary Chapman

Winn Claybaugh

Stephen M. R. Covey

Stephen R. Covey

Wayne Dyer

Rita Emmitt

Jentezen Franklin

Jeffery Gitomer

Billy Glynn

Malcolm Gladwell

Darren Hardy

Brig Hart

Louise Hay

Ed & Cheryl Henderson

Napoleon Hill

Spencer Johnson

Stuart Johnson

Brian Klemmer

Robert Kiyosaki

Tamara Lowe

Max Lucado

Og Mandino

Henry Marsh

John Mason

John C. Maxwell

Joyce Meyer

Myles Monroe

Beth Moore

Joel Osteen

Norman Vincent Peale

Bob Proctor

Anthony Robbins

Jim Rohn

Jennifer Rothschild

Don Miguel Ruiz

Brian Tracy

Rick Warren

Paula White

Bruce Wilkinson

Zig Ziglar

About the Author

Shelly Aristizabal is one of the world's leading Community Commerce Executives. She is an author, speaker, coach, and a passionate student of personal development and achievement. A product of the success principles she teaches, Shelly became a consummate entrepreneur early in life and now is committed to sharing the basic life skills and lessons of success with people of all ages and stages.

Shelly is committed to encouraging others to design and pursue the life of their dreams everyday. She has been on a mission to discover her own true purpose and to live a more meaningful life. This journey has led her to trust God completely and follow her heart. Now she encourages others to begin their own journey toward discovering and living a healthier, happier, more prosperous life. You can find inspiration and motivation through her blog, speaking, website, newsletter, and magazine articles.

Shelly lives in beautiful Naples, Florida with her husband, Edward, and their four children: Nicolas, Spencer, Alexander, and Emma.

For further information, activities, tips, and more, please visit

www.ThisIsYourYearBook.com & www.ShellyAristizabal.com